# DEFOE'S NARRATIVES
## *SITUATIONS AND STRUCTURES*

# DEFOE'S NARRATIVES

## Situations and Structures

JOHN J. RICHETTI

CLARENDON PRESS · OXFORD
1975

*Oxford University Press, Ely House, London W.I*

GLASGOW NEW YORK TORONTO MELBOURNE WELLINGTON
CAPE TOWN IBADAN NAIROBI DAR ES SALAAM LUSAKA ADDIS ABABA
DELHI BOMBAY CALCUTTA MADRAS KARACHI LAHORE DACCA
KUALA LUMPUR SINGAPORE HONG KONG TOKYO

ISBN 0 19 812067 2

© *Oxford University Press 1975*

*Printed in Great Britain
by Butler & Tanner Ltd
Frome and London*

*for*
*My Parents*

# Preface

THIS book grew out of my suspicion as I read Defoe that his books contained energies that historical and biographical studies of his work did not fully explain. I found myself persuaded by critics and scholars that Defoe was indeed an exactly practical realist and a man of serious beliefs and commitments, but I also found myself convinced as I read his novels that his characters are a wonderfully improbable and fantastically lucky company. I read with genuine admiration critical attempts to make Defoe an ironic narrator, or a thoughtful and even pious moralist, or best of all a cunning novelistic intelligence lurking behind that cheerful crew of criminals and adventurers who populate his books. But the feeling remained that the characters in those books are more important and more alive than any submerged intelligence which had perhaps created them to serve its own subtle purposes. The pleasures I renewed by re-reading Defoe included total acceptance of those characters, naïve involvement rather than ironic distance, in short a whole-hearted participation in their lives which did not seem to require special historical information about them or about Daniel Defoe.

And yet after the fact, after the experience of actually reading the books, I knew that I had been taken in, that Crusoe, Moll, Bob Singleton, and the rest were not only fantastic and even grotesque, but shallow-hearted and self-seeking, not really the sort of people one might trust or even care to know. This book is an attempt to reconcile my entire pleasures in reading Defoe's novels with my divided and contradictory reactions after the enjoyable fact. It is, in that sense, a commentary on my reading of Defoe rather than an effort to find a new handle with which to understand his books.

To be sure, as I explain in the opening chapter, my commentary is self-conscious and informed by the notion that Defoe's novels are inescapably 'novelistic', that they can best be understood in terms of a broadly conceived theory of the kinds of satisfactions that fiction uniquely delivers to its willing readers. My reactions to the various parts of these books are

conditioned, to some extent, by my idea of the whole to which
they belong, that is, by my idea of what novelistic narration is
and the particular kind of characters and situations that it
creates.

I have learned a great deal for which I am grateful from
recent Defoe scholarship and criticism, but I have often used
that body of work as a spring-board for my own speculations
and even as a handy pool in which to find adversaries. In other
ways, too, I have kept my own counsel and written a private
book about a set of exceedingly private characters. But I have
been encouraged in the enterprise by many. Professor James
Clifford introduced me to Defoe's works long ago and has
always supported this and my other efforts with total generosity
and unfailing enthusiasm. Professor James Sutherland encouraged my initial vague intention to write about Defoe, and
I took courage from that. George Starr, Leo Braudy, and
Robert Hopkins liked my other work and graciously wished me
well in this project. I am grateful to various friends and colleagues who helped in less direct but equally significant ways.
Hugh Babinski, Joe Cady, Fred Keener, Bob Kolker, and Myra
Riskin provided continuous intellectual stimulation and challenge while I worked on this book. Deirdre David helped me
live with this project, and with all things. My colleagues at
Rutgers, Maurice Charney, Thomas Edwards, Paul Fussell,
Dan Howard, John Huntington, Bill Keach, Bridget Lyons,
and Richard Poirier, encouraged me by their friendship and
confidence in my work. The Rutgers Research Council and its
wise Associate Director, C. F. Main, provided an indispensable
typing grant. Finally, I owe a great deal to Gordon Ray and
the John Simon Guggenheim Memorial Foundation for the
fellowship which supplied the leisure for writing the first draft
of this book.

# Contents

# I

## Defoe and the Problem of the Novel

I Converse with Presbyterian, Episcopall-Dissenter, papist and
Non Juror, and I hope with Equall Circumspection. I flatter my
Self you will have no Complaints of my Conduct. I have faithfull
Emissaries in Every Company And I Talk to Everybody in Their
Own way. To the Merchants I am about to Settle here in Trade,
Building ships etc. With the Lawyers I Want to purchase a House
and Land to bring my family and live Upon it (God knows where
the Money is to pay for it). To day I am Goeing into a Partnership
with a Membr of parliamt in a Glass house, to morrow with
Another in a Salt work. With the Glasgow Mutineers I am to be a
fish Merchant, with the Aberdeen Men a woollen and with the
Perth and western men a Linen Manufacturer, and still at the End
of all Discourse the Union is the Essentiall and I am all to Every
one that I may Gain some.

Defoe, to Robert Harley,
26 November 1706.

DEFOE has never lacked readers, and in the last century or so
he has acquired a great crowd of commentators. Most of these
have been drawn at first by the archetypal attractions of
*Robinson Crusoe* but then caught by that ultimately mysterious
personality which produced *Crusoe* and so much more. Since the
extent of Defoe's work began to be uncovered in the early
nineteenth century, that mystery has grown deeper.[1] Within

---

[1] We shall never know, apparently, just what Defoe wrote. Since George
Chalmers (*The Life of Daniel Defoe*, 1785) and Walter Wilson (*Memoirs of the Life
and Times of Daniel Defoe*, 1830) began the guessing, scholars have been contributing
attributions to an expanding canon. And from Chalmers to J. R. Moore (*A
Checklist of the Writings of Daniel Defoe*, Bloomington, Indiana, 1960), some of that
attribution, as R. M. Baine has pointed out, has been on very shaky ground, some
of it based on so-called stylistic evidence. Baine has estimated with mock exactness
that if the rate of attribution established between Chalmers and Moore persists,
Defoe before the end of the next century will have ghost-written 1,850 books,
pamphlets, and periodicals. Baine and Clinton S. Bond have recently done much
to correct that escalation and to expose the flimsy foundation upon which some of
the Defoe canon rests. They were anticipated in general terms by the polite
scepticism which greeted Moore's sometimes indiscriminate attributions in his

his mass of books and pamphlets and essays, Defoe performed what we can now recognize as extraordinary feats of literary ventriloquism. A talented and voluminous journalist, a consummate polemicist, and the victim of sharp economic necessity, he managed somehow to work for many and contradictory causes, to speak with many voices, to be like the Apostle, 'all to Every one that I may Gain some.'[2] His commentators have been at work now for about a hundred years, patiently trying to hear the real Defoe under the protean styles of these works, to isolate his actual opinions, to make him at last a presentable man not only of popular letters but of ideas.

The main source of scandal and difficulty is his fiction, for there Defoe seems to have identified himself to great and indeed powerful effect with characters who often strike modern critics as disreputable or inconsistent. For readers who think of a novelist as a heroic moralist-sage deeply concerned with personal and social problems, Defoe must often appear a fool or a knave. If, however, an intelligence or a covert sensibility can be found operating behind his limpid narratives, then the problem is fairly solved. Defoe becomes an ironist at least and perhaps a moral intelligence of high order.

But in the quest for the real Defoe, the personality we can imagine in some kind of imaginative interaction with his characters, critics have constructed various men. At the moment, Defoe exists in two rather distinct versions. The first and more traditional of these is a happy secularist, a proto-realistic novelist whose more famous creations such as Moll and Crusoe embody an ethos of expansive individualism and total possibility. This is the exuberant Defoe of the *Essay on Projects* and the *Tour of Great Britain*, Professor Moore's 'citizen of the modern world'. Recently, this secular Defoe has been spiritually rehabilitated. Some commentators have insisted that the moral and religious surface of the novels (to say nothing of the overtly religious and didactic works like *The Family Instructor, Religious*

---

*Checklist.* See R. M. Baine, 'Chalmers's First Biography of Daniel Defoe', *Texas Studies in Language and Literature*, 10 (1969), 547–68; and Clinton S. Bond, '*Street Robberies Consider'd* and the Canon of Daniel Defoe', *Texas Studies in Language and Literature*, 13 (1971), 431–45. Baine's *Daniel Defoe and the Supernatural* (Athens, Georgia, 1968) contains an exemplary displacing from the canon of the Duncan Campbell and Dickory Cronke pamphlets and books (pp. 131–97).

[2] *The Letters of Daniel Defoe*, ed. G. H. Healey (Oxford, 1955), p. 43.

*Courtship*, and the *History and Reality of Apparitions*) cannot simply be dismissed as the pious or opportunistic sugar-coatings of essentially secular material, that Defoe's works are indeed informed by a view of the world which is religious in a profound sense. At the least, these revisionist critics say, Defoe's narratives have a problematic nature, for they are about the paradox and anguish of surviving in a secular world with a religious ideology.[3]

Both of these views are plausible, persuasive, sound. But both, it seems to me, are necessarily incomplete by virtue of their larger attitudes towards literary history and towards the dynamics of narrative fiction. To begin with literary history, it is generally assumed (at least in Anglo-Saxon countries) that the more facts the better. The more we know about a writer's life and thought the better we will be able to understand his work. If only we knew exactly which books Defoe read, if only he had left a diary or a journal, if only he had written a theoretical essay on fiction or an explicit personal credo, then we should know what he meant more exactly, where he stood in that swirl of events and ideas he wrote about so well. We might know, that is, exactly what the intelligence behind the narrative voices in his fiction wanted us to think about them.

From such a perspective, there are two orders of facts that literary scholarship strives to recover: the personal and the ideological. Defoe seems forever out of reach on that first level; he had no Boswell and he left pathetically few and sadly unrevealing letters and personal papers. Those that remain are largely official and secret correspondence with the equally devious Harley: one master of deception dealing with and for another yields little evidence of personal convictions.[4] We do know the facts of his life—the business ventures and the

---

[3] The best and most extensive delineation of the spiritual Defoe is to be found in two fine studies: J. Paul Hunter, *The Reluctant Pilgrim: Defoe's Emblematic Method and Quest for Form* (Baltimore, 1966); and G. A. Starr, *Defoe and Spiritual Autobiography* (Princeton, 1965).

[4] One might add here that this necessarily devious and secret life Defoe had to lead as a merchant, political spy, and hack writer is the single most valuable and truly relevant fact we have about him. Secrecy is the common and pervasive obsession of all his fictional characters. Benjamin Boyce has observed that one of the neglected aspects of Defoe's novels is his 'representation of anxiety' and that his 'success in this latter phase of his art was a result of his own problems of morality'. There are, Boyce concludes, significant parallels between what we must assume was Defoe's own guilt and secrecy and that of his characters. (See 'The Question of Emotion in Defoe', *Studies in Philology*, i (1953), 45, 57–8.)

recurring failures, the imprisonment, trips taken, periodicals and books written, marriage settlement, children—but any attempt to unearth a coherent personality from those facts seems doomed to the kind of imaginative desperation committed by some of his biographers.[5] Defoe remains essentially a biographical puzzle. The only man to be seen and the only quality that it seems we can safely guess at is the elusive intelligence which somehow kept functioning brilliantly through disaster. The novels, more than any other of his works, defy explicit connection with his private life, even though we can sense emotional springs and private resonances in them. Since we know someone else is doing their talking, we suspect some sort of deep identification between characters and author in those narratives. Many of us would feel cheated of a valuable personality unless we had Daniel Defoe to insert in the experience of reading the books. But Defoe never did say that he *was* Moll or Crusoe or Roxana.[6]

There is more hope and there has been more success on the second level of fact. Defoe's library was sold at auction, teasingly mixed in with another's books. So we can at least guess reasonably at what he read. Of course, his works themselves fairly bristle with ideas, with the intellectual currency of the early eighteenth century at hand to a popularizer and purveyor of such wares. Defoe's didactic and religious works reveal clear beliefs and biases, an omnivorous and even discriminating intelligence. And those ideas do clearly figure in the narratives, occasionally in a quite explicit and discursive fashion.

In fact, the pursuit of those ideas, together with the granting to Defoe of the serious intelligence and complex sensibility he so obviously had, has been one of the most rewarding aspects

---

[5] That kind of frustration can be seen in J. R. Moore's brave attempt in his *Daniel Defoe: Citizen of the Modern World* (Chicago, 1958) to use the available facts about Defoe and to construct the real Defoe out of a synthesis of those facts. The result is a book which really adds nothing but conjecture to James Sutherland's *Defoe* (London, 1937).

[6] Such an insertion has some justification. Robert Scholes and Robert Kellogg say that the novel is really constituted by the unprecedented intrusion of the personality of the author into narrative. Montaigne, they argue, is the great origin and prime example of that new intensity, and 'even in less civilized, less sensitive England, is there not much of Defoe not only in Robinson Crusoe but in Moll Flanders and Roxana as well?' See *The Nature of Narrative* (New York, 1966), p. 191.

of the revisionist trend in recent Defoe scholarship. Previously, critics had pointed with a mixture of approval and condescension to Defoe's eye for the fact in his narratives and in some of his journalism, his immersion in the objects of his culture, and his instinctive ability to render the psychological truth about middle-class man.[7] But Defoe's truth in this reckoning was essentially a simple one: the conflict in the narratives between commerce and morality was resolved by his cheerful insertion of occasional tributes to ethics and piety.[8] He is now, happily, given more credit in these matters and allowed a more subtle response to complexity.[9] As Martin Price has put it, Defoe's narratives exemplify 'the troubled conscience of a Puritan tradesman, aware of the frequent conflict between the demands of commercial gain and those of spiritual salvation'.[10]

To validate that insight, scholars have gone to great and often fruitful lengths to prove that Defoe had extensive and fairly coherent views on God, man, and society, that he had read and absorbed Grotius, Cumberland, Pufendorf, Hobbes, Baxter, and various other repositories of late seventeenth-century thought, religious and secular. Moreover, implicit in the articulation of Defoe's mind is the idea that the narratives are informed by his learning and that they are in part quite serious attempts to dramatize and in some sense to resolve the central dilemmas of the age, between economics and morality,

---

[7] Leslie Stephen, for example, remarked that Defoe 'had the most marvellous power ever known of giving verisimilitude to his fictions; or, in other words again, he had the most amazing talent on record for telling lies'('Defoe's Novels', in *Hours in a Library* (New York, 1904), p. 4). Virginia Woolf agreed with her father and in an influential essay echoed by many later writers spoke of Defoe's 'genius for fact' (*The Common Reader* (New York, 1925), p. 57).

[8] A particularly smug and influential example of such reasoning can be found in Hans Andersen's article, 'The Paradox of Trade and Morality in Defoe', *Modern Philology*, 39 (1941), 46: 'The work of Defoe is an intimate revelation of the conflict between morality and commercialism in his age. He did not see the paradox with the complete intellectual detachment of Mandeville. He looked before and after. But he was consistent with reference to either direction and consistent also, finally, in voicing and supporting to the last the aspirations of England's increasing commerce, though he continued to pay morality the conventional, if economically inexpensive, tributes.'

[9] M. E. Novak's careful monograph, *Economics and the Fiction of Daniel Defoe* (Berkeley and Los Angeles, 1962), has been important in establishing Defoe's subtlety and complexity in these matters.

[10] *To the Palace of Wisdom: Studies in Order and Energy from Dryden to Blake* (New York, 1965), p. 264.

submission to the will of God and survival and/or prosperity in a secular society.[11] Under such a dispensation, obviously, even Defoe's much maligned piety can be rescued with confidence and linked to a tradition of religious exercise and perception of self: the narratives belong in part to a tradition of spiritual autobiography and their heroes want to find spiritual pattern and divine emblems in their lives as well as riches and power. Defoe's narratives are rescued from inconsistency by fitting into a background which provides some of them with unsuspected coherence and makes them expositions of their author's informed view of a complex reality. In a way, the books are no longer mere adventure stories but case histories which exemplify Defoe's psycho-religious view of the world.

Such scholarship is, on its own ground, highly illuminating and beyond refutation. Defoe's position as a moralist is apparently there for the reading in his various discursive works. For Professor Novak, who has read them all with care and deep sympathy, his resolution of the problems of human nature as understood by his age marks him as 'neither an original nor a profound thinker' but one possessed of a 'certain eclectic originality'.[12] What matters is that, given Defoe the moralist and amateur philosopher, we can understand Defoe the novelist; we can judge his characters through that moral theory and thereby recover the real Defoe underneath the narrative mimicry. Or, to use the more refined and flexible version of this approach lately put forward by G. A. Starr, we can recover Defoe's perspective on his characters by examining an informing tradition of moral casuistry within which Defoe's mind worked. Beginning with the existence and vogue of casuistical journalism and establishing Defoe's practice of it elsewhere, Starr moves to the novels and makes an excellent case for them as elaborations of this habit of mind. Casuistry is the source of both the fragmentation and coherence of Defoe's fiction; it is a habit of mind which operates on case histories by accepting and examining all the data of experience and finally extracting

[11] M. E. Novak's authoritative *Defoe and the Nature of Man* (Oxford, 1963) is the most comprehensive effort in this direction. More specialized and detailed examinations of Defoe's 'thought' include, Michael Shinagel, *Daniel Defoe and Middle-Class Gentility* (Cambridge, Mass., 1968), and R. M. Baine, *Daniel Defoe and the Supernatural* (Athens, Georgia, 1968).
[12] *Defoe and the Nature of Man*, pp. 157, 2.

the morally coherent possibilities, discovering moral structure in what seems to be randomly selfish or instinctive action.[13]

I do not propose to argue with this admirable line of thought but rather to raise some objections and to shift the terms of discussion somewhat. The most elementary difficulty is a critical commonplace: conscious intention is an important factor in the meaning of narrative, but it is by no means the whole story. Moreover, even the overt ideological content of Defoe's narratives (whether explicitly and consciously inserted by the author or introduced by the critic as an implicit set of assumptions and problems) is again a part of their meaning rather than some hidden whole truth. The historian of ideas who extrapolates themes out of Defoe's narratives as their ultimate content is in danger of ignoring at his peril the truism that story-telling is by its nature something different from discursive statement, something dynamic and relational in which discursive statement plays only a role, and a role in which it is often transformed into something quite unlike itself.[14] Professor Starr, it should be said, carefully avoids this danger by

---

[13] *Defoe and Casuistry* (Princeton, 1971), p. 32 and *passim*. Starr's persuasive point is that the casuistical habit of mind enabled Defoe to give his superficially disorderly books quite a revolutionary underlying coherence: 'Within the individual episode, however, casuistry often afforded Defoe both his subject matter and a distinctive way of treating it. Many scenes are not only based upon traditional cases of conscience, but organized internally in ways that reflect the casuistical method of posing and resolving moral dilemmas. There is a constant marshalling of motives and sanctions, choices and circumstances, precedents and hypothetical analogues; although this procedure can jeopardize any larger pattern or design a book may have it can also supply a kind of minimal consistency between episodes, and can give them a fullness and complexity lacking in earlier fiction.' (p. x)

[14] To be sure and to be fair, Professor Novak in a series of critical articles written after his two fine monographs on Defoe's 'ideas' has been examining the techniques to be found in the narratives. He has constructed Defoe's implicit 'theory of fiction' and concluded that Defoe had a moral or allegorical awareness derived from the biblical criticism of the time. That awareness, conjoined with his journalistic eye for the literal, produced 'a sense of the social, religious, economic, political and moral implications of events which had no parallel in fiction until the 19th century'. (See 'Defoe's Theory of Fiction', *SP*, 61 (1964), 668.) In subsequent articles, Professor Novak has focused on Defoe as an ironist and suggested that his frequent use of irony in his discursive works instructs us in how to read the novels. (See 'Defoe's Use of Irony', in *The Uses of Irony: Papers on Defoe and Swift Read at a Clark Library Seminar*, 2 April 1966.) Here and elsewhere, Novak asks us to treat Defoe as purely a self-conscious artist, a novelist like James and Conrad it would seem, who set out to create certain moral and psychological effects. Thus, in his most recent article, he tells us that 'Defoe's real technical achievement involved slowing down the pace of first-person narrative by focusing on single actions and

finding in casuistry not so much a content as a method of narrative perception and presentation. But even his brilliant essay is ultimately committed to the static proposition implicit in literary history that narrative meaning can be reduced to a single perspective or position of the author (however complex and flexible that position may be), whether more or less consciously articulated by the author. More generally, the historican of ideas *cum* literary critic is wedded to the particular facts surrounding a work, and no matter if those facts are dynamic and relational as Professor Starr's 'casuistry' is, they still emerge as static and essentially external determinants of the work. If we understand the facts around it, we are in a fair way to understand the work.

This view and the methodological assumptions it carries are what I propose to challenge, or rather, to refine. For, obviously, the historian of ideas is very much on the right track when he assumes that a work of narrative has to be returned to its historical context if its meaning is to be recovered. I agree fully with Novak and Starr and others when they assume that Defoe and his narratives inhabit a world somewhat different from ours, that they represent a consciousness of self and history distinct from our own. Meaning clearly resides, in an important sense, in the dynamics of the historical moment. The problem, as Scholes and Kellogg have put it without criticism's usual evasions, 'is the nature of the relationship between the author's fictional world and his real world'.[15]

For the historian of ideas that 'real world' is quite correctly the particular ideological world of the writer and his society, a constructed world necessarily opposed to a neutral or natural world. 'Reality', in every case, equals culture and society. We have access to that reality through a set of historical facts and documents which surrounds the work of fiction. We imagine

---

characters and through various devices of repetition offering new angles of vision.' (See 'Early Fictional Forms', *Novel*, 6 (Winter 1973), 132.) My point is simply that Defoe's stories obtain their real interest for us as structures that soon leave that sort of coherence well behind, that Defoe's effects (like Richardson's) have a resonance provided by the dynamics of the genre and the historical moment of which he could not have been fully aware and of which no narrator of fiction can ever be fully conscious.

[15] *The Nature of Narrative*, p. 83. See also Ian Watt, *The Rise of the Novel* (Berkeley and Los Angeles, 1962), p. 11.

that fiction aspires to 'reflect' that ideological world, that is, to sustain or prove it against the relatively disorderly energies of what can be called mere nature. But it is also generally agreed that Defoe's narratives form part of an emerging tendency in the history of narrative to render that world of mere nature, to dramatize the process whereby individuals and their society separate themselves from mere nature. The distinctive and heroic ambition of the novel as currently understood is to tell the literal truth about things and events and even people as they are, somehow, in themselves: circumstantial realism, to use Ian Watt's term. In similar fashion, Arnold Kettle has observed that the novel, more than any other genre, is defined by its commitment to 'life' over 'pattern'. The novels of a writer like Defoe, Kettle continues, provide what he calls 'the sense of what life as their characters live it really feels like'.[16] One can go further. The novel as a genre tends to be committed to the feeling that personal experience is nothing less than some sort of irreducible imponderable, that life properly apprehended is an object of experience rather than of knowledge in the abstract sense. Thus, the novel considered as a formal tendency is uniquely concerned to arrange a kind of participation for its readers in the events being described, for only the experience of experience can render it or communicate it. Implicit in these assumptions of modern realistic narrative is the idea that unmediated personal experience itself is a fundamental category, the ultimate material out of which the secondary sources of consciousness such as culture and society and even language itself are fabricated.

Such assumptions are quickly reduced to absurdity by a slightly more rigorous empiricism. To experience something is to stand in some sort of relationship to it, and to stand in relationship to an event or an object is to form part of a reciprocal structure: the subject imposes on the object and is himself imposed upon by the qualities of the perceived object. One can put the case even more sharply. Consciousness, as Hume noted drily, is always consciousness of something. The idea of a self always dissolves upon examination into a dependent relationship with something the 'self' perceives. 'When I enter most

[16] *An Introduction to the English Novel*, I (New York, 1960), p. 16.

intimately into what I call *myself*, I always stumble on some particular perception or other, of heat or cold, light or shade, love or hatred, pain or pleasure. I never can catch *myself* at any time without a perception, and never can observe anything but the perception.'[17]

What we recognize as novelistic narration involves the articulation of that ironic pattern or the re-creation of that field of movements. The novel, uniquely sensitive to context and situation, seems to be the best literary convention ever devised to present an acceptable or convincing version of the situation that Hume describes. It follows, therefore, that when we credit Defoe as we should with rendering the 'feel of experience', we are really saying that he succeeds in dramatizing the inner and necessarily reciprocal structure of all experience, or at least of a good deal of self-conscious modern experience. His narratives exist in the middle of the paradox uncovered by all intensely mimetic realistic fiction, what Scholes and Kellogg have nicely called mimetic-historical narrative.[18] Such stories may be said to claim to offer us life in all its disorder, 'as it is really lived' is the occasional boast; but what they in fact provide is a series of imaginary situations whereby we are at once in the actual and historical world of limiting and ironic reciprocity and out of it in a world where an unmediated personal experience is the ultimate category of being.

What emerges from such a shift in perspective towards the dynamics of fiction is the centrality of the process of narration itself. Whatever the content or the shape of the writer's 'real' world (his social ideology), fiction like Defoe's is inescapably involved in reconciling that world with the persistent feeling that personal experience is the final and determining category that in some way must precede ideology. The typology of the novel worked out by a Hegelian critic like the young Lukács thus fits these facts rather well. The novel, as Lukács remarked, involves the 'affirmation of a dissonance' between the immanence of being and empirical life. What Lukács called the essentially biographical form of the novel is the sign of a 'fluctuation between a conceptual system which can never completely capture life and a life complex which can never attain completeness because completeness is immanently utopian'.[19] Whatever its ideological content, whatever its attitude toward the material it narrates, the novel's energy as a form is essentially a matter of revealing that fluctuation and of preserving or asserting the authority over that fluctuation of the self that writes and, by extension, of the self that reads. From quite another philosophical perspective, Paul de Man has observed that fiction involves the assertion of an inescapable subjectivity, that an 'invented fiction, far from filling the void, asserts itself as pure nothingness, *our* nothingness stated and restated by a subject that is the agent of its own instability'.[20] We are left in a position by such theoretical statements to say that modern narrative has, therefore, to find ways and means for reconcilement of the dissonant opposites revealed by its primary operations. Ideology, whether secular or religious, is thereby part of the problem any novel faces rather than the answer to what it means. The real question in reading Defoe's narratives in this critical context is not the presence in them of rival and contradictory ideologies but the problem raised by the nature of mimetic narrative whereby all ideologies are potentially nullified by what Lukács called the abstract, solipsistic ambitions of the novel.[21]

Thus, the various inconsistencies and contradictions that several generations of commentators have found in Defoe's narratives and tried to resolve by putting him on one side or another of the controversy are really by these lights signs of the process of confrontation and mediation within the totality of perception and experience which mimetic fiction by its nature and tendency sets in motion. The ultimate way to understand Defoe's fiction is, I think, to be found in just these dynamics of that intensely mimetic fiction of which his narratives are among the earliest if somewhat imperfect examples we have in English.

[19] *The Theory of the Novel*, trans. Anna Bostock (London, 1971, first published 1920), p. 72.

[20] *Blindness and Insight: Essays in the Rhetoric of Contemporary Criticism* (New York, 1971), p. 19. Significantly for my purposes, de Man remarks later (pp. 34–5) that, 'The imagination takes its flight only after the void, the inauthenticity of the existential project has been revealed; literature begins where the existential demystification ends and the critic has no need to linger over this preliminary stage. Considerations of the actual and historical existence of writers are a waste of time from a critical viewpoint.'

[21] *The Theory of the Novel*, p. 70.

These stories may be said to record the transformation of the reciprocal world of perception that Hume describes so that it somehow admits the notion of personal experience as an ultimate category, so that the idea of a primary and irreproachable self that Hume sneers at can somehow be maintained.

This is not to say that this primary self ever achieves some sort of static existence in a compromise position clearly visible between the absolute and the reciprocal. The mediation between the two lies in the liberating and quite dynamic process of narrative itself; what effects the reconciliation (or attempts it) is the 'movement' of the characters (and, in another and parallel sense, the audience) through the fullness of reciprocity and into a sense of powerful but temporary autonomy, and then quickly back again to a somewhat less restrictive reciprocity. What happens is perhaps best described as a kind of rapid oscillating movement of narrative energy between those poles of experience which produces the high frequency signal that we read as literary personality or novelistic being. In this kind of situation, 'substance', to use the terms of a brilliant theoretical essay by Fredric Jameson, 'is replaced by relationship', and the reality of things by 'a sense of the identity of a given element which derives solely from our awareness of its difference from other elements, and ultimately from an implicit comparison of it with its own opposite'.[22]

There is an impeccable precedent for such an approach to fiction. This kind of dialectic between experience and ideology has long been recognized as the imaginative secret of *Don Quixote*. Critics no longer really need argue about which side Cervantes was on, whether Don Quixote is satiric butt or saintly hero. Cervantes's book can only be read, I think, as a meditation on the problem of consciousness and the irony of action facing late-sixteenth-century Spain, and as such as an adumbration of the characteristic problem of the novel. Just so, such an approach and such a model enable us to avoid sterile scholarly debate about the moral and ideological meanings surrounding Defoe's narratives. They too should be seen as meditations (admittedly less subtle, self-conscious, and consistent than *Don Quixote*) on the problem of a certain kind of

[22] 'Metacommentary', *PMLA*, 86 (Jan. 1971), 14.

early eighteenth-century English consciousness. The enormous differences between a late Renaissance master like Cervantes and an honest journeyman like Defoe hardly require comment. What they share is the perspective provided by mimetic-historical fiction, and therefore its problems.

In *Don Quixote* experience is ultimately rescued from its initial ridiculous status as absurd and derivative personal fantasy. But that rescue is not a matter of transcending or denying Quixote's shabby provincial circumstances; it is rather a question of moving through the two worlds mimetic-historical narrative uncovers (the visionary-free world of experience and the real-limiting world of reciprocity) so that eventually we perceive that Quixote's chivalric vision of himself and the world is inseparable from the refractory circumstances which provoke it. Quixote's chivalric fantasies are the result on the one hand of that complex of social and historical circumstances which makes him an impoverished hidalgo feverishly reading romances, but they are on the other hand an effective way of personal action and a way out of those circumstances without every denying them. The real world of arid La Mancha and the last predatory days of Spanish imperialism drive Don Quixote mad; they drive him by their moral and imaginative poverty into the golden dream of chivalry. His determinate fantasies are transformed by his actions into a kind of independence and of authentic if temporary personal meaning. The energy we call Don Quixote consists of a third term somewhere between the absurd personal fantasy and the dull reciprocity of normal ideology. But that third term, to return to my metaphor, cannot exist without the other two; they are the vibrating poles which constitute the mediating signal we call Don Quixote.

Defoe's various autobiographers are engaged in their several ways and on their distinct social and historical ground in a similar enterprise and quest for autonomy, if on a more parochial scale and at a lower stage of self-consciousness. Like Quixote, they begin by encountering themselves as the result of circumstances. Their narratives go on invariably to uncover unruly realities, the limiting reciprocity involved in those personal, social, natural, and historical determinants which threaten the autonomy and even the physical survival of the self. Their problem, again like Quixote's, is to transform this world of compulsion into an opportunity for freedom and self-assertion.[23]

Take Crusoe, for the best example. Like Quixote, he is 'mad', possessed by a mysterious inner compulsion to go to sea which in the course of the narrative emerges as a desire to acquire wealth and power of an extraordinary kind, that is, beyond the determined possibilities of that 'middle state' into which he is born. Crusoe seems to be choosing freedom, but his 'original sin', as he calls it, is what Ian Watt has labelled 'the dynamic tendency of capitalism itself, whose aim is never merely to maintain the *status quo*, but to transform it incessantly'.[24] So Crusoe is not, strictly speaking, 'free' in following his inner desire; what he experiences as his unique personality is at least partly the result of the ideology of capitalism. Indeed, in calling it a sin and classifying it as an inner and nearly irresistible compulsion, Crusoe recognizes its true nature if not its actual source. Like Quixote, he manages in time to exchange one set of circumstances for another and infinitely more promising set. In his madness, Don Quixote is the captive of a chivalric fantasy whose sources we can locate in the compulsions of his genteel poverty, in his particular history. His fervent acceptance of the fiction of chivalry utilizes the energies it potentially contains and liberates him from the deadening alternative of accepting normal reality. He acts in relation to 'history' in such a way that it becomes *his* history. Crusoe is likewise realized as a character in the conflict in him between two historical factors: the expansive ideology of capitalism and the conservative moral and religious ideology which is its logical opposite. His position as a consciousness aware of the claims of

[23] James Sutherland has lately reminded us of the necessity of shifting the critical issue from Defoe's realism to its purpose. 'If his characters are often criminal types, they only serve the better to let him explore the problem which seems to have interested him above all others—that of *necessity*; the will to survive that comes into collision with economic facts, that natural morality which is often in conflict with law and order.' (See 'The Relation of Defoe's Fiction to his Non-Fictional Writings', in *Imagined Worlds: Essays . . . in Honour of John Butt*, ed. Maynard Mack and Ian Gregor (London, 1968), p. 48.) M. E. Novak has also written about the importance of 'necessity' in Defoe's fiction. (See 'The Problem of Necessity in Defoe's Fiction', *Philogical Quarterly*, 40 (1961), 513–24.) What critics have failed to do, I think, is to see that the 'necessity' at work in the narratives is the comprehensive autonomy of the self that fiction implies, a necessity including and yet transcending the social survival critics describe as its source.

[24] *The Rise of the Novel*, p. 65.

those ideologies liberates him from them; his narrative is the result of his busy suspension between those competing ideologies. He acts in such a way in response to history that it becomes *his* history, not simply the impulses provided by capitalism or the repressions of conventional morality and religion which counter them, but his unique and shifting position between those ideologies, now an adventurer, now a penitent, and finally a grand synthesis of those positions. Both he and Quixote exist as characters because their narratives arrange for them to be coherently in history and yet outside it by virtue of their total personal appropriation of history's demands.

At this point, the differences history enforces between *Don Quixote* and Defoe's narratives are illuminating. Don Quixote has a model, an idea of chivalric coherence summed up in the famous Amadis de Gaul. To remove himself from degrading circumstances, he can imitate the career of Amadis and thereby escape mere self-consciousness and the fragility that implies. Amadis is for Quixote what René Girard calls an 'external mediator', a focus of and a means for the desire of the self to exist apart from its material and determinate being. Quixote imitates Amadis, Girard says, as the Christian imitates Christ.[25] Both acquire meaning and context for their otherwise randomly selfish and determined actions: to imitate the mediator is to possess the historically authenticated and meaningful world he represents. Defoe's heroes, on the other hand, sorely lack a mediator. Their obtrusive loneliness and secrecy are the clearest signs of that; their confessional and private narrative perspective another aspect of it. In place of the models of chivalry or the *imitatio Christi*, they have at various times the secular ideology of individualism and the religious ideology of free will balanced by providential arrangement. But neither of these provides a mediator. On the one hand, both seem to promise freedom and place the individual on his own at a point outside history. But on the other hand, both ideologies are ultimately restrictive and confining; both are committed to the paradox of a situation which resembles the conditions of market society. Such a society begins with the proposition that each man establishes himself by a process of personal

[25] *Deceit, Desire, and the Novel: Self and Other in Literary Structure*, trans. Yvonne Freccero (Baltimore, 1965), pp. 2–3.

acquisition, but, as the young Marx saw so clearly, that need to acquire is given by the structure of market society itself. 'Man himself is no longer in a condition of external tension with the external substance of private property; he has himself become the tension-ridden being of private property.' Marx saw that private property is thereby incorporated 'in the very essence of man, and it is no longer, therefore, conditioned by the local or national characteristics of private property regarded as existing outside itself'.[26] What appears to be the freest and most independent of acts, the acquisition of private property and the solid certification of a private self, becomes the inescapable manifestation of a social reality. The very freedom of the individual to acquire and possess is no more than the coherent and therefore confining expression of social necessity.

Such a society, moreover, requires that men be free and rational but creates at each moment of its existence a situation in which those men are confronted by compulsive forces. As C. B. Macpherson has put it, 'All men's choices determine, and each man's choice is determined by, the market.'[27] As below, so above. God requires each man to believe that he is free and to act as if he were, but confronts him at every moment with signs of compulsive arrangements in heaven and earth, arrangements which have been determined by men's free choice since Adam.

The novel is, of course, crucially aware as a genre of these dilemmas. In the broadest historical terms such as I have been using, the novel is one of the plainest manifestations of what Ian Watt has called 'the transition from the objective, social and public orientation of the classical world to the subjective, individualist and private orientation of the life and literature of the last two hundred years'.[28] In the broadest sense, eighteenth-century thought seemed always to return to an image of man as an essentially free individual; the primal scene was political, the signing of a contract by individuals who loaned their freedom to the state and erected institutions to suit their

---

[26] 'Economic and Philosophical Manuscripts', in *Early Writings* trans. T. B. Bottomore (New York, 1964), p. 148.

[27] *The Political Theory of Possessive Individualism* (Oxford, 1964), p. 106.

[28] *The Rise of the Novel*, p. 176.

needs.[29] Defoe's characters find themselves effectively outside those institutions and with nothing between themselves and their roles in heaven and on earth. But they also find themselves placed in a world thick with social and psychological compulsion, where necessity of all kinds is the absolute rule. Defoe's novels are not, as is sometimes asserted, naïve celebrations of individual possibility. They are most accurately described as dramatizations of what can be called the individualist dilemma. They communicate by their arrangements and strategies an implicit grasp of the tangled relationships between the free self and the social and ideological realities which that self seems to require. What they show us as we read is character carefully separating itself from that unsatisfactory tangle of private and public, personal and social, and establishing an unimpeachable selfhood, at least in the privileged space of the narrative.

In such a view, to describe the ultimate meaning of Defoe's narratives is to speak of their ultimate function. Narrative looked at in this way has the status and structure of what we are in the habit of calling myth. In encountering and trying to overcome the disparity between the experience of a free self and the demands of a restrictive ideology, the heroes of narrative perform a version of that traditional cultural function which is obvious in myth and visibly present in romance and epic. Northrop Frye has observed that Defoe's narratives are part of the emergence of what he calls the 'low mimetic mode' of fiction in which that function seems to disappear. In the low mimetic the hero is 'superior neither to other men nor to his environment'. We respond, Frye continues, 'to a sense of his common humanity, and demand from the poet the same canons of probability that we find in our own experience'.[30] But, as Frye himself notes, the modes go around in a circle. We violate the essential unity of all narrative fiction by separating

---

[29] The conservative sociologist, Robert A. Nisbet, underlines the contradiction between that individualist base and the rational surface that prevailed: 'But behind the rationalist image of society in this period there was always the prior image of naturally free individuals who had rationally bound themselves into a specified and limited mode of association. Man was primary; relationships were secondary. Institutions were but the projections of fixed, atom-like sentiments innate in man.' *The Sociological Tradition* (New York, 1966), p. 48.

[30] *The Anatomy of Criticism* (Princeton, 1957), p. 34.

too drastically the low mimetic from the primary fictional modes of myth and romance where the hero is superior to other men and to the environment. For what happens below the surface of the low mimetic in many cases is that the hero becomes as powerful as the heroes of myth and romance. We come at last to see that mimetic fiction is inevitably to one degree or another concerned with the covert re-establishment of the power of the hero.

Normally, critical discussion of a novel's function tends to be oblique and diffident. The novel, especially, has attracted moralizing critics who like to judge novels according to their capacity to deliver us from illusion and to show us the possibility of authentic experience. In other words, the novelist himself can be regarded, with some justice we should add, as a hero who asserts experience in the face of the falsifications of ideology, or who sees tragically that culture and society will always reassert themselves over authentic personal experience, or who observes ironically the failure of characters to come through to some kind of authenticity. The novelist may even, like Jane Austen and Fielding for example, dramatize the ironic inadequacy of self-contained experience in the face of the cultural realities which inevitably control it.

All these formulations illustrate the fundamental truth that the novelist is committed *qua* novelist first and simply to the revelation of that process whereby experience is separated from ideology and becomes conscious of itself as the powerful if often undirected opposite of ideology. The mimetic act in modern narrative begins in the imagination of a self which is somehow apart from the very things which define it, that is, from the constellation of causes and circumstances which it must use to present itself. Defoe's narratives seem to me in this way examples of nearly pure and certainly naïve mimesis, concerned to possess both experience and ideology with an exuberance and fullness that later and more self-conscious novelists reject as crude or simply untrue. To read Defoe requires a willingness to participate at one and the same time in thoroughly observed fact and in extravagant fantasy. The point of talking about Defoe as an important writer is not to congratulate him once again for his psychological perceptions, sociological acuity, and moral-spiritual sensitivity, but rather to see that such undeniable achievements are means of promoting the self by establishing its primacy as the perceiver and guarantor of reality. To a degree, the facts about themselves and about nature and society with which Defoe's characters present themselves are converted by the process of narration into emanations of the self and proof of its power. Defoe's narratives provide in fairly transparent fashion a sense of that autonomous and authentic self which later eighteenth-century aesthetic theorists thought the novel was uniquely equipped to sustain in its readers. As Lionel Trilling has observed, Rousseau especially admired the novel because it provided its audience with the 'sentiment of being', that is to say with energy interested not so much in aggressive and dominant action but in perfect self-possession.[31] We will see that Defoe's heroes are less exquisite and slightly confused. They attempt to reconcile extensive activity in the world with the kind of self-possession Rousseau was talking about.

All of this is not meant to deny the disorderly surfaces of Defoe's narratives or to suppose the existence in them of some hidden master plan or esoteric unity. Defoe's books are sloppy and opportunistic affairs, slapped together with skill and verve but with all the signs of obvious haste and relative indifference. They are not an *œuvre*, far indeed from the deliberately coherent and developing whole such as we can find in the works of other and much greater novelists. But Defoe's books do possess an imaginative unity, a set of common problems with a recurring solution. Indeed, partly because of their relatively spontaneous nature and their vulgar immediate purposes, they contain energies that more sophisticated fiction can never quite manage.

What I propose to do in the following pages is to read Defoe's major narratives with a particular care which will attempt to locate those energies and to find the sources of that imaginative unity that Defoe instinctively conferred on his books. I propose to that end to take the narratives with a seriousness not usually granted them, to see them as instinctively coherent and culturally functional acts of the mimetic-historical imagination. What such a procedure and perspective supply, I think, is a method rather than a thesis, a method which involves close reading of the narratives as they unfold, rather than generalizing from the

[31] *Sincerity and Authenticity* (Cambridge, Mass., 1972), p. 99.

superior heights of a particular and exclusive thesis. I intend in what follows to trace the exact line of each narrative and to re-create and summarize in their own sequence the local effects that occur. I propose to follow the plots and situations of the narratives, however inconsequential or meandering they seem at first. The overriding purpose of this extended particular analysis is the articulation of the larger structural patterns that emerge, but my attempt is to catch those patterns in the process of emerging by paying attention to what might be called the phenomenology of reading these particular narratives. The reading is necessarily my own and personal to some extent, but I wish to argue that the narratives contain and promote my response and others like it. My purpose is to watch the narratives at their various tasks rather than to impose some larger unity with criticism's usual sense of superiority. My hope is to catch the fictions as they rise and mark the self as it flies with them.

# II

## *Robinson Crusoe:* the Self as Master

You are not to take it, if you please, as the saying of an ignorant man, when I express my opinion that such a book as Robinson Crusoe never was written, and never will be written again. I have tried that book for years—generally in combination with a pipe of tobacco—and I have found it my friend in need in all the necessities of this mortal life. When my spirits are bad—Robinson Crusoe. When I want advice—Robinson Crusoe. In past times, when my wife plagued me; in present times, when I have had a drop too much—Robinson Crusoe. I have worn out six stout Robinson Crusoes with hard work in my service. On my lady's last birthday she gave me a seventh. I took a drop too much on the strength of it; and Robinson Crusoe put me right again. Price four shillings and sixpence, bound in blue, with a picture into the bargain.

Wilkie Collins, *The Moonstone*

NEAR the very end of his *Farther Adventures*, Robinson Crusoe visits China and allows himself to describe it as a poor, ignorant, and barbarous nation. That description strikes Crusoe as a departure from his usual procedure and he apologizes:

As this is the only excursion of this kind which I have made in all the account I have given of my travels, so I shall make no more descriptions of countrys and people; 'tis none of my business, or any part of my design; but giving an account of my own adventures, through a life of inimitable wandrings, and a long variety of changes, which perhaps few that come after me will have heard the like of; I shall therefore say very little of all the mighty places, desart countrys, and numerous people I have yet to pass thro', more then relates to my own story, and which my concern among them will make necessary.[1]

Such limitation is exactly why we now read Defoe. His achievement, as Ian Watt has rendered it fairly, was to assert the

---

[1] *Robinson Crusoe* (Everyman edition, ed. Guy N. Pocock), p. 387. All further page references in the text are to this edition.

'primacy of individual experience' by a 'total subordination of the plot to the pattern of the autobiographical memoir'.[2] Crusoe sees more of the world in his sequel than any ordinary eighteenth-century person could even hope to see, and yet he calmly denies his readers extensive knowledge of that extra-ordinarily varied world in order to deliver himself. This audacity accords perfectly with the egocentric preferences of the novel as a genre which really cares only for personality and its triumph over environment and circumstances. As Ortega y Gasset once remarked, characters in novels 'interest us not be-cause of what they are doing; rather the opposite, what they do interests us because it is they who do it'.[3] Such paradox seems borne out by the dismal fate of Crusoe's continuation. The tremendous variety of scene the sequel features is, perhaps, part of the reason for its failure. Crusoe himself tends to fade out of sight and the exotic locales take over to a degree. In the original, Crusoe is himself the actor and the stage, the whole theatre.

But even in Part One, it may be argued, there are events, actions of a fairly spectacular and clearly external kind. Crusoe, after all, is not ironically self-contained in the manner of modern heroes. The point is that those acts and events are sub-ordinate to the special event we call literary personality or character. The events do indeed seem to draw out personality, for some kind of event (or the deliberate absence of one) is clearly necessary to provide a field for achievement or exter-nalization of personality. But we always feel as we read that personality is radically primary, that it existed before events and continues to exist in spite of circumstances that seek to change or even to obliterate it. Finally, in fact, we are led back to Ortega's paradox when we realize that the result of the narrative is to convert events into vehicles for character; or, more exactly, that events gradually accommodate themselves to the emerging self as its power to deal with events increases. It is not simply that the self learns to manage events. Rather, events become as we read an appropriate expression of the self. Thus, what we are chiefly conscious of as readers of the first part of *Robinson Crusoe* is a world of initially controlling circumstances and events in

---

[2] *The Rise of the Novel*, p. 15.
[3] 'Notes on the Novel', in *The Dehumanization of Art and Other Writings* (New York, 1956), pp. 61–2.

which the narrative self somehow manages not simply to survive but to make survival a form of autonomy. That autonomy is acceptable because it is disguised, not presented as a simple heroic assertion but residing in the kind of complex and elusive being that the novel as such is uniquely equipped to create. In that being, the self does not dominate the world but manages to produce a version of the world which is perfectly aligned with itself and its desires.

As an archetypal personage of the last two hundred and fifty years of European consciousness, Crusoe seems to have achieved his popularity by virtue of precisely that versatility and adaptability, able as Wilkie Collins's Betteredge says to provide sage advice 'in cases of doubt and emergency'.[4] As the accumulated reports of more serious Crusoe watchers make clear, he seems at various times to be the embodiment of various ideologies. On the one hand, for observers from Marx to Ian Watt, he is a representative of capitalist ideology, driven to acquire, control, and dominate. On the other hand, if we read with patience the actual text of his story and listen to recent commentators such as J. Paul Hunter and G. A. Starr, he is quite convincing as a man intent upon discovering his ultimate limitations by seeking spiritual definition and divine pattern in his life. His goal is from this point of view to abdicate responsibility, to give God the glory and take whatever shame there is upon himself. I think we must concede the accuracy of *both* these descriptions; Crusoe is in my view neither exclusively a masterful economic individual nor a heroically spiritual slave. He inhabits both ideologies in such a way that he manages to be both at once and therefore to reside in neither. What we may call the real Crusoe, the existential Crusoe that the novel aspires instinctively to deliver, is the personal energy that experiences the contradiction implicit in mimetic narrative: control in a context of helplessness and helplessness in a context of control. Crusoe can be called a converter, turning an ideology to the uses of survival and autonomy by using what it gives and neutralizing its possessive effects. He survives physically on the island, as we shall see, by means of a resourcefulness and cunning well beyond probability, but the narrative tries to assure us in various ways that his control is a mere response to circumstances. For the sake of

---

[4] *The Moonstone* (Modern Library edition), p. 15.

what we must call psychological survival, to get away from the destructive effects of isolation, he realizes on the island that he is a part of providential design. He experiences and accepts divine control but that control can only be realized in the free context he has himself created. And that free context, the narrative makes us remember, is itself the result of determining circumstances stretching back to Crusoe's adolescence. In *Robinson Crusoe*, a position is always relative; the freedom and defining autonomy of the narrative self is in the consciousness (or, better, the enactment) of this dynamic relativity.

*Robinson Crusoe* begins with an advertisement which is a remarkably accurate adumbration of that structure of relations as it introduces some key terms and oppositions:

> If ever the story of any private man's adventures in the world were worth making publick, and were acceptable when publish'd, the editor of this account thinks this will be so.
> The wonders of this man's life exceed all that (he thinks) is to be found extant; the life of one man being scarce capable of a greater variety. (1)

We are used to valuing private experience. Much fiction since the mid-nineteenth century has explicitly and self-consciously set out to show how reality resides in subjective states and how public realities are mere superstructures, attenuated forms of institutions. The value of making such experience 'public' in a novel is really to deny the category of public experience[5] and to exalt the aggressively unique nature of private experience. This preface claims that Crusoe has connected the public and the private, implying that in being himself he has lived the kind of private existence that is of 'public' interest. But, as the next sentence of the preface makes clear, that interest does not arise because Crusoe's life resembles those of his contemporaries, not because he is the typical private man. Rather, his life is one of 'wonders' unparalleled, 'variety' without precedent. How, then, is Crusoe's story so worthy of public notice? It is, obviously, being sold as an extravaganza to people who like all of us value the exotic and the various as a pleasurable relief from the humdrum and uniform quality of daily life. Crusoe, however,

---

[5] The decline in the belief in the worth of such experience since antiquity is discussed by Hannah Arendt in definitive fashion. See *The Human Condition* (New York, 1958), p. 175.

domesticates wonder by industry and skill and discovers common providential arrangement in variety. He lives in an uncommon common fashion. His life is public, that is, attractive and meaningful to the typical private person, because he introduces private and common order into thrilling and uncommon events.

This special 'commonness' which Crusoe exemplifies is evident at once in the opening paragraph of the narrative. It is at once unique and conventional in the history of English narrative in its brief but exact attention to sociological detail. Seventeenth-century criminal biographies supplied sociological location for their heroes and speculated briefly on why they left conventional pursuits for lives of crime. Travellers sometimes did the same. We remember that Gulliver was the third of five sons of a father who had a small estate in Nottinghamshire.[6] But Crusoe supplies information which is at first merely neutral—date of birth, details of European immigration, and naturalization in England—undifferentiated data whose purpose is to certify Crusoe not simply as a real person but as a private person, one whose life begins in random, shapeless facts.

That opening goes on to record, again with a unique attention to exact sociological data, how these facts provide an explanation of Crusoe's subsequent behaviour which is the root of his story. He is a third son, bred to no trade and *therefore* given to 'rambling thoughts'. These facts provide something like an explanation of behaviour rather than an exact determinant of it. The issue remains uncertain. Young Crusoe is partly the result of these factors, partly the victim of a compulsive inner 'propension of nature' to wander. Crusoe, from the start of his narrative, is both in and out of its circumstances. The narrative seems to reserve a part of him which is really beyond social determinants, merely natural but triggered somehow by social factors.

Now we know, as Ian Watt has put it, that Crusoe's 'propension of nature' is really the internalized ideology of capitalism,[7] or rather, that dangerously dynamic aspect of capitalist ideology which must in the context of the early eighteenth century

---

[6] Gulliver has entirely rational and overt motives, at first certainly, for his travels. He, after all, has a legitimate and limiting professional identity as a ship's doctor. His later and more compulsive journeys come out of personal inclination and not out of that mixture of personality and social circumstance that the beginning of *Robinson Crusoe* tries to grasp.　　　[7] *The Rise of the Novel*, p. 65.

be denied and suppressed.[8] By its location here partly in circumstances and partly in the unruly nature of the individual,
such desire can be presented but disavowed. Moreover, it can
provide a plausible motion for its own eventual banishment to
Crusoe's island, where it will be able to surface and work itself
out fully but benignly. This wavering pattern of the opening
pages of the book is crucial in every respect. Not only Crusoe
but the nature of his world are being defined. It is a world
where 'nature' (a personal, internal reality, somehow given) and
circumstances (that is, external in some way, historical, social
facts) seem to be complementary causes of action. Again, the
self must in such a situation be both in and out of circumstances.
Its 'nature' becomes a shifting and complex thing, sometimes
given, sometimes partly 'caused', sometimes private, and sometimes sliding over into public patterns like the generalized
figures of fiction (the rebellious son, the ambitious traveller, the
heroic castaway, the repentant sinner). In his opening paragraphs, Crusoe is infected mysteriously by nature, but this
nature is at least partially rooted in the personal circumstances
Crusoe has just described. He himself tells us so, although he
puts it in such a way that circumstances seem responsible
primarily for the earliness of the desire to leave home: 'Being
the third son of the family and not bred to any trade, my head
began to be fill'd very early with rambling thoughts' (5).

'Rambling' is, then, a natural tendency which in Crusoe's
case is triggered or aggravated by circumstances. Young men,
psychological truisms permit us to agree with Crusoe, are
always potentially attracted to 'rambling', that is, to repudiat-
ing their fathers and establishing themselves as independent
beings. The destruction of the father implicit in such an
establishment seems to be what lies behind Crusoe's desire to go
to sea, that is, to become rich above his father's station. To sur-
pass him economically is in a real sense to destroy him. Capitalist ideology may be said to encourage this natural tendency
much more strongly than other ideologies, but at the same time

---

[8] C. B. Macpherson remarks on this pervasive hesitation in the face of new
implications: 'And however one interprets the Restoration and the Whig Revolu-
tion it cannot be said that support for traditional values had become entirely
insignificant by the end of the century, or even later. Locke tried to combine
traditional and market morality; so did Burke, in a more fundamental and more
desperate way, a century later.' *The Political Theory of Possessive Individualism*, p. 86.

it preserves a hesitancy about the destructive implications of such ambitious energies. The official and sanitized version of capitalist ideology represented by Crusoe *père* formally disapproves of a radical separation of son from father and of the consequent destruction of father by son in surpassing him. So Crusoe's father and Crusoe himself in his narrative portray as unruly nature and/or unfortunate circumstance what is really the central energy of capitalist ideology. Crusoe is a culture hero in the literal sense because he enacts this destructive separation by means of his narrative complexity, taking on himself and deriving from himself and his circumstances the responsibility for it. The long haul toward the island and back eventually is a journey into 'nature' to bring back an acceptable version of official ideology. Crusoe appropriates nature for his culture by experiencing it, that is, by deriving it simultaneously from personal reality and circumstances. The formal ambitions of his narrative to find the exact measure of will and circumstances which make up a life are a means to that cultural end. Moreover, that relativity whereby the self is presented creates by implication the autonomous self that masters that paradox.

Those formal ambitions are especially evident in the opening pages of the book. As we read we are confronted with a dance among various sorts of explanations—social, moral, and psychoreligious—for Crusoe's desire to roam. Crusoe's perspective is, of course, above these levels as analytic reporter, concerned, as his tone and manner inform us, primarily with reporting causes and conditions exactly. As his father concludes his homily, Crusoe reports rather stiffly but exactly: 'I observed in this last part of his discourse . . . I say, I observed the tears run down his face very plentifully, and especially, when he spoke of my brother who was kill'd' (7). He reports further that he 'was sincerely affected with this discourse, as indeed who could be otherwise' (7). But the next sentence records the wearing off of this impression in a few days. Crusoe notes the irrelevance of moral discourse in the face of irrational desire; in fact, he implies in his capacity as neutral recorder the primacy of mysterious internal impulse. The deliberate and impressive circumstantiality of his account is a means of proving the compulsive nature of that internal impulse.

But young Crusoe is hardly impulsive and his compulsion

seems furthered by craft. He tries to create conditions which will be favourable for his going away, working on his mother: 'However, I did not act so hastily neither as my first heat of resolution prompted, but I took my mother, at a time when I thought her a little pleasanter than ordinary' (7). He plans, in short, to go away, but neither impulsively nor formally and definitively. He wants his father's consent, he reasons with his mother, and will agree to a bargain: 'if she would speak to my father to let me go but one voyage abroad, if I came home again and did not like it, I would go no more, and I would promise by a double diligence to recover that time I had lost' (7). Such diplomatic cunning is perfectly plausible psychologically and reinforces our belief in Crusoe's real desire to go to sea. But it does lessen considerably our belief in the irrationality of Crusoe as agent or executor of his desires. Crusoe is effectively separated from his desires by his cunning in executing them. To put it another way which can serve as the cryptic summary of his secret as a successful character and culture hero, he acts but does not act.

That is precisely how he first goes to sea. Despite his manipulations, his actual departure is a matter of accident: 'But being one day at Hull, where I went casually, and without any purpose of making an elopement that time' (8). Even though he has been planning and resolving to go for over a year, he is finally moved by immediate impulse and circumstance. His career begins (as it is to continue) as mediation between action and control. His voluntary–involuntary beginning is a rough example and exemplar of his later career. He is both responsible and not responsible, and the convincing and specifically novelistic complexity thus evoked is a way to have action without full responsibility.

We need, perhaps, to remember the dangers and discomforts of seventeenth- and eighteenth-century sailing; most of us would choose gaol with Dr. Johnson. Understandably, Crusoe takes to the sea very slowly. And again, Defoe's commitment to the plausible is a means towards the structural consistency we are after. Crusoe in bad weather repents dramatically; when the storm subsides he responds to these new circumstances with equal complacence, only to return to even greater repentance when the storm returns. All this pathetic vacillation establishes

Crusoe as the absolute dupe of circumstances, a veritable weather-vane. Such a characteristic effectively weakens the subversive independence he aspires to and will eventually achieve. Paradoxically, it also establishes the irresistible force of his compulsion to go to sea, for he resolves to continue even in the face of absolute terror not only of violent death but of his own revealed moral weakness.[9] Psychologically, Crusoe is possessed by an imperious desire which is strengthened by his own weakness; structurally, this psychological plausibility is in the service of the contradiction his story seeks to enact. Weakness and strength, active control and passive submission are the antinomies being suspended by his narrative.

The ship sinks and Crusoe is provided with a substitute father to draw the moral. His comrade's sea-faring father warns him that these are palpable tokens of divine will. That traditionally transparent world of religious meaning, complete with biblical figure, presented by the old sailor is followed directly in the narrative by a world of casual but pressing social and psychological particulars. Crusoe explains that he had some money with him, so he went to London by land, and that fear of ridicule kept him from taking the divine warning. The commonplace realities of psycho-social circumstance are, however, endowed by Crusoe with a mysterious significance. They are part of that inscrutable inner drive which Crusoe the narrator can only account for at this point by speculating about 'a secret overruling decree that hurries us on to be the instruments of our own destruction, even tho' it be before us, and that we rush upon it with our eyes open' (13). Crusoe is tentative in offering this; he says that nothing else seems quite adequate to explain the persistence of his drive. He rejects, as we perhaps do not, the merely random and self-serving psycho-social particulars which lead him on and with which he co-operates. We know from our historical perspective what those energies are up to; we realize that the trivial facts and circumstances of personality are ultimately governed by a will to power which lies behind

[9] 'But if I can express at this distance the thoughts I had about me at that time, I was in tenfold more horror of mind upon account of my former convictions, and the having returned from them to the resolutions I had wickedly taken at first, than I was at death it self; and these, added to the terror of the storm, put me into such a condition, that I can by no words describe it.' (11)

narrative and dream. Crusoe's baffled explanation is an instinctive and protective reversal of that will to power into a self-
destructive internal mechanism or an external fate.

Throughout this first voyage and its aftermath, Crusoe remains 'ignorant' in the literal sense. During the shipwreck, he is
just a passenger, does not quite understand what is happening
to the ship because nautical terms like 'founder' mean very
little to him, cannot help the crew fight the storm, and sits
quaking in his cabin. He even swoons, frightened and bewildered by a gun the ship fires as a distress signal (11–12).
During his second voyage, his first real trading voyage, this
ignorance continues. In retrospect, Crusoe regrets that he
sailed as a gentleman-adventurer-trader rather than as a sailor,
in which 'tho I might indeed have workt a little harder than
ordinary, yet at the same time I had learn'd the duty and
office of a fore-mast man; and in time might have quallified my
self for a mate or lieutenant, if not for a master' (14).

Preliminary ignorance of self is a prerequisite for autobiographical protagonists; unlike picaros who begin with
infinite cunning and thorough cynicism, they exist to show us
the self growing and expanding in one way or another. Crusoe
is thus required to be ignorant that we may experience his
acquisition of wisdom. And yet, we know that Crusoe's subsequent wisdom is fully implicit in his initial desire to go to sea.
In this light, Crusoe's ignorance is a strategy for ideological
coherence as well as narrative satisfaction; indeed, in *Robinson
Crusoe* these two ends are always exactly parallel. It is not
necessary to worry about which came first; the technique of
autobiographical narrative of this kind is the working out of the
implications of the ideological position it describes. The urge to
acquire is given, as Marx noted, by the structure of market
society, where the individual incorporates within himself the
idea of private property.[10] But the narrative is out to establish a
pattern whereby the self can gradually discover outside itself
that which it carries within. Thus, the assertion of a pre-
existing self is always what is meant by the development of the
self. Crusoe is necessarily ignorant of the implications of his will
to power, and his overt technical ignorance of seamanship is an
intensifier which covers up those implications, or at least dis-

[10] See above, Chapter I.

tracts us from them. The real task of this kind of narrative seems to be not the development of a new self but the discovery or establishment of an environment where the self can emerge without blame as a response to reality rather than as the creator of it.

In spite of his ignorance, Crusoe prospers on his voyage and learns navigation into the bargain. He acquires social identity for the first time: 'this voyage made me both a sailor and a merchant' (15). The security and stability are temporary, and the next trip ends in Moorish captivity. On one level, this captivity is part of the variety of event to which the book is committed.[11] On the level of structure, it is part of the shift which takes place in Crusoe's situation from internal to external compulsion. An objective and technical problem of survival and freedom replaces the subjective need for powerful self-assertion implicit in Crusoe's original desire. In escaping from Sallee, Crusoe is free to master his environment without apologies. In narrative terms, this liberates the story to elaborate that environment with precision, not simply because it is exotic but because it is morally neutral. It is only at this point in the story that Defoe begins to place before us in any abundance the fascinating details for which he is famous. That precision is the most obvious manifestation at the level of language of the will to power that informs the book. The environment is handed over to Moors and monsters and can therefore safely be dominated and elaborated by Defoe's language and Crusoe's acts.

This is not to say that there is a melodramatic shift from that novelistic ambiguity we have observed to heroic simplicities. Here and indeed throughout *Robinson Crusoe* what we experience as readers is that sense of freedom only within circumstances already observed. Consider the escape itself. Crusoe meditates for some two years but forms no definite plans. Specific plans involve the arrival of proper circumstances, of what Crusoe calls 'an odd circumstance . . . which put the old thought of making some attempt for my liberty again in my head' (17). Out fishing one day with Crusoe and another slave, his master finds himself nearly lost at sea. He resolves for the future to

[11] The narrative convention to which this part of the book belongs has been isolated by G. A. Starr in 'Escape from Barbary: A Seventeenth-Century Genre', *Huntington Library Quarterly*, 29 (Nov. 1965), 35–52.

refurbish a captured English longboat with a cabin, a compass, and provisions against an emergency. Crusoe, by virtue of his dexterity in taking fish, always accompanies him. It happens further and more particularly that his master is to go out in this boat 'with two or three Moors of some distinction in that place, and for whom he had provided extraordinarily' (17). So the boat this time has extraordinary provisions, guns as well, since they plan to shoot as well as fish. The last crucial circumstance arrives when Crusoe's master finds that his friends are unable to go and orders him to go out in the ship thus provisioned and catch some fish for their dinner that night. Crusoe's escape is a matter of hugely fortunate circumstances combined with his eye for the main chance. This set of circumstances (a regular set-up) anticipates those that surround his survival on the island a little later in the narrative and announces his central talent: an ability in the midst of captivity to act at precisely the right moment. The structure of this escape is the same as that implicit in his 'escape' from paternal restriction and the land-locked 'upper station of low life', a question of waiting patiently for the inevitable fortunate moment.

A key transition is at stake here. Moorish captivity and escape mark the first conversion of Crusoe's original impulse to dominate into a will to survive. The inevitability of such a conversion and justification of the will to power is a commonplace for anyone who looks at a competitive market society. Crusoe must be taken out of the way and placed in an environment whose inhuman (or non-European) hostility converts self-aggrandizing dominance into a completely justifiable will to survive. The real function of the exotic locales in the book is to provide a suitable ground for Crusoe's energies. The process forms what Roland Barthes in another context has called the naturalization of the social and historical which is behind what he calls bourgeois myth.[12]

The capture and escape thus function as a means of setting Crusoe free for the first time from the negative responsibilities of his internalized drive to power. His story once started cannot be

---

[12] *Mythologies*, trans. Annette Lavers (New York, 1972), p. 141. All of Defoe's stories, but especially *Crusoe*, fit Barthes's notion of 'myth' very well, for they may all be said to convert the historical world they describe into 'natural' arenas where survival is the defining problem.

stopped. His inner compulsion is largely transferred to the series of external accidents and coincidences which constitute the rest of his adventures. His initial capture creates a chain of events with their own inevitable sequence. Nature and narrative logic create a liberating circle of compulsion within which Crusoe can act with an innocent desperation which gives him great power.

That power seems almost too great and the escape situation seems a melodramatic study for the more plausible and even struggles to come on the island. Here, doubtless responding to convention in such matters, Defoe drags in mysterious monsters, hideous howlings which keep Crusoe and Xury awake at night.[13] Crusoe is obtrusively original and boldly self-conscious as he fires his gun at these monsters: 'But it is impossible to describe the horrible noises, and hideous cryes and howlings, that were raised, as well upon the edge of the shoar as higher within the country, upon the noise or report of the gun, a thing I have some reason to believe those creatures had never heard before' (21). Similarly, when he and Xury meet friendly Negroes, Crusoe asserts himself by shooting a monster which is about to attack them. The Negroes then skin the brute, taking the meat and giving Crusoe the skin. They display in the process their skills and native crafts; they bring him water in 'a great vessel made of earth, and burnt as I suppose in the sun' (25). Once Crusoe establishes his power and technological superiority, anthropological observations are possible. Clearly, all this anticipates the sequence of events on the island, although in hasty, crude, and sketchy form. Such repetition and elaboration of pattern are signs of the story's affinities with myth so often remarked upon. What is novelistically crude is appropriate in myth, where, as Levi-Strauss observes, 'the function of repetition is to render the structure of the myth apparent'.[14]

However, Crusoe is a crypto-hero and his story true rather than mythical; his power and autonomy are only permitted to emerge within the world of circumstances that the novel specializes in and myth excludes. So he is 'delivered' by a Portuguese ship and returned to the chain of circumstances that

---

[13] See Starr, 'Escape from Barbary'.
[14] 'The Structural Study of Myth', in *Structural Anthropology*, trans. Claire Jacobson and Brooke Grundfert Schoepf (New York, 1963), p. 229.

constitute his life. Luck and accident in this case complete
heroic escape and European self-establishment among beasts
and savages, as indeed they are to conclude matters later on in
the story. These conclusions point to a recurring problem. The
central fantasy of the book has to be grounded somehow in
those social and psychological realities to which the book is
committed. Crusoe therefore is given solid reason to continue in
his quest for satisfaction in the facts surrounding his prosperity
as a planter in Brazil. He describes with characteristic clarity
how he and his neighbour planned their crops and cleared their
ground but also how his old desires thereby returned: 'I had no
remedy but to go on; I was gotten into an employment quite
remote to my genius, and directly contrary to the life I delighted
in, and for which I forsook my father's house and broke thro'
all his good advice; nay I was coming into the very middle
station or upper degree of low life, which my father advised me
to before' (28). The repetition which myth requires is here the
plausible result of the reawakening of Crusoe's initial desires
among the social realities of farming in Brazil, cunningly
turned into the acceptable cycle of psycho-social probability.
The indefatigable desires of the self that Crusoe so clearly if
casually describes are not gratuitously asserted but made to
grow out of the handy and opposite circumstances which repeat
his original situation in England. In a sense, the circumstances
exist to provoke the self and return it to its mythic direction
without violating the mimetic decorum of the novel, indeed by
paying exact attention to it.

This survey of the preliminary situations of Crusoe's career
reveals, I think, the central and essentially double view the
narrative takes toward its incidents. Reality is richly served,
and my commentary necessarily violates the thick texture of
inner and outer circumstance the narrative delivers. But that
convincingly tangled surface invariably resolves itself into situations which propel Crusoe forward, which seem to be obstacles
but which are as we read remarkably similar occasions for self-
display. Beneath the mimetic fullness and apparent variety,
there is what can only be called an energy which may be said to
turn each situation toward a variation on the theme of self-
assertion.

That energy and its capacity for turning the randomly

varied world of mimetic narrative into a self-expressive structure emerge in their fullness on the island, where fidelity to
mimetic decorum is naturally more prominent than ever. On
the island Defoe's exact rendering of things and events is at its
clearest and most intense, partly because exactness becomes
most necessary here as an opposite to the formlessness of the
island. In other words, the technique of self-analysis combined
with scrupulous external observation that Defoe gives his hero
reveals itself here clearly for what it is: a means of blameless
self-assertion. That technique is often praised as an end in itself,
an achievement that speaks for itself; but I think it is more important and critically relevant to analyse Crusoe's talents as
analytic reporter in the context of their function in the narrative
considered as a whole. Crusoe isolated so dramatically is in a
position to speak about himself and his circumstances in a new
way which eventually allows him that maximum of freedom and
virtual autonomy as a character that his narrative aspires to
achieve for him. I think we can say that in time he becomes on
the island a contemplative consciousness who can literally
observe himself at work, resembling in that fruitful split the
master in Hegel's formulation who interposes the slave between
the thing and himself and thereby achieves freedom.[15] Indeed,
the point of my commentary from here on is to observe Crusoe's
expanding but carefully qualified power, to see how precisely he
extracts control within the limitations of circumstances.

To be sure, Crusoe's control is partly an aspect of the retrospective narrative position which he shares with Defoe's other
autobiographers. They are writing their own stories, and we are
conscious of them as masters of their autobiographies, above
events in that elementary sense. But Crusoe's relationship to
events has a dynamic quality that we have already experienced
if we have read this far in his book, but which becomes more
regular and even obtrusive when he reaches the island. Consider the shipwreck itself, a rush of meticulously rendered
descriptive details but preceded and indeed punctuated by a
phrase which is characteristic of Defoe's narratives at moments
of stress. The ship in the storm suddenly strikes a sand bar: 'It is
not easy for any one, who has not been in the like condition, to

---

[15] *The Phenomenology of the Spirit*, trans. J. B. Baille, in *The Philosophy of Hegel*
ed. C. J. Friedrich (Modern Library edition), p. 405.

describe or conceive the consternation of men in such circumstances' (33). What is implicit in such a statement is a world of
pure compulsion *as experienced*, that is, of the frenzied simul-
taneity of a reality which admits of no human mediation at all
and which taxes the limited linear resources of the novel.
Crusoe's next step is to violate the blurred reality of such a
sentence by outlining the situation as a set of possibilities:
'. . . we knew nothing where we were, or upon what land it was
we were driven, whether an island or the main, whether inhabited or not inhabited; and as the rage of the wind was still
great, tho' rather less than at first, we could not so much as
hope to have the ship hold many minutes without breaking in
pieces, unless the winds by a kind of miracle should turn immediately about' (33). To provide shape and calm sequence in
the middle of the disasters of experience is a function of any
retrospective narrator, but Crusoe is also aware of the desirability of conveying the emotional immediacy of the situation.
His recourse to the initial formula of the impossibility of rendering experience is evidence of that. What he is in fact doing is
establishing a narrative point between the world of experience
and the world of narrative, that is, between the unruly and
actually incommunicable world of reality as experienced and
the lucid, controlled world of narrative. Throughout his narrative, Crusoe will continue to allude to that inchoate world of
experience and indeed succeed in making us see it to some
extent, but only by constantly giving up the attempt to describe
it and rendering it in the solid sequences of orderly narrative.
What we read is not simply the sequence but the sequence
offering itself again and again as a partial description and evocation of the experience itself. The eventual result of that delicate
balance is to give us the world of experience as such where the
'slave' exists and to allow us at the same time to occupy the
privileged position of the 'master'.

To continue the example: Crusoe's ability to evoke confusion and render a convincing and potentially involving version of experience is beyond question here in the shipwreck
scene. (Compare Gulliver's calm and totally emotionless descriptions of similar disasters.) But in that rush of detail, we
observe signs of the control that keeps us sufficiently in control
to read and sufficiently out of control to participate. 'Nothing

can describe the confusion of thought which I felt when I sunk into the water' (34), says Crusoe at once. He leaves us to insert or to charge what follows with the appropriate turmoil, but the invocation of that turmoil is necessary. What follows is an almost completely objective description of action, of how Crusoe survives, what he does and the tactical reasons for doing it: 'I had so much presence of mind as well as breath left, that seeing my self nearer the main land than I expected, I got upon my feet and endeavoured to make on towards the land as fast as I could' (35). At this point in the paragraph, there occurs the only metaphor for several pages, one of the few figurative moments in the language of the shipwreck scene: 'I saw the sea come after me as high as a great hill, and as furious as an enemy which I had no means or strength to contend with' (35). His business, he tells us, is not to contend but to co-operate, to hold his breath and try to maintain the kind of neutral position which will use the force of the surf as a propellant towards the shore. The simile is exactly appropriate at this point: its first part is a way of measuring and describing and its second has a tactical rather than emotional content. It is a way of figuring Crusoe's refusal to over-step himself either in action or in language. Even this figurative moment is of a piece with the rigorously descriptive and analytic function of these paragraphs. The figurative surface contributes to the deeper opposition between control and participation, reminds us of the initial compulsion and confusion, and reinvokes the emotional tone set some sentences before at the beginning of the sequence.

We are conscious here and elsewhere in the book of a world of unruly and therefore fascinating forces—experience, in short. But in the midst of all that welter of observation are the occasional analytic details which establish human understanding and implicit control of that world. That is the discernible shape and disposition of Defoe's narrative prose: a series of descriptive clauses and then the analytic phrase, the clarifying insight which makes the previous clauses cohere. 'I stood still a few moments to recover breath and till the water went from me, and then took to my heels, and run with what strength I had further towards the shore. But neither would this deliver me from the fury of the sea, which came pouring in after me again, and twice more I was lifted up by the waves and carried forwards as

before, the shore being very flat.' (35). Crusoe's understanding
of the relationship between surf and shore anticipates his
shrewd understanding in time of the island. We are conscious in
the very arrangements of Defoe's prose of a continuous and
dynamic movement between experience exactly observed and
the experiencing and narrating self, and that swing in the prose
is a metonymic reflection of the substance of the narrative in its
most profound sense.

That dynamic substance is clearest in what Crusoe tells us
about how he came to keep a journal, only beginning to keep it
after he had achieved some mastery of himself and the island. If
he had kept it from the first, the journal would have been full of
what he calls 'many dull things'.

For example, I must have said thus: 'Sept. the 30th.

After I got to shore and had escap'd drowning, instead of being
thankful to God for my deliverance, having first vomited with the
great quantity of salt water which was gotten into my stomach, and
recovering my self a little, I ran about the shore, wringing my
hands and beating my head and face, exclaiming at my misery, and
crying out, I was undone, undone, till tyr'd and faint I was forc'd to
lye down on the ground to repose, but durst not sleep for fear of
being devour'd.' (52)

In this passage from the journal that he chose not to write
Crusoe is merely what other historically authenticated lone
survivors became. This hysterical, formless, and naturally self-
destructive aspect of Crusoe is only touched upon, although it is
the threatening chaos implicit in his subsequent ordering of
things. His paranoia, of course, continues unabated, but it is as
much a fear of this formless, self-destructive self as it is of
external enemies.[16]

---

[16] Here is one passage among various that illustrates the presence of a disorder
which is potentially threatening, constricting and stifling as this description implies:
'I have already observ'd how I brought all my goods into this pale, and into the
cave which I had made behind me. But I must observe too, that at first this was a
confus'd heap of goods, which as they lay in no order, so they took up all my place,
I had no room to turn my self; so I set my self to enlarge my cave and works
farther into the earth, for it was a loose sandy rock, which yielded easily to the
labour I bestow'd on it; and so when I found I was pretty safe as to beasts of prey,
I work'd side-ways to the right hand into the rock, and then turning to the right
again, work'd quite out and made me a door to come out, on the out-side of my
pale or fortification.' (51.) The disorder of the goods is overcome by the elaborate

Nature and the natural self are overcome by a form of self-assertion of which the journal is only the most obvious manifestation. Crusoe's gradual discovery of God and his acquisition of what he identifies as spiritual consciousness of God's presence and operation in his life are ways to enforce that self, to acquire a self which is, like God, beyond nature and yet in nature. Crusoe's spirituality does not, therefore, contradict his talents as survivor; it is a formalization, in effect, of his own masterful relationship to the environment.

If we look at Crusoe's survival after the initial shocked stupidity of being thrown upon the beach, it is a continuation of his behaviour in the water: clear-eyed co-operation with circumstances. As the Spaniard remarks after hearing of all this in the *Farther Adventures*, this is a remarkable achievement: ' "had we poor Spaniards been in your case, we should never have gotten half those things out of the ship, as you did: nay," says he, "we should never have found means to have gotten a raft to carry them, or to have gotten the raft on shore without boat or sail; and how much less should we have done," said he, "if any of us had been alone!" ' (294.) Crusoe works with unbelievable care, and the secret of his success lies in watching the tides and co-operating with their flow. But even in the middle of heroic ingenuity and improbable steadiness, there are unstable forces at work, a portion of that formless and hysterical self that threatened him when he landed. In the middle of his tide-watching and planning, Crusoe begins to wonder 'why Providence should thus compleatly ruine its creatures, and render them so absolutely miserable, so without help abandon'd, so entirely depress'd, that it could hardly be rational to be thankful for such a life' (47). But 'something always return'd swift upon me to check these thoughts' (47). Crusoe casts up an account at this point and ends rumination with a proverb: 'All evils are to be considered with the good that is in them, and with what worse attends them' (48). By themselves, such ruminations are uninteresting; proverbs like this one are normally excuses for inaction. But in the context of Crusoe's remarkable feat of survival, the division of experience into good

---

and intricate system of Crusoe's tunnels, not just a large space in which to range goods but a larger space in which Crusoe himself can participate in his externalized order.

and bad, useful and destructive, and the analysis of circumstances implicit in the proverb are heroic acts which are the centre of Crusoe's character. Just as God co-operates with natural process and even employs disasters to further his mysterious ends, Crusoe finds meaning in flux, holds back his own potential hysteria, and converts disaster and accident into fortune and plan.

His casting of accounts is as admirable a feat in his context as mastering the tides and building a raft to get the goods from the ship. Both are analytic acts, both involve a separation of the self from circumstances in order to master them by co-operating with their flow. It is no accident that Crusoe begins to speak at this point as if he operated on himself as well, as if he had a self which dealt in various ways with another part of himself. This is perhaps an existential inevitability which is perceived in common speech: 'I made myself do it', we say, meaning really that there is a part of us that is self-consciously apart from our functioning self. Crusoe exists at this point in his narrative in that world of self-consciousness that we ordinarily conventionalize; indeed, it is for him a means of survival rather than a manner of speaking: '. . . as my reason began now to master my despondency, I began to comfort my self as well as I could, and to set the good against the evil, that I might have something to distinguish my case from worse, and I stated it very impartially, like debtor and creditor, the comforts I enjoy'd against the miseries I suffer'd' (50). In the context of his exertions, such reflections are more than pious platitudes; the 'I' that performs this operation has asserted itself impressively and coherently. The other self that is negated is like the potentially destructive world of tides and winds that surrounds him.

Crusoe's techniques of self-assurance can be derived from the methods of Protestant self-consciousness, but the meaning and ultimate function of these spiritual techniques are inseparable from Crusoe's position in his book and on his island. Although Crusoe has to learn certain specific techniques such as building, pot-making, baking, etc., he is essentially knowledgeable in the over-all technique and internal disposition for physical survival. He seems to know *how to learn*. He tells us that such is not the case when it comes to spiritual survival; he pictures himself as insensible to God's mercy and goodness, occasionally confused by his bad fortune and indifferent the rest of the time to God's role or presence in his life. The casting of accounts is an effective but temporary stay against confusion, that is against the psycho-spiritual uncertainty that Crusoe tells us was a real danger until his 'conversion'. That conversion occurs slowly, surrounded by the continuing details of survival, and, given the efficiency of Crusoe's proceedings, we may wonder why that conversion is necessary at all. We may easily be tempted and forgiven for dismissing all this religious rigmarole as Defoe's cunning or boring insertion of piety. But Crusoe's story is coherent and whole and the religious experience is part of his total survival. The answer to our unease with it lies, I think, in his solitude, an untenable human situation but a necessary one for the needs of this particular narrative. In our context as readers of the narrative, 'conversion' is an informative pun on what really happens. To be that delicately powerful master-slave the narrative requires, Crusoe has to be converted in part into a passive figure who is delivered by God, that is, whose active survival and the identity which that involves have to be guaranteed by some outside force beyond the random flow of circumstance, some force that is on the side of order and pattern and meaning. Crusoe's competence at survival is a sign of his potentiality for virtual autonomy, but he can hardly be the only one who establishes order and pattern and meaning. Thus, before his conversion he suffers from what we may call with R. D. Laing a form of 'ontological insecurity'. Laing's description of that state is useful and relevant here:

The individual in the ordinary circumstances of living may feel more unreal than real; in a literal sense, more dead than alive; precariously differentiated from the rest of the world, so that his identity and autonomy are always in question. He may lack the experience of his own temporal continuity. He may not possess an over-riding sense of personal consistency or cohesiveness. He may feel more insubstantial than substantial, and unable to assume that the stuff he is made of is genuine, good, valuable. And he may feel his self as partially divorced from his body.

. . . the ontologically insecure person is preoccupied with preserving rather than gratifying himself: the ordinary circumstances of living threaten his *low threshold* of security.[17]

[17] *The Divided Self* (London: Penguin edition, 1965), p. 42.

Now Crusoe is not in 'ordinary circumstances'; his singular
situation makes him liable to the symptoms of schizophrenia
that Laing describes but at the same time facilitates by its
externality his ability to correct those symptoms. To that end,
he establishes identity and his own temporal continuity: he
makes his own calendar and his own house and clothing and so
on. He is forced to be preoccupied with survival, so that, to use
Laing's terms, surviving becomes a form of gratification. But in
order, finally, to feel more substantial than insubstantial and to
establish his value and worth, in order definitively to avoid the
schizophrenia Laing describes, he needs a God who enforces his
new way of living, whose ways are his ways. He has already
left behind the God of his father back in England, a God who
rewards complacency in a complacent fashion. This new God
is to be an ingenious artisan, a force who in fashioning Crusoe's
life is both in and out of nature, like Crusoe in building and
expanding continuously. Looking at the economy of the novel,
we can say that what happens is Crusoe's conversion of God
from an antagonist into an ally.

   That kind of God begins to be revealed to Crusoe early in his
journal. There he records how he was astounded to find one day
ten or twelve ears of green barley growing by his cave and how
he took this for a miracle: '. . . that God had miraculously
caus'd this grain to grow without any help of seed sown, and
that it was directed purely for my sustenance on that wild
miserable place' (59). But then the world of mere circumstance
is discovered to be responsible; the barley has grown from some
chicken feed Crusoe shook out of a bag he wished to use.
Crusoe's 'religious thankfulness to God's providence' abates
'upon the discovering that all this was nothing but what was
common' (59). Now the mature Crusoe of a bit later in the
narrative learns to see this as a virtual miracle. God has used
this devious chain of circumstances to provide corn, 'as if it had
been dropt from heaven' (59). The mature Crusoe learns to see
the dialectic between secular detail and divine order and to see
that God works his uncommon ways with common things. It is
miraculous that some corn should have remained unspoiled,
that Crusoe should throw it out at that place, 'it being in the
shade of a high rock . . . whereas, if I had thrown it anywhere
else at that time, it had been burnt up and destroy'd' (59). The

world of mere circumstance is not transcended, but rather intensified in its importance. Just as Crusoe survives physically by watching for favourable forces in the chaotic appearances of nature, he survives on a psycho-spiritual level by learning to see God's presence in the minutest disposition of his circumstances. For us as readers, this is effectively a reinforcement and validation of our delight in the details of the narrative. Our attention is a means of participating in that world of richly satisfying order at every level, from Crusoe's domestic arrangements to the divine arrangements Crusoe perceives.

Crusoe's need for that God as something which validates his solitary being and provides an analogue for his order becomes evident in the next sequence as he falls ill with a fever and describes a dreadful dream of religious warning in which he sees a powerful and mysterious figure who threatens him with death. But the nightmare does not precipitate his religious crisis; it is simply a symptom of his bodily and spiritual confusion. Defoe makes Crusoe travel towards his conversion through the clinical reports of his physical illness. It is impossible even for us (practised as we are at such reactions) to experience that illness as a reductive comment on his spirituality, mainly because the narrative is so firmly committed to the factual aspects of Crusoe's survival and this 'spirituality' is so manifestly a necessary consequence of that factual survival. For the main conversion experience is not the dream, which as such belongs to the shapeless and potentially unmanageable aspect of experience that the book is out to dominate. The dream is clearly presented as the kind of experience that can be evoked but not described: the destroying angel in the dream is 'all over as bright as a flame, so that I could but just bear to look towards him; his countenance was most inexpressibly dreadful, impossible for words to describe' (65). What actually effects the conversion is Crusoe's search for tobacco, which he explains, with the solid verification the book specializes in, the Brazilians take 'for almost all distempers' (69). He finds the tobacco, along with a Bible, and then tells us in great detail how he experimented with taking the tobacco and, in a fuddled condition from his fever and the tobacco, opened the Bible 'casually' and read, 'Call on me in the day of trouble, and I will deliver, and thou shalt glorify me' (70). Even at so dramatic a moment, Crusoe continues to report circumstances and to describe alternatively his physical treatment and its results and the accompanying clarity and leisure for religious meditation: 'while I was thus gathering strength, my thoughts run exceedingly upon this scripture, *I will deliver thee*' (71). Crusoe delivers himself at last be meditating upon the situation and the text; he has been delivered from sickness, if not from the island.

Once again, Crusoe's immersion in the minutest facts of his existence provides the solution and enables him to survive. Sickness, the most obvious kind of victimization of an individual by circumstance, becomes a means of self-knowledge and eventual freedom. Sickness gives Crusoe the opportunity to report his symptoms, to distance himself from his physical and psychological self, for his sickness induces a kind of delirium. Crusoe is able in his narrative to treat himself as a thing, as something which because of its weakness can enter into the flow of objects and events which constitutes natural reality. Once in that reality, Crusoe can be led by an exact and complicated but entirely visible chain of circumstances stretching back in his history towards the tobacco and the Bible; he can observe himself getting better and see himself in the process of regaining health as participating in the partially benign forces that God inserts into nature. Heretofore, Crusoe observed for his own survival, marked carefully how external phenomena can be made to yield human direction and bent carefully to human purpose. Now he himself, body and soul, joins that company of natural phenomena. He observes 'himself', he achieves by sickness the perspective that Hegel called the 'master'. Part of himself remains the 'slave', indeed the point is that part of him becomes for the first time entirely perceived in his narrative as the slave of circumstance, committed fully and clearly to a chain of events going back to his origins. He has always been part of that chain, but as readers of the sickness–conversion sequence we are being involved in the operative reality of that chain and in the simultaneous freedom implicit in our and Crusoe's consciousness of that necessity and co-operation with it. We and Crusoe join God in co-operating with that chain of circumstances, for God inserts his purpose (i.e. Crusoe's conversion) into circumstances without violating their natural logic.

Crusoe's exact description of his return to health and his examination of the word 'deliverance' are worth looking at, since they reveal quite explicitly how he achieves freedom by perfect submission to those circumstances:

But as I was discouraging my self with such thoughts, it occurr'd to my mind that I pored so much upon my deliverance from the main affliction, that I disregarded the deliverance I had receiv'd; and *I was, as it were, made to ask my self* such questions as these, viz. Have I not been deliver'd, and wonderfully too, from sickness? from the most distress'd condition that could be, and that was so frightful to me? and what notice had I taken of it? Had I done my part? God had deliver'd me, but I had not glorify'd Him; that is to say, I had not own'd and been thankful for that as a deliverance, and how cou'd I expect greater deliverance?

This touch'd my heart very much, and immediately I kneel'd down and gave God thanks aloud for my recovery from my sickness. (71, my italics)

Necessarily, Crusoe talks to himself, but it is circumstance that forces him to ask the crucial questions of himself. He is no longer casting an account, as we observed him earlier in a more independent and crude ethical phase; he is himself part of an account. Before, Crusoe had balanced circumstances, splitting them into positive and negative, debit and credit. Here he becomes part of God's ledger, owing certain services for certain services. It is a tremendous relief, a validation of what had been an entirely personal survival. And the next day while reading the New Testament, Crusoe reads another text whose relevance completes the conversion experience: '*He is exalted a Prince and a Saviour, to give repentance, and to give remission.* I threw down the book, and with my heart as well as my hands lifted up to heaven, in a kind of extasy of joy, I cry'd out aloud, "Jesus, thou son of David, Jesus, thou exalted Prince and Saviour, give me repentance!" ' (72.) Crusoe is 'converted' into a petitioner, changed from an omnicompetent engineer into a primitive and fearful supplicant. But we know as readers that he experiences this extravagant and conventional dependence in a position of radically complete security. He does not, we remember, fall ill until his habitation is complete and secure: his walls have been finished; the wrecked ship has been systematically stripped of all that can be used and we hear no more of it. Structurally, his sickness can be regarded as a guilty response to his assertive survival, the complete opposite of the miracle of independent action, a kind of compensatory withdrawal into formless passivity and a desire for validation of the order established by the self.

The conversion, in fact, enables Crusoe to leave his paranoid seclusion and to convert his island from a prison into a garden. From this point on, Crusoe turns to the island itself, exploring it, domesticating it, and indeed enjoying it in various ways. The self, liberated from survival by a reciprocal relationship with an 'other', is free to gratify itself. Crusoe experiences power for the first time, 'a secret kind of pleasure (tho' mixt with my other afflicting thoughts) to think that this was all my own, that I was king and lord of all this country indefeasibly, and had a right of possession' (74). Now the countryside appears 'so fresh, so green, so flourishing, every thing being in a constant verdure or flourish of spring, that it looked like a planted garden' (74). In all this, the structure emerges only as something which is suspended in the tentative resolutions of the narrative. Crusoe's condition 'began now to be, tho' not less miserable as to my way of living, yet much easier to my mind' (72). In time (eleven days we are told) and within the qualifications of psychological relativity, he takes a survey of the island and begins to enumerate its positive side. Like Marvell's sojourner in the garden, he finds 'mellons upon the ground in great abundance, and grapes upon the trees; the vines had spread indeed over the trees, and the clusters of grapes were just now in their prime, very ripe and rich' (74). But quite unlike Marvell's Adam, he notes that this is an equivocal paradise, the grapes are dangerous if eaten as they are. He remembers several Englishmen in Barbary killed by 'fluxes and feavers' from eating such. Crusoe converts them into raisins by drying them, 'wholesom as agreeable to eat' (74).

That detail of Crusoe's Eden can stand as a perfect example of Crusoe's new condition: the recipient of divine deliverance, he understands that God is only partially present in what he gives, and so he converts or refines nature into that which sustains and nourishes. Having himself experienced pure activity and pure passivity, he can now in his lordship of the island set about reconciling or balancing the contradiction to be found everywhere upon it. It is a new step from the cunning observation and defensive building he did when he first arrived, and it is also unlike the passive stasis of his sickness. His new condition is the synthesis which results from the thesis and antithesis of pure action and pure passivity. This part of the book can therefore display Crusoe as the perfect mediator. Having reconciled contradiction in himself, he moves among contradictions, resolving them. He discovers that the island has wet and dry seasons, he builds a 'villa' for pleasure to balance his secure fortress for survival, he tames wild things (a parrot, then goats), he despises the surplus value of his gold and celebrates useful things but keeps his gold anyway, in effect reconciling the two systems of value. He is able to speak jauntily 'of my reign or my captivity, which you please' (101). Such activities enable us to see a meaning in Crusoe's new condition which makes it more than the simple religious tranquillity he claims it is. Crusoe sings a *contemptus mundi* tune even while we rejoice in his expanding and ever more orderly island world. Crusoe's independence is really his achievement of the Hegelian mastership; he has done with the thing and is not contained in its being as a thing but 'enjoys it without qualification and without reserve. The aspect of its independence he leaves to the servant, who labors upon it.'[18] There is a part of Crusoe which 'labors' upon the island in these various and fascinating ways, but the true gratification Crusoe derives from it is a matter of his freedom from the fact of the island, the island as a constellation of forces and things which threaten his being in their natural formlessness, their character as undifferentiated and (as we know) potentially dangerous phenomena. It is his mastership and the authentic gratification it implies that are being asserted when Crusoe describes his spiritual indifference:

In the middle of this work [he has been building what will be an unusable boat], I finish'd my fourth year in this place, and kept my anniversary with the same devotion, and with as much comfort as ever before; for by a constant study and serious application of the word of God and by the assistance of His grace, I gain'd a different knowledge from what I had before. I entertain'd different notions of things. I look'd now upon the world as a thing remote, which I had nothing to do with, no expectation from, and indeed no desires

18 *The Phenomenology of the Spirit*, p. 405.

about: in a word, I had nothing indeed to do with it, nor was ever like to have; so I thought it look'd as we may perhaps look upon it hereafter, viz. as a place I had liv'd in, but was come out of it, and well might I say, as Father Abraham to Dives, *Between me and thee is a great gulph fix'd.* (94–5)

Significantly, it is at this point that Crusoe's self-consciousness develops to the extent that he is able to think in coherent autobiographical terms. Previously, he had only been able to look back at flashes of his past, to regret this or that imprudence or to bewail a present deficiency. Now he reviews his life, considers the causes of his wandering and of his relative in-difference to God and finds at last that God has forgiven him and is in process of showing him mercy. His new sense of self, his new mastership, provides access to the Puritan world-view, with its emblems, types, allusions, and metaphors,[19] and that scheme provides his autobiography with a shape by giving him a coherent past. But that world-view is in Crusoe's case expres-sion of an inner coherence which can now recapture the past and enjoy the spectacle of the self surviving into the present. He spends, he tells us, 'whole hours, I may say whole days' thinking what would have become of him without the goods from the ship. The picture that holds Crusoe's attention is his significant anti-type, either dead or worse, a 'meer savage; that if I had kill'd a goat or a fowl, by any contrivance, I had no way to flea or open them, or part the flesh from the skin and the bowels, or to cut it up; but must gnaw it with my teeth and pull it with my claws like a beast' (96). The graphic insistence of this vision in the context of Crusoe's order and what we know of its establishment tells us that Crusoe's thankfulness is an indirect expression of his triumph and satisfaction over avoid-ing that hideous alternative. Crusoe can safely invoke Elijah's survival as a type of his own; he intends no irony and considers the relative benignity of his environment as quite the equivalent

---

[19] Crusoe comes to these meanings only gradually, but J. Paul Hunter is certainly justified in complaining that past emphasis upon Defoe's 'realism' has 'obscured the emblematic meaning of Crusoe's physical activities.' Hunter's point, however, that Defoe's realism 'continually makes his hero express his spiritual condition by physical actions' is implicitly reductive and neglects the situation in which the self comes to earn the right to indulge in such exegesis. See *The Reluctant Pilgrim: Defoe's Emblematic Method and Quest for Form in Robinson Crusoe* (Baltimore, 1966), pp. 189–90.

of the prophet's ravens. Praising the mildness of his God-given environment is a way of neutralizing what Crusoe fears most, what he stands most clearly against and what we have already defined as the turbulent world of experience *per se* that the novel posits and then refines: 'I found no ravenous beast, no furious wolves or tygers to threaten my life, no venemous creatures, or poisonous, which I might feed on to my hurt, no savages to murther and devour me' (98). What is chiefly of interest, what we as readers experience through Crusoe's thankful auto-biographical pause, is the antithesis between Crusoe as atavistic savage or beast and Crusoe as orderly master of himself and his island. That is the opposition that informs this section, and our calm experience of it is the culmination of our experience so far as readers and satisfied onlookers. In fact, what Crusoe really learns to do in every way through his conversion is to experience by means of contradiction, to keep before himself (in his terms) what he might have been if God had indeed abandoned him. To experience anything properly, that is to see through it and understand its meaning, the event must be doubled, seen as part of a system of alternatives. Of course, what that comes to for Crusoe is keeping before himself the image of various anti-Crusoes, the beast and savage at his fiercest, but also the Crusoe who fails to plan (building a boat too large to move to the water) or the 'rash and ignorant' pilot who finds his boat carried out to sea. In this temporarily hopeless state, Crusoe looks back at the island and reproaches himself with his 'unthankful temper, and how I had repin'd at my solitary condition; and now what would I give to be on shore there again! Thus we never see the true state of our condition till it is illustrated to us by its contraries, nor know how to value what we enjoy, but by the want of it' (102–3).

We are never very far from that central antithesis, especially in that stretch of the book from Crusoe's conversion to his discovery of the footprint. Crusoe in that time provides us with the most extensive descriptions of his technology; making clothes, boatbuilding, pot-making, basket weaving—culminating, within his own hierarchy, in the taming of wild goats. This last achievement is crucial for his comfort if not his survival, because his powder has run out. In his context, meat or game is not only an important food but a defining food; it is culturally superior to fish and grain and is part of his sustaining order. Crusoe's informal recapitulation of the history of civilization appears here at its most coherent, and the transition from the hunting to the domestication of animals for food is a momentous one in terms of establishing human control and regularity. It is at this point that Crusoe can speak, jokingly to be sure, of political power and of total domination of his island. In taming the goats, he possesses nature in a thoroughgoing way, exceeding the dominance implicit in agriculture, which is after all something of a co-operation with natural forces. 'It would have made a stoick smile to have seen me and my little family sit down to dinner; there was my majesty the prince and lord of the whole island; I had the lives of all my subjects at my absolute command; I could hang, draw, give liberty, and take it away, and no rebels among all my subjects' (109).

But to attend to the symmetry of this act and its place in the narrative is to see another and even more coherent principle in operation. Like all his technology but more clearly than any other act, the taming of the goats repeats Crusoe's own story; it is a re-enactment of the conversion of his own unruly nature (that fatal propension for wandering which began it all) by God, who catches Crusoe on the island and tames him the same way that Crusoe catches goats in a pit and tames them. Crusoe's entire career on the island as a bringer of order is, by extension, a taming of his externalized self. I am not suggesting that Defoe intended the goats as a 'symbol', or that Crusoe in any way transfers his guilt to them as scapegoats. As elsewhere in this study, I am positing a level of coherence which is below the consciousness or explicit intention of author and character and which is, rather, implicit in the reader's experience and which constitutes the system or language by which the book exists.

And it is precisely at this point in the narrative, when the island has been totally possessed by Crusoe, when it is fully an extension of himself, that he discovers the footprint on the beach. Crusoe has all along feared others, although his paranoia has diminished with his growing powers. That he should now find that he has indeed been in danger all along, that his possession and rule of the island are in some sense illusory is a recapitulation of the primal bourgeois scene. The free individual discovers that he is threatened by other individuals whose claim to freedom is as total as his own. Crusoe's fear and ultimate rage are compounded of classic Hobbesian aggression and jealousy. Moreover, those rivals will turn out to be cannibals, that is, nothing less than full-fledged embodiments of the anti-type of himself that haunts Crusoe's imagination and sustains him in his drive for order and towards civilisation. Crusoe has established 'culture' in nature, but nature returns with a vengeance in the person of the cannibals.

It is worth noticing that there is no novelistic preparation for the footprint, no transition is offered, merely an abrupt new topic: 'But now I come to a new scene of my life' (113). The abruptness is appropriate in several ways, the first and most obvious one of which may be described as psychological. It is accurate and inevitable that Crusoe's serenity should lead to turbulence, that he should face the greatest danger when he is totally secure. But the inevitable irony of desire thus uncovered is really a way of proving the inevitability of bourgeois society: serenity need not be eternally followed by its psychological opposite, but it must always be so in a bourgeois society where the price of freedom, as politicians still stay, is eternal vigilance. Psychological patterns are insisted upon when they coincide with social patterns.

On another level, the abruptness reveals the structure I have been talking about. *Robinson Crusoe* deals in extremes; it presents a world where one state is transformed into its opposite and where the secret of survival is a talent for changing violent transpositions into gradual adaptations. Crusoe is here once again literally hurled back on to the world of mere nature, and that thrust from absolute solitude to dangerous society, from pastoral isolation and mock empire to a realistic state of war, is enacted and heightened dramatically by this violent shift in the action. What Crusoe must learn to do in this section is to repeat the stabilizing and possessive operation he has performed first upon himself and then upon his island, and now upon others, that is, upon society.

That situation and the beginnings of the controlling operation are implicit in Crusoe's rendition of his shock upon seeing the footprint:

But after innumerable fluttering thoughts, like a man perfectly confus'd and out of my self, I came home to my fortification, not

feeling, as we say, the ground I went on, but terrify'd to the last
degree, looking behind me at every two or three steps, mistaking
every bush and tree, and fancying every stump at a distance to be a
man; nor is it possible to describe how many various shapes affrighted
imagination represented things to me in, how many wild ideas were
found every moment in my fancy, and what strange unaccountable
whimsies came into my thoughts by the way. (113)

Characteristically, Crusoe refuses to reproduce confused
emotions and delivers a careful rendition of the external
facts of behaviour; he sketches a scenario of movements and
alludes to internal disorder too vast to render. Note the apology
('as we say') for the imprecise, colloquially figurative expression
he needs to describe the physical feeling of terror: 'not feeling
. . . the ground I went on' (113). He is out of himself and surrounded by others; the most intense subjectivity induced by the
fear of others eliminates the balanced, 'objective' subjectivity
Crusoe has painfully acquired, and he experiences himself as a
subject pure and simple, a wildly erratic collection of responses
to threatening stimuli. The re-introduction of 'spontaneous'
subjectivity reveals definitively for us and Crusoe the dangers
and the persistence of nature.

The ensuing long debate that occupies Crusoe for many pages
until the last defeat of the cannibals is still another kind of
accounting whereby Crusoe seeks to escape this destructive
spontaneity, to exhaust reality by listing its alternative formulations, hoping to stand at last quite apart from their world of
cause and effect. What Crusoe really seeks, in short, is to re-
enact the mastery he has already achieved. The beginning of
that distancing, the theoretical underpinning for his autonomy,
is laid out at the beginnings of the internal debate: 'How strange
a chequer work of providence is the life of man! and by what
secret differing springs are the affections hurry'd about as
differing circumstances present! To day we love what to morrow
we hate; to day we seek what to morrow we shun; to day we
desire what to morrow we fear, nay, even tremble at the
apprehensions of; this was exemplify'd in me at this time in the
most lively manner imaginable' (114–15). On one level, this
is mere sententious verbalizing, Christian stoicism of an un-
interesting sort. But in the imaginative context of Crusoe's
problem within the narrative, it is an anatomy of experience

which enables him to stand both in and out of experience, to be in those contraries and eventually to stand apart from them in the moment of action which is a magical combination of both.

For what Crusoe does in the debate is to explore those contradictions by verbalizing them intensely. After seeing the cannibals, he jumps rapidly from violent and eloquent moral disgust and elaborate schemes for destroying them to impeccably enlightened anthropological and historicist tolerance to clear-headed self-preservation. He embraces all these positions with equal fervour, seems to hold them all with equal if temporary conviction. His final decision is to do nothing, to leave it all to God, to obey impulse: in his words, to obey 'a secret hint . . . a strange impression upon the mind, from we know not what springs' (128). Thus, when the moment for action finally comes, none of the coherent plans or postures is quite relevant. Crusoe acts, to be sure, but he acts because of the totally unforeseen and purely haphazard circumstances he is by this time so at home in. Action is a reflex which has little to do with consciousness. Action, in fact, is a matter of watching the unpredictable flow of events for an opening, of co-operating with events at the moment when they will serve, that is, of observation and submission such as Crusoe has used in his previous triumphs. Throughout this long period of suspenseful watching and contradictory planning, Crusoe is changed from a planter-colonist into a fearful observer as much of his own shifting desires and fantasies as of the coastline for cannibal enemies. He comes close to disastrous action, almost reverts to his first condition as a man of naïvely aggressive action: 'All my calm of mind in my resignation to providence, and waiting the issue of the dispositions of Heaven, seem'd to be suspended, and I had, as it were, no power to turn my thoughts to any thing, but to the project of a voyage to the main, which came upon me with such force, and such an impetuosity of desire, that it was not to be resisted' (144). Such direct human assertion is a vulgar surrender to nature; it reduces reality to a simple challenge issued by nature and places the actor in an impossible heroic situation in which he must struggle directly with oppressive circumstances. Survival in Defoe's narratives typically involves a strong temptation towards such action. Indeed the central problem of all the narratives is to find a mode of action which mediates between the impossible heroic and the untenable actual.

Crusoe is saved from the novelistic disaster of simple heroism by a dream, a remarkably prophetic one. He dreams of 'two canoes and eleven savages' who bring another one to kill and eat. The prisoner escapes and Crusoe takes him in: '. . . he came running into my little thick grove before my fortification, to hide himself; and that I seeing him alone, and not perceiving that the others sought him that way, show'd myself to him, and smiling upon him, encourag'd him; that he kneel'd down to me, seeming to pray me to assist him; upon which I shew'd my ladder, made him go up, and carry'd him into my cave, and he became my servant' (145). In his dream, Crusoe hopes this servant will guide him to the mainland and escape. His dream strengthens him in his resolve to do nothing directly, for it is a curiously unreal dream in which Crusoe does not really participate but simply watches action with a cool detachment totally foreign to normal dream experience. Crusoe's smile in the dream is a sign of the serenity he is about to achieve, a pleased instinctive recognition of the resolution of his dilemma: doing nothing will involve him in the ultimate act of control— escape. The frantic internal debate over a course of action is resolved by the dream; the ultimate danger represented by the cannibals is to be converted into the source of ultimate deliverance. By standing still and watching the most extreme of his circumstances, Crusoe will be liberated from them. Awake, he realizes that planning is useless, circumstances will provide: 'But as I could pitch upon no probable means for it, so I resolv'd to put myself upon the watch, to see them when they came on shore, and leave the rest to the event, taking such measures as the opportunity should present, let be what would be' (146).

Crusoe's resolution is the most explicit statement of the central satisfaction of his book. His strategy for survival is a means of establishing a relationship between the free self and the determined event so that the self can act upon events and in reaction to events without losing its autonomy. Indeed, the deep fantasy that Crusoe and his story serve is the dream of freedom perfectly reconciled with necessity, the self using

necessity to promote its freedom. Crusoe builds up at this point
to his greatest and most daring exploit in the enactment of the
dream of freedom, and the pervasive antithesis between circumstances and freedom is here at its sharpest. What he proposes (fittingly in a dream, proposing without asserting) is the
startling exploitation of his own anti-type, for the cannibals
are an externalization of an anti-Crusoe, the natural man he
has repressed by various means.

For once, Crusoe is eager, and his readiness endures through
the year and a half he tells us he had to wait. Time of this sort
is meaningless in *Robinson Crusoe*; the 'years' serve as breaks
and transitions between crises. As readers, we feel the stress
of ordering experience which rushes by Crusoe: a world of moving details and obstacles rather than the lingering static existence he claims he endured. But even Crusoe's record at this
point is of impatience: '*But* the longer it seem'd to be delay'd,
the more eager I was for it; in a word, I was not at first so
careful to shun the sight of these savages, and avoid being seen
by them, as I was now eager to be upon them' (146).[20]

The long break in Crusoe's personal time between his resolve and his opportunity does work, however, to make him
surprised when the cannibals actually appear. Moreover,
opportunity when it comes never matches plans, so Crusoe
finds not the eleven of his dream but thirty. These and subsequent events Crusoe perceives through his telescope, and he
reports everything he sees by that means in suitably distanced
language, full of the tentative and objective features of vision
from a distance. He is really in this scene physically apart from
events even as he is tremendously concerned in them; his
perspective is literally necessary but structurally coherent as
well. Crusoe is on his way to enacting literally what he has been
doing thus far in various indirect ways. He becomes at the
moment of Friday's deliverance exactly like the deity who

---

[20] In one sense, this is a mere psychological truism, the natural shape of behaviour
for a person in Crusoe's circumstances. But the psychological truth of Crusoe's
moments is merely the top layer of his reality for us. The ultimate source of his
excitement is the hope of deliverance, and that deliverance in the light of his
status as a hero of narrative must be a deliverance with freedom. Crusoe, I think
we have to remind ourselves, cannot be experienced simply as a man on an island;
he is *the* man on *the* island. The critical *locus classicus* for that point is Watt's chapter
in *The Rise of the Novel*, 'Robinson Crusoe, Individualism and the Novel', pp. 60–92.

delivered him: suddenly visible, powerful, and obviously mysterious in that power. He acquires at the moment of action, that moment when he sees the lone savage pursued by two others, a sense of divine purpose, or, better, his impulses are for the first time in his story fully acceptable as divine urges. Crusoe here begins his final transformation into a quasi-divine, autonomous hero whose desires are no longer self-destructive in their determinate independence but fulfilling and self-constructive in their free dependence on reality. Friday swims from his pursuers (two of them), and at that precise moment when the unmanageable three pursuers are reduced to a workable two, Crusoe is struck with the inevitability of his action: 'It came now very warmly upon my thoughts, and indeed irresistibly, that now was my time to get me a servant, and perhaps a companion or assistant; and that I was call'd plainly by Providence to save this poor creature's life' (147). The universe has been dramatically realigned; the inevitable is now exactly parallel to Crusoe's desires and needs. By mastering the art of observation, by rejecting in effect all assertive and personal action, Crusoe (telescope in hand) achieves a divine perspective and his action coincides perfectly with the bizarre swing of events.

As a reconstructed cannibal, Friday in his conversion repeats the taming of the goats. He is Crusoe's heretofore menacing anti-type now completely domesticated, and Crusoe is now literally the master in acquiring an actual slave. The split whereby part of him worked on nature is now healed, as Friday is easily taught the various techniques for running the island's economy that Crusoe had previously mastered. Crusoe retains the mastery, of course, in every sense. They are his techniques and his island; Friday works, but Crusoe possesses the labour and its meaning. Moreover, Friday retains enough of his ferocity and tribal hatred to assist Crusoe in his last acquisition of real political power in the defeat of the cannibals when they return with European captives.

Having in a real sense defeated the last recalcitrant part of himself in domesticating Friday, Crusoe is now able to treat the cannibals who return as an objective force which can be freely destroyed. In terms of the coherence of the narrative, it is for this reason that the cannibals appear this time with European captives. The sight of a white man bound and awaiting horrid consumption galvanizes Crusoe into action. He is released by his total mastery of himself from the complicating moral alternatives he posed when he first saw the cannibals. True, he gives us a highly condensed repetition of those moral alternatives when he first learns of the cannibals' arrival from Friday. But he places himself with new confidence in an aggressively close position (within range of his weapons) to their feast, 'that I might observe their barbarous feast, and that I would act then as God should direct; but that unless something offer'd that was more a call to me than yet I knew of, I would not meddle with them' (169). To say that Crusoe's immediate and impetuous attack to save a white man is a racist instinct is true but not the whole truth. The hapless Spaniard about to be devoured is a surrogate Crusoe in a way, for Crusoe can now view the island as entirely his, and an attack on another white man is an attack on himself, on a community that he is now fit to preside over by virtue of his mastery. He recognizes himself in that bearded man, for at that moment he becomes the proprietor of the island and his sovereignty is threatened by the atrocity. Friday hates these cannibals already; he is, Crusoe notes, 'in a state of war with those very particular people; and it was lawful for him to attack them' (169). Crusoe enters into a state of war with those cannibals because he has achieved the requisite freedom for meaningful opposition to them, what Friday has by means of his history and membership in a community. Crusoe now has his own equivalent to that history, a coherent being in his island rather than a mere defensive relationship to it.

The huge battle with the cannibals and their bloody defeat is only the first in the climactic series of consistently one-sided triumphs which marks this last phase of Crusoe's career.[21] Crusoe admits that his enemies are so surprised and so frightened by the action of the fire-arms that they 'had no more

[21] Crucial throughout this analysis is the simple fact that things happen in *Robinson Crusoe* in a certain sequence rather than in any other order. The sequence we read yields a coherent progression of transformations, much as a sentence is what linguists call a transformation of raw information into the resolving order of language. Crusoe's book presents a series of experiences—both the events themselves and the narration which delivers those events to us—and that series constitutes a coherent sequence, an extended sentence. The trouble up to now is that critics have used the partial perspectives of religion, economics, psychology, and literary history and missed or blocked out important parts of that sequence.

power to attempt their own escape, than their flesh had to resist our shot' (171). In other words, Crusoe's triumph is not really or at least not completely the result of bravery but of the power and surprise he commands and the technological world over which he alone on his island presides. He moves, once again, like his God, unexpectedly and irresistibly. On the surface, Crusoe's new political power which follows the battle is adventitious; he refers to it in jest: 'My island was now peopled, and I thought my self very rich in subjects; and it was a merry reflection which I frequently made, how like a king I look'd' (175). His real power is in his confident movements: his absolutely sure sense of what to do and where to station himself in relation to events and phenomena. His power has the techno-logical-natural inevitability of the bullets which pierce the flesh of the terrified cannibals.

When his last great adventure on the island arrives, when a ship suddenly appears in his harbour, Crusoe's caution is thus appropriately a divine instinct: 'I had some secret doubts hung about me, I cannot tell from whence they came, bidding me keep upon my guard' (182). He argues darkly that such in-tuitions are proof of a world of supervising spirits. No matter that Crusoe's reasons for caution are absolutely sound: 'it occurr'd to me to consider what business an English ship could have in that part of the world, since it was not the way to or from any part of the world where the English had any traffick; and I knew there had been no storms to drive them in there, as in distress; and that if they were English really, it was most probable that they were here upon no good design; and that I had better continue as I was, than fall into the hands of thieves and murtherers' (182). Crusoe is able to jump neatly from the natural cunning explicit in such observation to the ideological coherence which transforms such sagacity into a link between heaven and earth. Crusoe feels his power, feels a kind of current of energy running through him from natural fact and random circumstance to divine ordering. He is the centre, a heroic mediator of a special kind at this point.

That mediation is nowhere clearer than in the subsequent events. Crusoe sees three men put ashore by mutineers, and their condition, he remarks, is exactly like his when he first landed on the island. He is now in a position to rescue them

just as he was rescued by providence in various ways; he becomes providence in effect. When he confronts them, the
marvellous audacity implicit in Crusoe's new part in the drama
of deliverance surfaces in the dialogue:

'Gentlemen,' said I, 'do not be surpriz'd at me; perhaps you may
have a friend near you when you did not expect it.' 'He must be
sent directly from heaven then,' said one of them very gravely to me,
and pulling off his hat at the same time to me, 'for our condition is
past the help of man.' 'All help is from heaven, sir,' said I. (185)

Naturally, Crusoe disavows his powers and expresses only formal
confidence in God's wisdom. But the serene efficiency with
which he masterminds the fight against the mutiny is an
unmistakable token of the power he now embodies. Crusoe
invokes desperation as the psychological source of that serenity,
but we know that he has long ago in our experience of him
passed through desperation, that his entire story is an effort to
exclude the kind of frantic movement within circumstances that
desperation implies. His very description of desperation changes
it into the calm power we as onlookers are given. Crusoe senses
that he is part of a larger pattern, that his story has taken its
final shape and established its inevitable direction, and that
his and God's purposes are inseparable. The captain is ap-
prehensive, but Crusoe smiles.[22]

I smil'd at him, and told him that men in our circumstances were
past the operation of fear: that seeing almost every condition that
could be, was better than that which we were suppos'd to be in, we
ought to expect that the consequence, whether death or life, would
be sure to be a deliverance. I ask'd him what he thought of the
circumstances of my life, and whether a deliverance were not worth
venturing for. 'And where, sir,' said I, 'is your belief of my being
preserv'd here on purpose to save your life, which elevated you a
little while ago? For my part,' said I, 'there seems to be but one
thing amiss in all the prospect of it.' 'What's that?' says he. 'Why,'
said I, ''tis that as you say, there are three or four honest fellows
among them, which should be spar'd; had they been all of the
wicked part of the crew, I should have thought God's providence
had singled them out to deliver them into your hands; for depend

---

[22] J. R. Moore notes that 'Defoe smiled often and laughed rarely' and attributed
that habit to many of his characters. See *Daniel Defoe: Citizen of the Modern World*,
p. 73. Crusoe, at least, only smiles at moments of power.

upon it, every man of them that comes a-shore are our own, and shall die or live as they behave to us.' (189)

We know from following the sequence of Crusoe's career and watching his successive elevation to higher and higher forms of mastery (the self, the environment, animals, natives, and now Europeans) that he is speaking out of more than a desperate need to leave the island. What we enjoy most as readers and what is truest in all this sequence against the mutineers is our sense of Crusoe's serene omnicompetence, his ability to be above circumstances while immersed in them. Crusoe is so much the master in this passage that he can speak of their situation as only superficially dangerous; it looks dangerous only to an ignorant observer: 'almost every condition that could be, was better than that which we were *suppos'd to be in*'. Crusoe knows his power so exactly that he wonders that some of the mutineers on shore are honest fellows who must be spared. The whole lot, in his view, seem clearly meant to be instruments in his plan rather than individuals with their own fates and power to save themselves.

The actual battle with the mutineers repeats the strategies and satisfactions of the two encounters with the cannibals, although here the manœuvres are appropriately more complicated and extensive, given the higher sophistication of his adversaries. In directing this battle, Crusoe is still quite recognizable as a human imitation of providence: distant, inscrutable, and omnipotent. Matters are arranged so that the captain represents Crusoe as the 'governor and commander' of the island; the effectiveness of their counter-attack depends upon Crusoe's exactly engineered fiction of irresistible power, both military and legal: 'In a word, they all laid down their arms, and begg'd their lives; and I sent the man that had parley'd with them, and two more, who bound them all; and then my great army of 50 men, which, particularly with those three, were all but eight, came up and seiz'd upon them all, and upon their boat, only that I kept myself and one more out of sight, for reasons of state' (194–5).

The pretence continues past the victory. We and Crusoe and his allies from the ship are all in on the elaborate masquerade in which Crusoe is not only transformed for immediate strategic purposes from castaway hermit to colonial proprietor but in which he is given the ship as his political right, clothed by the captain in appropriate European garb, and in which he even extends these outward ceremonies to actual judicial power over the mutineers. Crusoe's transformation is utterly complete; he dispenses justice as it was, in a sense, dispensed to him at the beginning of the island episode. He gives the mutineers the penance of island exile: 'I accordingly set them at liberty, and had them retire into the woods to the place whence they came, and I would leave them some fire arms, some ammunition, and some directions how they should live very well, if they thought fit' (200). Through all this, Crusoe's acting is suspiciously perfect. He shows them (twice) as evidence of his power the captain of the mutiny hanging at the yard-arm of the ship. He pretends to correct the real captain and reminds him that these men are 'my prisoners, not his; and that seeing I had offered them so much favour, I would be as good as my word; and that if he did not think fit to consent to it, I would set them at liberty, as I found them; and if he did not like it, he might take them again if he could catch them' (200). Crusoe plays at power and never has to take it quite seriously, simply because he has achieved so much of it. One must never admit to one's power and freedom, since that would falsify their essentially dynamic and relational nature. Power and freedom are states of equilibrium between the self and a constantly unruly and threatening environment and/or society. The elaborate games that Crusoe plays as he ends his story are not only strategies for managing the mutineers; they represent an awareness in the narrative of the nature of freedom. They repeat on that trickiest and most difficult level of reality—the social and political—the games that Crusoe has had to master all through his story in order to 'survive', that is, to achieve a special kind of autonomy.

Once Crusoe leaves the island (now a full-fledged colony), the rest is rather tedious accounting of the wealth he richly deserves for his extraordinary feat of survival and mastery. It is wealth which has earned itself in Crusoe's absence. He has only innocently fought for his life but has been rewarded with great wealth he did not directly seek. That is a perfect and beautifully appropriate conclusion for a capitalist hero, combining freedom and innocence in a manner rather difficult to achieve in the real economic world. But Crusoe is faced with a dilemma now that he is back in the world where that inno- cence can hardly hope to be preserved: 'I had more care upon my head now, than I had in my silent state of life in the island, where I wanted nothing but what I had, and had nothing but what I wanted: whereas I had now a great charge upon me, and my business was how to secure it. I had ne'er a cave now to hide my money in, or a place where it might lie without lock or key . . . on the contrary, I knew not where to put it, or who to trust with it' (207). Crusoe never solves that problem. In his sequel, he goes wandering and trading, moving incessantly to maintain his (and our) sense of innocent mastery. But having lost the island and its free space, he loses our interest.

# III

## Captain Avery and Captain Singleton: Revisions of Popular Legend

Rome the Mistress of the World, was no more at first than a Refuge for Thieves and Outlaws; and if the Progress of our Pyrates had been equal to their Beginning, had they all united, and settled in some of those Islands, they might, by this Time, have been honoured with the Name of Commonwealth, and no Power in those Parts of the World could have been able to dispute it with them.

'Captain Charles Johnson',
*A General History of the Robberies and Murders of the most notorious Pyrates* (1724). Attributed to Defoe.

ROBINSON CRUSOE is the complex hero of what everyone now admits is a complex book. He inhabits a number of distinct eighteenth-century roles, secular and religious, active and contemplative: intrepid traveller, planter, entrepreneur, repentant sinner, and visionary contemplative. The case seems remarkably otherwise with *Captain Singleton* (1720), whose characters and events are nothing if not simple and direct: a series of adventures in Africa and on the high seas of piracy, starring Captain Bob and featuring a large and colourful cast. *Robinson Crusoe* obviously cares about moral questions and treats experience as an interaction of motives and circumstances. But *Crusoe's* ultimate concerns may be properly described as existential rather than moralistic, and underneath its diversity and moral ambiguity it is most about self-assertion and the accommodation of nature to man and of social ideology to personal reality. *Captain Singleton*, a few moralistic touches aside, is a fantasy of power and joyous acquisition, revealing in more direct fashion the energies and ambitions of the bourgeois self that are obliquely rendered in *Robinson Crusoe*. The narrative problem in the latter is to allow Crusoe to achieve and enjoy freedom and power without violating the restrictions of a moral and religious ideology which defines the individual as less than autonomous. The formal and ideological problem in *Captain*

*Singleton* is of the same kind but with a greater degree of difficulty: to participate in the extravagant power and freedom of the pirate adventurer within the limited universe of mimetic historical narrative.[1] Such overt autonomy as the pirate possesses subverts the limitations of realistic narrative, and those limitations are the guardians of the central fantasy of secret and indirect power delivered by Defoe's fiction. The solution his fiction provides here and elsewhere is a mediating consciousness, a narrative which sees to it that its hero is both in and out of circumstances, placed in his personal history so that he can work his way out of it. *Captain Singleton* is thereby a work of some complexity, concerned like *Robinson Crusoe* to enact events in order to place its hero within the liberating dialectic of mimetic narrative.

Crusoe, we have seen, is a 'converter', a character who transforms the erratic energies of the self and of nature into acceptable and useful currents. But he has that large repertory of roles to play and safe positions to occupy; the will to power that he represents can safely retreat and reside in the active and contemplative sterotypes of the story as it unfolds. *Captain Singleton* is, in this way, a much bolder attempt, for the story it begins with is the folk myth of piracy, a fantasy which seems to have acquired its particular resonances of demonic power in the early eighteenth century. The late seventeenth- and early eighteenth-century European pirates apparently became in the popular imagination an extension, utterly logical and therefore thrilling, of the implications of economic individualism. The task in *Captain Singleton* is to deliver that pirate fantasy but to deliver us as well from its crude and unacceptable demonism, crude because of its vulgar heroic asssertion of self and its thorough denial of limitation and imperfection. The pirate and his story defy circumstances openly. He acquires fabulous sums and commits unspeakable crimes with splendid

---

[1] Manuel Schonhorn has observed that *Captain Singleton* 'bears little similarity to those piratical records it was intended to resemble'. He concludes that the disposition of events in the story 'dilutes beyond distinction what is falsely represented as a traditional buccaneering narrative filled with daring adventures and piracies'. My point in this chapter is to observe the way that 'dilution' takes place and to suggest that it is more of a significant blending of two narrative types and purposes. See 'Defoe's *Captain Singleton:* A Reassessment with Observations', *Papers on Language and Literature*, 7 (1971), 39, 47.

and guiltless ferocity. He establishes a free society of pirate comrades in which the power of the group and the autonomy of the individual coexist perfectly. In short, the pirate denies reality on every level: moral, economic, and political. The novel can hardly tolerate any of this, since its public task (and justification) is to establish reality, to insist upon limitation, imperfection, and derivation. *Captain Singleton* accomplishes this public task by the various sequences and limitations of mimetic narration, but in so doing it achieves its other goal of promoting the immanently utopian consciousness that is the real end of fiction. More clearly than in any other of Defoe's narratives, mimetic technique is here revealed for what it is, an instrument for achieving the pleasures of total control, an acceptable means for reader and hero to dominate the world.

Scholars have long realized that Defoe's operations on his source materials were in the direction of credibility, in this case explicitly away from the thrilling improbabilities of pirate legend. Arthur Secord noted that *Captain Singleton* was based largely on the life of Captain John Avery, perhaps the most notorious pirate of the early eighteenth century.[2] But Defoe's immediate source seems to have been a version of Avery's story which he had himself published the year before, *The King of the Pirates* (1719). The sources for that work were what Secord calls 'common rumor' and an anonymous pamphlet life of Avery of 1709, *The Life and Adventures of Captain John Avery, the Famous English Pirate, (rais'd from a Cabbin-Boy to a King) now in possession of Madagascar*.[3] The progress from that short pamphlet and the common rumour implicit in it to Defoe's *King of the Pirates* and thence to *Captain Singleton* is a highly revealing one. The total movement is not only from the fanciful to the documentary, but from the naïve and unconscious force of a popular hero to the complex freedom of a novelistic hero, in short from folk tale to sophisticated bourgeois myth. Moreover, the movement from the *King of the Pirates* to *Captain Singleton* is itself of interest; the latter, much longer and elaborate,

[2] *The Narrative Method of Defoe* (New York, 1963, first published 1924), p. 161.
[3] Secord, p. 140. Another possible source has been suggested, a pamphlet of 1696: *The Tryals of Joseph Dawson, Edward Forseith . . . For Several Piracies and Robberies by them Committed, in the Company of Every the Grand Pirate, near the Coasts of the East Indies . . . Giving an Account of their Villainous Robberies and Barbarities*. See Manuel Schonhorn, 'Defoe's Pirates: A New Source', *RES*, 14 (1963), 387.

represents a subtle and gradual version of the rather abruptly intelligent consciousness of the former.

As its title makes clear, *The King of the Pirates: Being an account of the Famous Enterprizes of Captain Avery, the Mock King of Madagascar; with his Rambles and Piracies, wherein all the Sham Accounts formerly published of him are detected*[4] has specific targets, not simply rivals in the presentation of wonders but liars, distorters of the plain truth. The work is a small example of the autobiographical mimicry of a quasi-historical character which was Defoe's master strategy. This convention by its very nature requires a plain frankness and un-heroic introspection which clashes immediately with the established popular legend surrounding a notorious pirate like Avery. Defoe's 'editorial' preface to these memoirs shows that he is aware of the deflation implicit in the method itself, for he remarks that 'there is always a great difference between what men say of themselves, and what others say for them, when they come to write historically of the transactions of their lives' (xv). Personal history and actual commerce ('transactions') are opposed to legendary vagueness. From the first, the reader is informed in every way possible that this is to be a sober and judicious account which will appeal to him because he has the clear perception and steady judgement which the giddy and easily-put-upon world lacks. Defoe's sense of reality is here partly a polemical strategy which flatters his hypothetical reader by carefully establishing another and obviously unsound approach to reality to which he and the knowing reader are clearly superior.

It has been enough to the writers of this man's life, as they call it, that they could put anything together to make a kind of monstrous unheard-of story as romantic as the reports that have been spread about of him; and the more those stories appeared monstrous and incredible, the more suitable they seemed to be to what the world would have been made to expect of Captain Avery. (xvi)

This is not to say that Defoe is misrepresenting the legend which had gathered around Avery and his exploits. The Avery of the 1709 pamphlet is as much Dick Whittington as he is a pirate captain. He begins as the son of a prosperous Devonshire

---

[4] In *The Works of Daniel Defoe*, ed. G. H. Maynadier (New York, 1904), vol. XVI. All page references in the text are to this edition.

sea-captain, but when his father dies he is tricked out of his patrimony by his evil guardian. Left alone and totally disenfranchised, he goes to sea to seek status and fortune. In the navy, the relentlessly evil and envious world conspires against him still in the person of a jealous and therefore unjust officer. Avery wounds him in a duel to which he is provoked and is dismissed from the navy. He resolves to become a merchant-captain, returns to Devon, and tries to establish himself as such by marrying. He is cheated by his bride's father out of the promised dowry and fooled by the lady herself, she producing six months after the wedding a baby who looks just like the local apothecary. So, he turns pirate, the victim only of his own courageous ambition thwarted repeatedly and unfairly by the scheming and deceitful world.

Like any folk hero, his rise is sudden and spectacular, the result of magical luck: he captures a ship belonging to the Great Mogul which is carrying that potentate's daughter on her way to be married with a fabulous dowry. Avery marries her, takes the dowry, and, to complete the familiar fairy-tale pattern acquires, a kingdom along with his princess. He decides, that is, to found a colony on Madagascar, which will 'be secure enough from all the Attempts that the Universe could make against it' (10).[5] Here he reigns secure, his empire mustering, we are told, 15,000 men and 40 large ships, and he himself supreme and absolute commander 'with such a Power as the Doges or Dukes of Venice and Genoa are now possessed of' (11). But absolute power, in this case at least, corrupts not at all, and Avery never becomes a tyrant, and his kingdom is a pirate utopia. The pamphlet concludes with a palinode, but one which purifies Avery's heart and redeems his piratical career without destroying his empire:

But as, amidst all the Prosperities of Life, Reflexions on the short Duration of it, will sometimes intervene, and the Inclinations of Mankind are not so sunk in Vice, as to admit no Thoughts that border upon Virtue, so the Captain could not but lean after a Prospect of his own native Country, the Desire of finishing the Remainder of his Days where he first had the Happiness of seeing the Light, which was increas'd by looking into his past Crimes, and a just Survey of what he must one Day answer for at a Heavenly

[5] All references in the text are to the anonymous 1709 pamphlet.

Tribunal, tho' he found himself out of the Reach of one that was Earthly. (14)

Avery gets everything a reader would want, including comfortable repentance, in this brief and transparent popular fantasy. A pamphlet hero like Avery is naturally a stylized and sketchy figure. His story is a popular morality tale, exposing the world as a viciously competitive place and celebrating the power of the individual like Avery to establish a better world all for and by himself. The individual responds to universal depravity by asserting his total innocence (in relation to man, not to God) and total capacity for self-creation. The utopian pirate king, in short, is a pure bourgeois fantasy, individualism triumphant and superbly unaware that it commits the same sins it scorns.

Defoe's Avery ultimately provides these same gratifications, for he achieves everything this popular Avery does. But those gratifications are delivered within an extended and complicated narrative.

Like Defoe's other heroes, he possesses for a start an introspective clarity about himself which is far from the stylized and superficial psychologizing of the 1709 pamphlet. We all know how well Defoe can render the interplay of secret motive and conscious rationalization. His Captain Avery is endowed with a winning kind of moral clarity which makes him declare that he had 'seen something of the immense wealth which the buccaneers and other adventurers met with in their scouring about the world' and had 'for a long time meditated in my thoughts to get possessed of a good ship for that purpose' (4). Where the hero of the pamphlet is passive, the victim of an aggressive world and the child of great good fortune, Defoe's Avery is deliberately active, self-possessed, and controlled. Simple ambition, he tells us, to escape from the life of a common sailor led him on, 'and therefore night and day I applied myself to study how I should dismiss myself from that drudgery, and get to be, first or last, master of a good ship, which was the utmost of my ambition at that time' (5). Avery is established as a level-headed and practical schemer, but Defoe is careful to make certain that such moral and psychological naturalism retains its sensational and legendary opposite. Avery in the same passage reminds us once again that 'being bred to the sea from a youth, none of those romantic introductions published had any share in my adventures, or were in any way the cause of my taking the courses I have since been engaged in' (4).

Two things, it seems to me, are happening here. Avery insists (and we believe him) that he has been in control, has chosen to turn pirate, seen the opportunities, and worked out a conscious plan to make himself into a pirate. On the other hand, Avery as realistic narrator is an instinctive novelist, aware of the necessary relationship between the environment and the self; he has, he notes for us, been bred to the sea and has therefore been heavily influenced in the direction his life has taken. It is a small point and quickly made, but as we have seen, it is the characteristic insight as well as the chief problem of Defoe's narratives. His heroes are self-generated, essentially purely active, self-creating personages, and yet the implicit logic of their stories, the deterministic realism which derives them from history and circumstance, commits them to a necessity larger than themselves.

This paradox is at the heart of Avery's early career. He and a few companions begin as legal if unofficial privateers against the Spaniards and eventually find themselves stranded and in danger of capture in the Spanish West Indies. They meet with an English ship and agree to sail on it and soon discover that they have fallen in with real pirates. Avery emphasizes the crucial legal distinction between pirate and privateer:

When we came there we found they were a worse sort of wanderers than ourselves; for though we had been a kind of pirates, known and declared enemies to the Spaniards, yet it was to them only and to no other; for we never offered to rob any of our other European nations, either Dutch or French, much less English; but now we were listed in the service of the devil indeed, and like him, were at war with all mankind.(7)

This is, of course, the pirate as demonic folk hero, the pirate as he appears in the 1724 *History of the Pirates*, the satanically attractive figure who separates himself from any exising human community and creates his own world by declaring unconditional war on all mankind.[6] The pirate as folk hero frequently

[6] For a discussion of these implications of piracy, see my *Popular Fiction Before Richardson* (Oxford, 1969), pp. 75–7.

has cause for his separation; like the hero of the 1709 Avery pamphlet he has discovered that the world and mankind are untenable organizations. The pirate, in such pure and naïve manifestations, expresses a myth of total individualism; every authentic man can ultimately and simply create his own world and live well in it. But total individualism, with its radical denial of communal restrictions and loyalties, is hardly a theory that Defoe's narratives can endorse specifically or explicitly. So Avery is first forced by circumstances into taking up with a group of pure pirates, forced in spite of an earlier resolution 'not to prey upon my own countrymen' (5). The force of circumstance quickly habituates Avery and 'in a little time the novelty of the crime wore off and we grew hardened to it like the rest' (7).

An awareness of specific and determining circumstances is obviously the key to Defoe's revision of the Avery legend (and with it the pirate legend *per se*). Madagascar, the legendary Avery's utopian pirate kingdom, is here a poor and desolate retreat from a hurricane where the pirates find themselves stranded without a large ship in which to ply their trade. Avery manages to escape and to return with a suitable ship, but Madagascar itself remains a depressing place and Avery sees life there as burial 'among savages and barbarians' (42). Even after the capture of the Great Mogul's daughter and the acquisition of fabulous wealth, the island remains a prison from which all the pirates long to escape: 'We really knew not what to do with ourselves or with our wealth; and the only thing we had now before us was to consider what method to take for getting home' (59).

Not only, I might add, is their fabulous wealth reduced to merely another limiting circumstance, but the absolute power the pirates possess over their captives, the racial-sexual fantasy (marriage with a dusky princess) that is part of Avery's legend, is also translated into an inhibiting factor. Avery says pointedly that he never ravished the Great Mogul's daughter of anything but her dowry. But Defoe is smart enough to include an attractive drunken orgy; Avery's men lie with the inferior women captives, get drunk on 'arrack', and 'all sorts of liberty was both given and taken' (57). All this turns into a near-disaster, an almost destructive set of circumstances rather than an assertion of subversive and anarchic freedom:

. . . if the women made our men drunk before, this arrack made them quite mad; and they had so little government of themselves with it, that I think it might be said the whole ship's crew was drunk for above a fortnight together, till, six or seven of them killed themselves; two fell overboard and were drowned, and several more fell into raging fevers, and it was a wonder, on the whole, they were not all killed with it. (58)

Like the sexual licence, the gratuitous savagery which was so important a part of the fascination of piracy is something that Avery does not have and does not want. But Defoe's narrative is again careful to supply it, here in the person of Redhand, the captain for a time of the pirates, who is given his name 'because he was so bloody a wretch that he scarce ever was at the taking any prize, but he had a hand in some butchery or other' (7). Avery rejects this ferocity, but as much for its wastefulness as anything else. When they engage a fully-laden ship, and its captain offers to yield, 'Redhand would have given them no quarter, but according to his usual practice, would have thrown the men all into the sea', but Avery prevails 'with him to give them quarter, and good usage too, and so they yielded, and a very rich prize it was' (9). Such a passage looks two ways. It reminds us of the necessary savagery of the archetypal pirate, the logical and thrilling result of his secession from the human community. But the incident also celebrates that self-serving prudential calculation whereby Avery asserts his freedom in the midst of circumstances, the circumstances here being the logical amoral ferocity to which piracy has committed him.

Within this context of carefully evoked habituating and limiting circumstances, Avery is always superbly conscious and in control, as here, above circumstances and able therefore to describe them clearly. Upon first joining the pirates, he quickly distinguishes himself for his practical wisdom. The pirates go to Cuba to get meat, but since the wild cattle there have to be chased and then shot, Avery explains that the heated flesh is not able to be pickled or salted for keeping. Not realizing this, the crew is about to sail far out of their way to North America to get provisions when Avery explains why their meat is bad. By the simple precaution of not salting heated cattle they cure 'one hundred and forty barrels of very good beef' (8). Such details are a literary universe away from the pamphlet career of the folk hero Avery, but such circumstantial realism is not its own end but really a means towards producing another kind of hero for another kind of folk. What matters here is not only that Avery is knowledgeable efficiency and control embodied, but that he is always such within a predetermined context. Given a situation which he cannot help and a world he has not made, Avery like Defoe's other heroes co-operates with necessity, learns to use it carefully in order to preserve himself from it.

This same interplay between necessity and freedom can be observed at length in Defoe's handling of statistics, or rather in his introduction of statistics into a world of fabulously and essentially round numbers. In the preface, Avery is made to protest that the booty he has taken in his career 'though infinitely great in itself, yet has been so magnified beyond commonsense, that it makes all the rest that has been said of those things ridiculous and absurd' (xvi). The early adventures become in the narrative a series of inventories, interesting and detailed lists of those items that Avery and his associates need to establish themselves as pirates: 'We got in all those ships, besides the provisions above mentioned, about two hundred muskets and pistols, good store of cutlasses, about twenty ton of iron shot and musket ball, and thirty-three barrels of good powder, which was all very suitable things to our occasions' (13).

There is nothing like this in the legend; those who attend to legends have neither the patience nor the need for proof. Defoe's famous lists are part of the documentary apparatus of his books; they certify the otherwise improbable or at least singular situations he describes. The lists here also have a context, an opposite in the fabulous vagueness of the pirate myth in which pirates acquire treasure well beyond the dreams of avarice. But again, Defoe's narrative is cunning and opportunistic; the list is a strategy, not an absolute value or a simple quantity. Avery and the boys take a prize shortly after they have finished outfitting themselves.

Our men found in the ship six brass guns, two hundred sacks of meal, some fruit, and the value of 160,000 pieces of eight in gold of Chili; as good as any in the world. It was a glittering sight, and enough to dazzle the eyes of those that looked upon it, to see such a quantity of gold laid all of a heap together, and we began to embrace one another in congratulation of our good fortune. (16)

Here exactness prepares us for rapture and keeps rapture under control. The exact sum is in one sentence, the emotional reaction to it in another. There are other such occasions treated in the same fashion, and as we go from prize to prize it becomes more difficult to use statistics; the legendary begins to take over, begins to emerge from the statistical. The next prize, for example, is a Spanish ship whose yield is so great that Avery informs us that 'it is not easy to give an exact account of the prodigious variety of things we found' (21). The ultimate prize is the Great Mogul's daughter and her dowry, and here the legendary takes over, but the statistics have prepared us by this time to accept it: 'We had now wealth enough not only to make us rich, but almost to have made a nation rich; and to tell you the truth, considering the costly things we took here, which we did not know the value of, and besides gold and silver and jewels—I say, we never knew how rich we were' (59). It is a perfect example of exact psychological observation—confusion in the face of fabulous wealth—co-operating with and certifying legendary vagueness. The ordinary folk hero is as calm as a demi-god when faced with the fabulous. Defoe's pirates are astounded by it all; so are we, and we therefore tend to believe it all.

Throughout the mounting excitement, the gradual approach of the legendary and the fabulous, Avery remains consistently cool and separate. He not only devises lists in telling his story but within the narrative he brings order and analysis to bear upon fabulous whole sums, normally indivisible ones. After taking a large Spanish prize, he oversees the sharing of the booty:

... as keeping such a treasure in every man's particular private possession would have occasioned gaming, quarreling, and perhaps thieving and pilfering, I ordered that so many small chests should be made as there were men in the ship, and every man's treasure was nailed up in these chests, and the chests all stowed in the hold, with every man's name upon his chest, not to be touched but by general order. (23)

Such a passage epitomizes the strategy of the book. Avery is a hero because he handles the legendary by analysis, by breaking wholes into manageable parts. Here he sees the dangers of economic individualism and creates a system (pirates' savings bank!) which preserves individuality while neutralizing its dangers. He himself is the ultimate individual, controlling the individuality of others in asserting his own. Avery is thus both above and within individualism; he negates its bad effects and affirms a higher and more stable version of it. This operation on the world reflects the operation of the self, enacts the relationship between the self and the world. For Avery is crucially apart, from his legendary self, from his fellow pirates, from all his history and his circumstances.

All along, in fact, Avery as narrator of his own story has emphasized his separateness, and even his own duplicity in maintaining it. When they are at first stranded in Madagascar he proposes that they try to capture a ship large enough for all of them, but his real motive is his own escape. He tells us of his 'secret design' that the boat 'should not go without me' (33). At the same time, he is aware of the necessity of concealing himself from his men and pretends to want to stay as a means of assuring his escape. The men see through this double reverse and think the entire plan a scheme to 'run away from them, and so indeed it was' (33). Avery then proposes that any man who goes will leave his share of the booty as security. The result is, naturally, that no one is especially anxious to go and Avery is able to leave with a crew of forty men. But like Moll at the end of her story, he has something in reserve, a treasure that he and some other comrades buried long ago. He tells us that he resolved to go to England, except that he 'had too many men, and did not know what to do with them' (36). This time at least, Avery does not get away and eventually returns to Madagascar with a suitably large ship.

At the very end of the story, he describes his final escape. He sends out a crew from Madagascar but becomes fearful that they will return and guide enemies there. He is careful, however, to conceal such apprehensions from his men and sends out bulletins to the opposite effect: 'I gave it out that I was resolved to live and die here; and therefore, a little before I resolved upon going, I set to work to build me a new house, and to plant me a pretty garden' (76). He gathers a select few around him and uses the house—his evidence of permanence—as a base from which to escape. They run away as far as Baghdad, but even there Avery meditates solitary escape: 'Walking one morning upon the bank of the river Euphrates, I mused with myself what course I should take to make off, and get quite away from the gang, and let them not so much as suspect me' (81).

All this separateness is intensified, indeed given its real meaning, by the pirate legend which is its context. The legendary Avery is the head of a coherent anti-society of pirates and is as a pirate inseparable from the communal enterprise piracy invokes. Defoe's Avery is a king all right and the island, he tells us, attracts pirates from all over the world. But Avery remains alone, calculating for himself, only pretending to be their emperor: 'As for me, I discovered my intentions to nobody, but made them all believe I would stay here till some of them should come and fetch me off' (59).

This reserve is enacted literally when Avery and his men capture some Dutchmen who land on Madagascar. At Avery's urging these captives repeat the legend he and his men have acquired in Europe. Avery carefully presents himself to these men as one of his own captains and cunningly plays on the legend, thinking, he tells us, of possible future profit from such public relations. When he hears that the English have vowed to capture and hang him, he issues in his disguise a wonderful threat:

I smiled at that, and told them Captain Avery would give them leave to hang him and all his men when they could take them; but that I could assure him they were too strong to be taken; that if the Government of England went about to provoke them, Captain Avery would soon make those seas too hot for the English, and they might even give over their East India trade, for they little thought the circumstances Captain Avery was in. (66)

This and other speeches carefully recorded for us, says Avery, were 'the ground of the rumor you have heard in England' (69). The legend is perpetuated and exploited deliberately by a smiling Avery, who later tells another set of captives for the same public relations purpose that his pirates may in time become a great nation. In this Defoe anticipates his own huckstering of the pirate legend several years later in the preface to his *History of the Pirates* by saying that the 'Romans themselves were at first no better than such a gang of rovers as we were; and who knew but our general Captain Avery, might lay the foundation of as great an empire as they?' (73).

The legend, in short, is real; it has been deliberately created by Avery himself to serve his own ends. Or perhaps more accurately and in line with what Avery has done throughout the book, he has co-operated with the reality of the distortion of his career by others, exploited it by intensifying it and enacting it.

Defoe's story of Captain Avery is, then, a revision of a popular myth, one which preserves the myth's essential features and delivers its various gratifications but makes them acceptable by means of a rearrangement of emphasis. At its crudest, this is merely a matter of displacement. Avery lets others do his dirty work; slaughtering, raping, rioting, and even the act of turning pirate in the full sense are all there but distanced and ostensibly disdained by the narrator, who is both in and out of situations. In a more subtle fashion, the story accommodates the significant fantasies implicit in the pirate legend to an empirical and mundane view of the world; Avery's freedom as a pirate, the ideological resonance of his career and his utopian colony, is explained and derived from circumstances. That freedom is therefore acceptable, somewhat short of its overtly subversive and anarchic meanings. But last and most important is the separation implicit between Avery the narrator and Avery the hero. For Avery by demonstrating how he is himself (even as he lives the events he narrates) aware of circumstance, aware that is of his own necessity, exploits and promotes his own legend and thereby asserts his freedom. He is conscious that he is neither the utopian pirate king of the legend nor the logical antithesis, the sordid and petty ruffian. He is thus necessarily a free mean point somewhere between those extremes. The reality of his consciousness, then, as we experience it in reading his story, is that he is actually neither of those roles, although he can assume them. His talent for realistic narration is primarily a means of freedom, a self-assertive mediation between those limiting (and unreal) extremes and between other opposites which are the materials of his story: the legendary and the historical, the limitless and the numerical, the anarchic and the orderly. Avery 'smiles' because he is essentially and absolutely his own man.

*Captain Singleton* contains a version of most of these incidents and much more. Secord explains that Defoe seems to have added material he derived from travel writers such as Knox,

Dampier, Misson, and others.[7] Those materials are used chiefly in the spectacular march across Africa, which plays no part in *The King of the Pirates*. But obvious expansion aside, the most important difference between the two narratives is the character of the hero. Avery, as we have seen, is omnicompetent; he pays crucial but necessarily brief service to circumstances.[8] That relative brevity allows only the simplest of assertions of helplessness before we get on to action and conquest. Singleton has narrative space to elaborate that helplessness, but the result of the longer narrative is not simply more attention to circumstances but the creation of another and total kind of dependence.

The larger book uses its time to invoke a character who is literally a commodity, purchased for 12 shillings by his 'mother' and then passed from hand to hand in the course of a childhood and adolescence which have no parallel in the story of Captain Avery. That elaborate addition to Avery's story has several obvious narrative purposes. Singleton's deprived childhood establishes a moral innocence for him that Avery has no time to develop. It also ensures the ideological satisfactions implicit in the notion of personal development; Singleton's beginnings allow the discovery and gradual acquisition of a personal self in an objective world that is rendered at extensive length rather than out of the internal disposition given by the nature of market society. Moreover, Singleton's initial innocence acts like Crusoe's physical isolation on his island, placing him in a set of absolute circumstances which demand certain exertions for simple survival.

Singleton's 'unconcern', as he calls it more than once at the beginning of his story, looks like picaresque detachment. He is passed from master to master in the opening pages, the second of these as brutal as any of Lazarillo's. But as Robert Alter has pointed out, the classic European picaro's isolation is largely physical and social rather than moral or metaphysical. Lazarillo is on the outskirts of society, but he is part of that society in never questioning its values, in being peripheral to it rather than actually outside of it. In similar fashion, Gil Blas's position of servitude is a genial satiric perspective rather than an isolated

---

[7] *The Narrative Method of Defoe*, p. 114.
[8] See above, pp. 68–9.

distance.[9] Both of them participate fully and naïvely in their beings; they take joy in their rogueries and express themselves through them. Singleton's isolation is both more and less. It is a preliminary exposition of the self as quite apart from responsibility and consciousness; young Bob is a nullity, not so much outside society as outside any coherent being of his own. Defoe's narrative is so arranged that the Singleton who narrates can only present himself as a boy, cannot attribute any being, purpose, or consciousness to himself.

Consider the following dialogue at the very beginning of the book. After being rescued from pirates by a Portuguese ship, Bob is 'almost reduced to my primitive State, *viz.* of Starving', when his sea-captain master dies in Lisbon. The other men of the ship leave to find employment, but Bob is too young and inexperienced to know what to do:

. . . at length one of the Lieutenants seeing me, enquired what that young *English* Dog did there, and why they did not turn him on Shore?

I heard him, and partly understood what he meant, tho' not what he said, and began then to be in a terrible Fright; for I knew not where to get a Bit of Bread; when the Pilot of the Ship, an old Seaman, seeing me look very dull, came to me, and speaking broken *English* to me, told me, I must be gone. Whither must I go (said I?) Where you will, (said he), Home to your own Country, if you will. How must I go thither (said I?) Why have you no Friend (said he?) No, (said I) not in the World, but that Dog, pointing to the Ship's Dog, (who having stole a Piece of Meat just before, had brought it close by me, and I had taken it from him, and eat it) for he has been a good Friend, and brought me my Dinner. *Well, well,* says he, *you must have your Dinner: Will you go with me? Yes,* says I, *with all my Heart.*[10]

Young Bob's location in Lisbon is obviously similar in its effects to Crusoe's shipwreck on the island. Defoe's instinctive sense of structure places Bob in a foreign and hostile locale and makes him like Crusoe confront something close to bestiality as the basic alternative to self-determination. He hears sounds (the

---

[9] *Rogue's Progress* (Cambridge, Mass., 1964), pp. 5, 23.

[10] *The Life, Adventures and Piracies of the Famous Captain Singleton,* ed. James R. Sutherland (Everyman edition), pp. 4–5. All further references in the text are to this edition.

lieutenant's threatening Portuguese) and only understands them as signals of danger. Not only is language partly menacing sound, but the world has neither distinct meaning nor shape. His 'own Country' means little to him; he has been shifted from parish to parish as a child and as an adolescent been on three or four long voyages with his first master. Having no friends, he has no place; having no place, he has in effect no being except that provided by the necessity of the moment: '*you must have your Dinner*'. The strange simplicity of Bob's dialogue with the Portuguese pilot is partly the result of the desire to render the pilot's broken English, but the simplicity has a quasi-absurdist effect, underlining and emphasizing Bob's radical isolation from his surroundings.

Unlike the picaro who, as Alter observes, never changes,[11] Singleton is during his brief but formative *enfance* an infinitely malleable quantity who assumes the shape of the time and the milieu. His Portuguese pilot takes him on a voyage to Goa and Bob becomes exactly like his corrupt fellow seamen. But he claims at the same moment that he despised them. Part of them but not really of them, he resembles Avery who is a pirate and yet not piratical. We can, perhaps, account for Singleton's claim that he despised his fellows while being one of them by assuming that he is correcting his autobiography as he writes it, giving himself in retrospect more consciousness than he actually had. But such an analysis violates the naïve immediacy of the narrative. As readers we are encouraged to read Singleton's career and its narrative as a continuous whole, without any ironic lag between the two parts.

I was exactly fitted for their Society indeed; for I had no Sense of Virtue or Religion upon me. I had never heard much of either, except what a good old Parson had said to me when I was a Child of about Eight or Nine Years old; nay, I was preparing, and growing up apace, to be as wicked as any Body could be, or perhaps ever was. Fate certainly thus directed my Beginning, knowing that I had Work which I had to do in the World, which nothing but one hardened against all Sense of Honesty or Religion, could go thro'; and yet even in this State of Original Wickedness, I entertained such a settled Abhorrence of the abandon'd Vileness of the *Portuguese*, that I could not but hate them most heartily from the Beginning,

[11] *Rogue's Progress*, p. 31.

and all my life afterwards. They were so brutishly wicked, so base and perfidious, not only to Strangers, but to one another; so meanly submissive when subjected; so insolent, or barbarous and tyrannical when superior, that I thought there was something in them that shock'd my very Nature. Add to this, that 'tis natural to an *English-man* to hate a Coward, it all joined together to make the Devil and a *Portuguese* equally my Aversion. (7–8)

Like Avery and indeed like Crusoe looking back at his early youth, Singleton finds himself in circumstances and then discovers a surprising coherence in the events of his life. The nullity of the person is part of a plan, something comes from nothing. 'And yet', he adds, he remained in some sense apart from those brutish circumstances. The historian of ideas *cum* literary critic might well see at work here some aspect of Defoe's ideas on natural or residual goodness. Singleton is, after all, responding to necessity; it is either this or starvation. Or he might see this as part of Defoe's fidelity to the statistics of eighteenth-century crime: Defoe as liberal criminologist.[12] He might even in a trivial mood see Singleton's instinct as merely amusing English chauvinism. We can speculate about Defoe, but we can be reasonably objective about the structure of the story. Singleton is reserving a part of himself as free from circumstances; his expression of aversion to the brutish sailors is the first of a series of separatist and self-assertive gestures in his narrative. The sailors are despised, note, for their complete submission to circumstances. Their excess is really a total enslavement to the moment: 'so meanly submissive when subjected; so insolent, or barbarous and tyrannical when superior'. Singleton resembles Defoe's other criminals in that he is appalled not so much by evil as by the disorder of mere nature, that is, by a total loss of control to the desires of the moment. This opposition between control and anarchic natural evil occurs, as we have seen, in *The King of the Pirates*. In *Captain Singleton*, the opposition is naturally more extensive, but it is also more exact and intricate. For in practice Singleton does not simply, like Avery, oppose

[12] Thus, M. E. Novak say; that Singleton, 'like most of the pirates who people the pages of Defoe's biographies of real pirates, is a man of constitutional courage, that kind which may be found in both villains and heroes. But Defoe did not necessarily classify the pirate as a villain, for he knew that the best and bravest seamen turned to piracy when they could not find work.' See *Defoe and the Nature of Man*, p. 146.

competence and control to slovenly nature. Rather, he manœuvres himself (or is manœuvred by the facts of his story) into
events where survival depends upon competence and control.

That intricate movement is especially clear in the subsequent
facts of Bob's estrangement from his master and from 'lawful'
society. Much more a victim of direct circumstances than
Avery, he is involved in a mutiny and punished with the others
by being left on Madagascar. His involvement in the con-
spiracy, as he observes, has been slight. Indeed, Bob has just
finished telling us about his essential helplessness in the matter,
for he has nursed a frustrated homicidal hatred for his vicious
Portuguese pilot-master. But looking back at his exile, Bob now
contradicts this helplessness and says that exile saved him not
only from murdering his master but from the habituating implications of such a free and violent act: 'This was therefore a
good Providence for me, to keep me from dipping my Hands in
Blood, and it made me more tender afterwards in Matters of
Blood, than I believe I should otherwise have been' (13). Bob's
narrative arranges matters so that the cancelling of a free
moral act (the murder of his vicious master) by circumstances is
a liberating movement. Bob is released into the world of his
adventures where freedom can operate against a necessity of
tremendous variety and moral neutrality. Left on the ship and
in society with its inherent injustice (his master), Bob would
have been doomed to a life where the free moral act is turned
into an enslaved necessity: a life of crime in a morally biased
environment.

Bob stresses here and regularly afterwards that his radical
emptiness of personality renders him immune to the anxiety
suffered by his companions. His 'unconcern' at fate he describes as a mixture of ignorance and confidence, and it is (one
notices the heavy emphasis) precisely what separates him from
the others. They are mutineers, active conspirators in their fate
as Bob is mostly passive victim. Bob is free by virtue of his
radically flexible kind of non-being. They are committed to an
already failed self-assertion:

This thoughtless, unconcern'd Temper had one Felicity indeed
in it; that it made me daring and ready for doing any Mischief, and
kept off the Sorrow which otherwise ought to have attended me
when I fell into any Mischief; that this Stupidity was instead of a

Happiness to me, for it left my Thoughts free to act upon Means of Escape and Deliverance in my Distress, however great it might be; whereas my Companions in the Misery, were so sunk by their Fear and Grief, that they abandoned themselves to the Misery of their Condition, and gave over all Thought but of their perishing and starving, being devoured by wild Beasts, murthered, and perhaps eaten by *Cannibals, and the like.* (14)

The absolutely thorough nature of Bob's commitment to circumstances becomes fully visible in a dilemma which follows shortly and which Bob significantly refers to as a 'Miniature of my future Enterprizes' (29). Lacking proper materials, they find themselves unable to build a boat, and conclude that a canoe such as they can build will not hold them and their provisions and will not take them over the sea. Bob speaks for the first time in general council, and what he says is at first a transparent riddle. He notes that a canoe is inadequate for their purposes and that 'to make such an Adventure would be nothing but meer running into certain Destruction, and yet that nevertheless I was for making a Canoe' (30). The climax of Bob's speech is the answer to his riddle: 'our Business was to cruise along the Coast of the Island, which was very long, and to seize upon the first we could get that was better than our own, and so from that to another, till perhaps we might at last get a good Ship to carry us whither ever we pleased to go' (30). What Bob suggests both in the rhetorical sequence of his speech and in the substance of his proposal is that they can only do what is put before them, embrace the chain of circumstances present and future as a way out of them. The indirection of Bob's aggressive suggestion is the exact nature of his cunning and of his novelistic being. His essential innocence is preserved by it; his energies are directed formally toward pure survival even though the story will see to it that survival leads to expansion and acquisition of a fabulous surplus. It is left for Bob's cruder comrades to be explicit about just what it is they are thus embarking upon: 'You may call us Pyrates, says another, if you will, and if we fall into bad Hands, we may be used like Pyrates; but I care not for that, I'll be a Pyrate, or any thing, nay I'll be hang'd for a Pyrate, rather than starve here; and therefore I think the Advice is very good; and so they cry'd all, Let us have a Canoe' (31).

Their position as committed pirates in Madagascar is thus a double one which expresses the contradiction all of Defoe's narratives try to live with. In the immediate context of Madagascar they are powerful, fierce, and dangerous: 'We were a little Fleet of three Ships, and an Army of between Twenty and Thirty as dangerous Fellows as ever they [i.e. natives they meet] had among them; and had they known what we were they would have compounded to give us every thing we desired, to be rid of us' (39). But they are also, Bob reminds us with his emerging exactness, vulnerable and confused: 'On the other Hand, we were as miserable as Nature could well make us to be; for we were upon *a* Voyage and *no* Voyage, we were bound *some* where and *no* where; for tho' we knew what we intended to do, we did really not know what we were doing' (39).[13] The clearly perceived purpose of movement for Defoe's characters is survival. The effect of survival is invariably spectacular and blameless self-assertion. But those explicit and implicit ends of movement are always surrounded by the whirl of circumstances, random and unpredictable, that mimetic narrative provides so well. Such a structure is in operation in these scenes.

Madagascar, like Crusoe's smaller but tighter operation, provides materials both for penitence and building. Their carpenter erects 'a great Cross of Wood' on a hill overlooking the sea with these words inscribed: *Point Desperation. Jesus have Mercy!* (41). And at the same time Bob communicates the involving joy of building a settlement: 'I shall never forget the little City we built, for it was no less; and we fortify'd it accordingly; and the Idea is so fresh in my Thought, that I cannot but give a Short Description of it' (41–2). This easy alternation between the technical despair and their actual joyful movement is the key to the African journey, the most remarkable and imaginative trek in the whole history of the eighteenth-century English novel.[14] Bob begins by refusing to go, that is, by

[13] This obviously significant and peculiar construction occurs only at this point in *Colonel Jack* but is used several times with some insistence in *Moll Flanders*. See below, Chapter IV.

[14] Gary J. Scrimgeour has underlined the originality of the journey by pointing out that Defoe cunningly restricts the group's wanderings to those parts of Africa that were unexplored. See 'The Problem of Realism in Defoe's *Captain Singleton*', *HLQ*, 27 (Nov. 1963), 23.

declining the expedition as a hopelessly heroic gesture, more than survival warrants. He advises going north by sea to the Arabian Gulf or the Red Sea and seizing a ship. But then he agrees that to go north is to risk almost certain capture by Turks or Arabs. The trans-African journey is impossible, but there is no alternative. Bob's extended reluctance to undertake it marks the journey as necessity rather than enterprise. His reluctance is a preliminary apology for his astonishing competence in accomplishing it.

For Bob does grow more and more competent, or rather, in the manner of Defoe's heroes, he suddenly becomes omnicompetent, the leader of the group. There is no real preparation for this, no series of graduated psychological scenes. He simply becomes 'Captain Bob' when they get to the mainland of Africa and wonder how to carry their essential luggage overland. Bob suggests that they quarrel with some of the natives and take ten or twelve prisoner-slaves in the ensuing battle. This plan resembles Crusoe's dream of finding a guide-servant among the cannibals. As usual and necessarily, Bob's plan is overwhelmed by circumstances; there is no need to start a quarrel, the natives take the offensive. Bob can then say, 'It presently came into my Head, that we might now by the Law of Arms take as many Prisoners as we would, and make them travel with us, and carry our Baggage' (66). Bob's competence is, again, made into a response to necessity, although here necessity is the shameless slave of freedom. This reminds us of Crusoe's placing himself, after extended tactical rumination, in position and trusting to providence. Singleton as a thoughtless and decidedly unspiritual adventurer does not invoke providence, but the strategy of his narrative is exactly the same as Crusoe's. Courage and ruthless cunning are possessed and disavowed almost simultaneously. The 'Law of Arms' is a euphemism made possible by the narrative's conversion of a nakedly aggressive situation into a purely defensive and necessary one.

It is here, when he becomes suddenly competent, that Bob becomes just like his model, the Avery of *The King of the Pirates*. For his competence equals his consciousness of superiority to the others. In *Captain Singleton* (as in *Moll Flanders* and *Colonel Jack*) consciousness is separation; Bob passes from person to personality at the moment he realizes that his comrades are cowards. And, again, even at this initial swelling moment of control as Bob discourses on the strange weakness of Portuguese in general and particular, he tells us that he learns from them, that indeed he is part of an élite which emerges among them. The gunner (their original leader) takes him in hand, flatters him, and fills him with the ambition to become learned in a nautical way: 'I resolved, if ever I came back to *Europe*, and had any thing left to purchase it, I would make my self Master of all the Parts of Learning needful to the making of me a compleat Sailor' (69). Even as he leads, in short, Bob tells us in exact detail how he is being led.

Bob's leadership is of a piece with this shifting reality. His salient quality as we read is not really courage, not even in the battle with the natives where he earns his title. There Bob is a tactician, weighing odds and the alternative and bowing to necessity rather than asserting his courage. 'I was indeed forced to command,' he says, for the men were about to fly 'from a Parcel of naked Savages, tho' even by flying they could not have saved their Lives' (67). On the trek itself, he is first among them because he is radically aware of contingencies and multiple possibilities. For example, they find gold and Bob realizes immediately the potentially divisive effects of the discovery. Like Avery, he presides over the formation of a financial co-operative, appealing to the men to put all they find into a common stock, not just out of fairness but to preserve themselves from destructive competition. There is a great deal more of such rational discourse throughout the journey, enough to let us see quite clearly that the unruly natives and threatening fauna are there primarily to provoke cunning and caution, to give us the pleasure of seeing Bob especially master complication of a staggering sort. Critics and readers sometimes complain that Defoe's stories are tangled and confusing, an overgrowth of complication and gratuitous detailing. They are right in a way, for the heroism of characters like Bob and Moll and Jack and the others is their ability to hold extraordinary complication in mind, to keep the strings taut as they move through and around circumstance, never quite entangled in it all. Circumstances, therefore, do not add up to anything plausible or even coherent. They are there to provoke and to test the heroes, to enable them to display powers that would otherwise go unrevealed.

All this agility has survival as its declared purpose, but real survival in a market society means the accumulation and establishment of wealth in order to escape the vagaries of the market. All of Defoe's heroes want to have money, spend a great deal of their time talking about it, and nearly all their time acquiring it in one way or another. In *Crusoe*, that perfect fable, the hero despises money at length (even though he saves it) and jokes about its uselessness, but it is being accumulated for him in his absence back in Brazil. In general, the rest of the narratives follow that pattern, although in less satisfactory ways, for accumulation is never an explicit achievement for Defoe's characters while they are in motion through their stories. Real accumulation would grant them a stability and permanence that they cannot, after all, have as characters. The moment they achieve that stability they declare that their stories are over. The point is that Defoe's narratives dramatize in their various ways the paradox implicit in a market society, where the actual stability promised by accumulation is rare, where in fact accumulation is a dynamic and continuing process which equals survival. To survive, Defoe's characters must accumulate; the frequent lists and inventories are one of the stylistic results of that need. Another and opposite result is the rapid movement of the narratives, even to the point of confusion and irrelevance; that movement is a method of rendering the dynamics of accumulation, of endowing lumpish commodities and sums with the whirling life they actually have in society.

With the discovery of gold, grim survival seems to slide easily into ecstatic accumulation. Singleton himself, however, is not allowed to be the chief instigator of that accumulation. Just as the Quaker William Walters enters later to give focus to and to share responsibility for Bob's career as a pirate, here another outsider enters magically to take over the leadership of the search for gold. Singleton in command in any sense must always be Singleton serving as well, so they encounter an Englishman, an unregenerate Crusoe living quite naked among savages, who shows them where gold can be panned in great lumps from the rivers. This Englishman wants them to stay and reap a great harvest of gold and ivory. Bob and the others are reluctant, as improvident adventurers should be: 'none of the rest had any Mind to stay, nor I neither, I must confess; for I had no Notion of a great deal of Money, or what to do with my self, or what to do with it if I had it' (161). But they do stay and they do accumulate huge amounts of gold and ivory, 'two and twenty Ton of Teeth' (165). The Englishman continues, rather fantastically, to chide their reluctance: 'he told us he would not press us to any further Stay, since we did not care whether we got any more Gold or no; that we were indeed the first Men ever he met with in his Life, that said they had Gold enough, and of whom it might be truly said, that when it lay under our Feet, we would not stoop to take it up' (165). In the dialectic of responsibility and freedom which operates in the narrative, the Englishman's greed, suitably punished later we are told,[15] preserves Bob's innocence and makes his accumulation by contrast a blameless aspect of survival. Singleton and his men 'know' that they have to keep moving and that the kind of static accumulation the Englishman counsels is the end of survival. We can add that it is also the end of narrative and remind ourselves that survival and mimetic narration add up to the same thing. Less gnomically, we can say that a sequence of events such as this in *Captain Singleton* exemplifies the imaginative secret of Defoe's stories: the hero's magical domination of an environment is accomplished by the strictest attention to the demands and dimensions of that environment; the hero seems to obey the rules of nature, history, and society so exactly that he absorbs their independence, and they become aspects of his narrative personality. To stop and pile up gold as the greedy Englishman tries to do is to put yourself at odds with the fluid and open nature of the world of narrative where different things have to keep happening, where the narrative self keeps pressing on toward an always immanent being and never stops to claim any particular, and therefore restricting, activity or identity as its own.

Thus, when the African adventure ends abruptly, Bob in the space of several pages and two years gets to England and both

---

15 'Our *Englishman* remained in the *Dutch* Factory some time, and, as I heard afterwards, died there of Grief; for he having sent a Thousand Pound Sterling over to *England* by the Way of *Holland*, for his Refuge, at his Return to his Friends, the Ship was taken by the *French*, and the Effects all lost.' (167)

squanders and is cheated out of his fortune. We expect this kind of double description by now. Its plausibility is, again, not simply the neutral result of a realistic moral and social view of the world but a way of preserving Singleton's essential innocence, as free of static character or definable personality as of real guilt. The piracy which is the next and greatest phase of Bob's career is manifestly a continuation of that aversion to restrictive identity and that drive towards the possession of experience as a dynamic process.

Here, Defoe follows the general outline of the Avery story he told in *The King of the Pirates* but with the modifications necessary for the greater complexity and complication natural to a longer work. Bob goes to sea again after losing his money, but the near mutiny he is involved in is someone else's idea. The mutiny fails and he and his associates merely escape, joining with mutineers from another ship. All of these circumstances may be said to represent a compromise between the heroic piracy of the folk hero Avery and the self-serving cunning of *The King of the Pirates*. Singleton's subsequent career as a pirate is the usual series of triumphs, and victory in his story as in Defoe's other books is expressed frequently by enumeration of material and techniques. It needs to be emphasized that Defoe's adventure stories are peculiarly reticent about action itself. Most of their time is spent in detailing preparations for action and counting its material profits. The coherent satisfactions of a loose narrative sequence such as this part of *Captain Singleton* are precisely those of exciting enumeration; the vulgar assertive freedom of the pirate myth evident in *The King of the Pirates* is here refined to the excitement of technological and mercantile expertise. First, an example of the latter. The lists of provisions we are given regularly seem to be the bourgeois equivalent of epic detail; the equipment in the following description contains, like the armour of Homeric chieftains, the pattern of the adventure of acquisition:

The next Morning two Barco Longo's came off to us deep loaden, with five *Spaniards* on board them, for Traffick. Our Captain sold them good Pennyworths, and they delivered us sixteen Barrels of Powder, twelve small Runlets of fine Powder for our small Arms, sixty Musquets, and twelve Fuzees for the Officers; seventeen Ton of Cannon Ball, fifteen Barrels of Musquet Bullets, with some

Swords, and twenty good Pair of Pistols. Besides this, they brought thirteen Butts of Wine (for we that were now all become Gentlemen scorn'd to drink the Ship's Beer) also sixteen Puncheons of Brandy, with twelve Barrels of Raisins, and twenty Chests of Lemons: All which were paid for in *English* Goods; and over and above, the Captain received 600 Pieces of Eight in Money. (172)

The ironic, self-deprecatory insert about wine is perhaps the result of an implicit awareness of the libidinal triumph of such an inventory. Bob (he becomes captain later) and his fellows are trading stolen goods, receiving everything for nothing, gaining not only total profit but their identities as pirates in that splendid inventory of material.

Later, after Bob has become captain with William the Quaker as his mate, their ship is severely damaged upon some rocks. The description of the techniques of repairing the ship is a fair example of the main energy of the book, a response to its recurring situation of danger, survival, and skilful recovery:

We immediately unbent all our Sails, sent them ashore upon the Island, and set up seven or eight Tents with them: Then we un-rigged our Topmasts, and cut them down, hoisted all our Guns out, our Provisions and Loading, and put them ashore in the Tents. With the Guns we made two small Batteries, for fear of a Surprize, and kept a Look out upon the Hill. When we were all ready, we laid the Ship a-ground upon a hard Sand, the upper End of the Harbour, and shor'd her up on each Side. At low Water she lay almost dry, so we mended her Bottom, and stopt the Leak which was occasioned by straining some of the Rudder Irons with the Shock which the Ship had against the Rock. (234)

This is no ordinary dockyard. The first half of the paragraph reminds us that Singleton and his men have to be vigilant as they work. Their skills are always exercised in a thrilling context of constant danger from without. But that danger never excludes the exactness of the repairs. The hole is not the result of a simple collision with the rocks, but of the 'straining some of the Rudder Irons'. The precision of such remarks is intended to be a considerable achievement in the context of constant danger. Precision in the context of danger and the confusion implicit in it is one way to describe the structure of Defoe's prose and, by extension, the organizing tension of the books themselves.

This precise control that Singleton and his men exercise repeatedly has, like Crusoe's efficient ordering, a menacing opposite, an ignorant helplessness that they encounter directly at one point in a slave ship like the one in Melville's *Benito Cereno*. Through William's influence, the revolted slaves who man this ship are rescued and one of them tells their story to an incredulous Singleton:

. . . they threw all the Powder and Shot they could find, into the Sea, and they would have thrown the great Guns into the Sea, if they could have lifted them. Being ask'd how they came to have their Sails in such a Condition, his Answer was, *they no understand, they no know what the Sails do ;* that was, they did not so much as know that it was the Sails that made the Ship go; or understand what they meant, or what to do with them. When we asked him whither they were going, he said, they did not know, but believed they should go Home to their own Country again. (198–9)

Obviously, in the context of the story, this kind of passive helplessness and total ignorance of the technology of survival is the opposite of the active intelligence which Singleton and his mates embody. But they, we should remember, are outlaws, radically free beings whose activities have, strictly speaking, to be disavowed by the superficial moral ideology which governs the narrative. Radically active, the pirates should be passive, obedient prisoners in the circumstances they originally rebelled against. The pathetic slaves may be said to redefine passivity and make it unacceptable; their condition transforms passivity in the narrative context into barbarous immobility. *Captain Singleton* may be said at this point to conform to a pattern of transformations resembling that which Levi-Strauss has observed in myth. Active and passive represent two irreconcilable facts, one a fact of nature and one of culture: activity, a necessity of physical survival; passivity, a demand of moral ideology. Just so, Levi-Strauss observes, in myth 'two opposite terms with no intermediary always tend to be replaced by two equivalent terms which admit of a third one as mediator'.[16] The irreconcilable illegal activity and the blessed passivity of the original opposition created by piracy are converted by the operations of the narrative into the ignorant helplessness of the

[16] 'The Structural Study of Myth', in *Structural Anthropology*, p. 224.

slaves and the heroic dexterity of Singleton and his men. Bob himself embodies the mediating term in this new set, for he remains along with William apart from his men; his position as narrator and as a leader who negotiates constantly with the various forms of necessity they encounter places him self-consciously between the extremes of action and passivity. And finally, to confirm that position as mediator, Bob and William return at their end to society and accept its restraints, placing themselves like Crusoe in a position where providence may make use of them.[17]

It may be objected that William is merely a comic figure, a cunning Quaker whose smiling self-possession and excessively smooth casuistry provoke at once admiration and satirical laughter at his expense. William is more truly cunning, more effectively ruthless, and much more confident in his power than any of the other pirates, Bob included. But his wry power requires laughter, ours and his. Crusoe smiled when he described his real political power on the island, and we smile as William demands a certificate from the pirates to the effect that he was taken by force and serves with them against his will. When power really emerges in Defoe's narratives, it must be treated as a joke; that seems to be a way of defusing its subversive accuracy. For what William does in extracting this preliminary certificate of innocence is to repeat in a dangerously explicit way what Singleton's narrative implicitly does for him. William is in thrall to necessity; he has it in writing. Lest anyone see this as revealing parody of the narrative's strategy, the narrative anticipates and controls that reaction by making William a humorous character. Satire lets us discover absurdity in others; the self-mocking comedy of *Captain Singleton's* Quaker pirate disarms our criticism and makes us accept William as a blameless and winning character.[18]

[17] Bob wonders what they are to do with their stolen wealth. 'Nay, *says William*, the Answer to it is short; to quit what we have, and do it here, is to throw it away to those who have no Claim to it, and to divest our selves of it, but to do no Right with it; whereas we ought to keep it carefully together, with a Resolution to do what Right with it we are able; and who knows what Opportunity Providence may put into our Hands, to do Justice at least to some of those we have injured, so we ought at least to leave it to him, and go on, as it is, without doubt, our present Business to do, to some Place of Safety, where we may wait his Will.' (322)

[18] Manuel Schonhorn notes that William 'brings comic relief to a situation rife with expected violence and potential brutalities' and that 'Quaker William makes

Moreover, as the time approaches to end the adventures and retire, William is a crucial ally. Avery in *The King of the Pirates* simply runs away from it all. Bob undergoes a series of quick transformations. He suddenly acquires some religious forebodings; he is now rich enough to feel guilty. Guilt is a function of success, and Bob is once again the perfect reflector of circumstances. In the middle of piracy, opportunity presents itself when they capture three Chinese merchants on their way to Formosa to trade and decide to turn merchants, again following circumstances perfectly. After they resolve to liquidate their holdings totally, they wind up selling stolen goods in the South Seas where they have stolen them. This trick requires various stratagems, culminating in their actual disguise not simply of themselves but of their ship. In other words, they remain alive to the necessity of totally co-operating with circumstance in their transformation into merchants. The joy of power, as elsewhere, is in its subtle techniques of manipulation and indirect action. Thus, William dresses two of the sailors like Quaker merchants and transforms the ship by minutely described alterations into an innocent trading vessel. And the final trick in the series is the transformation of Bob and William into 'Merchants of Persia', rendered with gleefully exact details as an exercise in the art of powerful survival.

I should have observed, that we had new cloathed our selves here after the *Persian* Manner, in long Vests of Silk, a Gown or Robe of *English* Crimson Cloth, very fine and handsome, and had let our Beards grow so after the *Persian* Manner, that we past for *Persian* Merchants, in View only, tho', by *the Way*, we could not understand or speak óne Word of the Language of *Persia*, or indeed of any other but *English* and *Dutch*, and of the latter I understood very little. (319–20)[19]

It is appropriate that the book should end with a series of

---

piracy a joke, an agreeable and spiritedly humorous operation.' Schonhorn sees this as a new direction in the book, a way of saving it from the morally unpleasant. What strikes me as new is the overtly comic tone that William initiates. The direction he furthers by that comedy is the book's over-all ambition to have the energies of piracy without their subversive implications. See 'Defoe's *Captain Singleton*: A Reassessment with Observations', 45.

[19] Defoe and Bob have forgotten that he speaks Portuguese. This is, perhaps, an appropriate lapse, since the point at the end is to show how thoroughly outrageous and therefore impressive their impersonation is.

dazzling and speedy disguises. These transformations are the most visible aspect of the central energy of the book, which is best described at every level as a series of conversions. Most obviously, Bob himself is transformed by his own energy at first and later, with the help of William's cunning, from waif to adventurer to pirate and finally to a 'Grecian' merchant residing in suburban London and married to William's sister. From the beginning, as we have seen, Bob has himself been at the centre of various generalized transforming operations; on the African trip and on the high seas he has in each role he plays helped to convert the necessity of survival into a version of freedom. His narrative is itself a conversion of the pirate myth into a bourgeois narrative which records the establishment of an effectively private and therefore autonomous self, able as Bob is to be beyond the various roles it plays. Thus, his final triumph in overt disguise emphasizes that Bob himself, like smiling Avery at the end of *The King of the Pirates*, is his own man, something else behind the disguise, as he was really something else behind his various other roles. That 'something else', that myth of a residual person behind the visible social personality, is precisely what sets *Captain Singleton* apart from ordinary pirate story.

# IV

## *Moll Flanders:* The Dialectic of Power

I care not whether a Man is Good or Evil;
all that I care
Is whether he is a Wise Man or a Fool. Go!
put off Holiness
And put on Intellect.

Blake, *Jerusalem* (Chapter IV,
Plate 91, ll. 54–6)

I

MOLL has become in the last forty years or so the most popular
of Defoe's characters, at least with critics. The source of that
popularity seems to lie in her wonderful inconsistency, a contradiction between the sordid facts of her story and the attractive
vitality of her personality.[1] Summing up the matter recently,
G. A. Starr has remarked on the ultimate inconsistency: 'So if

[1] *Moll Flanders* is the centre of the critical debate surrounding Defoe's irony. In
that argument, Ian Watt's distinction between a consciously ironic work with a
coherent ironic structure and a work like *Moll Flanders* which is primarily ironic in
our perception of it as such strikes me as conclusive. Watt admits that there are
occasional ironic situations, but he argues persuasively that the deep moral
inconsistencies in the book derive not from Defoe's moral plan but from related
formal and ideological problems. The implicit ethical neutrality of the realistic
mimic autobiography led Defoe to portray a character who shared with him that
'unresolved and largely unconscious' conflict 'typical of the late Puritan dis-
engagement of economic matters from religious and moral sanctions'. (See *The
Rise of the Novel*, Chapter IV, 'Defoe as Novelist: *Moll Flanders*', and p. 127.)
Some replies to Watt's argument have rested on Defoe's journalism, which
makes it clear that he used irony more clearly (and more effectively) elsewhere
and therefore must be employing it in *Moll Flanders*. (See M. E. Novak, 'Defoe's
Use of Irony', in *The Uses of Irony: Papers on Defoe and Swift Read at a Clark Library
Seminar*, April 1966, and his 'Conscious Irony in *Moll Flanders*: Facts and Problems',
*College English*, 26 (1964), 198–204.) Others have based their argument on internal
and textual rather than historical grounds, in effect qualifying Watt's point that
Defoe's novelistic sensibility is not informed by the modern ironic mode. (See
H. L. Koonce, 'Moll's Muddle: Defoe's Use of Irony in *Moll Flanders*', *ELH*, 30
(Dec. 1963), 377–94; and John Preston, *The Created Self: The Reader's Role in
Eighteenth Century Fiction* (New York, 1970), pp. 8 ff.)
I think that Watt has himself provided a fair compromise in his genial survey

Moll is in some ways the product of sociological and psychological conditioning, in other ways she is quite untouched by
experience, a free spirit whom no pitch can defile.'[2]

More clearly than his other narratives, *Moll Flanders* allows us
to see the precise dynamics of the literary event we are dealing
with in reading Defoe's fiction. Strangely enough, to do that we
need to remind ourselves that the narrative self in the autobiographical novel is not a person in the ordinary sense and that
the events in a narrative do not add up to that cumulative
entity emerging from an actual person experiencing the events
of a life, which we call 'personality' in the domesticated psycho-
analytic terms of our time. It should hardly need saying that
literary character constitutes a kind of event, a more definable
entity than the expanding mystery that 'person' implies. The
experience we have as we read is of language describing certain
events and thereby invoking the special kind of 'world' implicit
in that language and those events. 'Character' is a name we
give to the beings who seem to possess that language and promote those events. As Martin Price has said, character in a
novel exists within it 'as persons in a society, but the "society" of
the novel is one with intensive and purposive structure'.[3] Character, in other words, is most often a means towards expressing
the structure of a novel in a way that a person in a society is not
a means of expressing the nature of society.[4] Character in

---

of the controversy. The point that I think we should begin with in any discussion
of *Moll Flanders* is, as Watt puts it, that 'Defoe's genius as an observer, together
with a narrative technique that did not force him to prejudge his material, may
well have produced a masterpiece which is, unintentionally but enduringly, a
comprehensive image of the ambiguous and dehumanizing conflicts into which
modern civilization plunges its unhappy natives.' (See 'The Recent Critical
Fortunes of *Moll Flanders*', *Eighteenth-Century Studies*, 1 (1967), 126.)

[2] *Moll Flanders* (Oxford English Novels, 1971), Introduction, p. ix. All further
references in the text are to this edition. Starr's shrewd discussion in his *Defoe and
Casuistry* points out how we are consistently distracted by the 'novelistic process'
from the 'moral implications' of Moll's various acts (pp. 151–2). 'We may recoil
momentarily from her heartlessness, but so does she, with disarming humanity:
once again, in a manner typical of the entire book, Defoe portrays Moll as both
reprehensible and sympathetic' (p. 164).

[3] 'The Other Self: Thoughts about Character in the Novel', in *Imagined Worlds:
Essays . . . in Honour of John Butt*, ed. Maynard Mack and Ian Gregor (London,
1968), p. 288.

[4] The presence of a thematic unity and structure in the novel has been discussed
by Terence R. Martin, 'The Unity of *Moll Flanders*', *MLQ*, 22 (1961), 115–24.
A different sort of structure, a loose arrangement of topics within the novel's

fiction tends to mimic the complex of problems implied in the term 'personality', but novelistic character is primarily a means towards a large structural end rather than an end in itself.

That notorious contradiction the character of Moll Flanders embodies is the most visible expression of the structure of her novel. Her narrative self is a means of enacting for us independence of the 'other', that is, of society, history, and circumstance in general. Novels like Defoe's, of course, pretend to begin with the opposite proposition that the self is precisely defined by the 'other' and claim to spend their time showing us just how the self is indeed derived from the other. We have seen, however, that there is a simultaneous push to assert self at the expense of other, that the real movement of Defoe's novels is not simply towards the determinants of character but rather towards the depiction of a dialectic between self and other which has as its end a covert but triumphant assertion of the self.[5] In *Moll Flanders*, that dialectic is at its clearest; the self is visibly apart from the other. This seems a paradoxical state of affairs, for the other is in this case no longer the exotic circumstances and characters which prevail in *Crusoe* or in *Singleton* but what is intended as a version of the real world of bourgeois society. But perhaps the values of personal freedom and individual consciousness that bourgeois culture values most are most possible in the exotic spaces Crusoe and Singleton inhabit and are most endangered in the actual streets of eighteenth-

chronology, has been suggested by William B. Piper, '*Moll Flanders* as a Structure of Topics', *SEL*, 9 (Summer 1969), 489–502. Both these essays are valuable correctives to the tendency to read the book in naïve moral-psychological terms as the appropriately formless case history of a person.

[5] That self-assertion is, of course, an obvious and important feature of the book. Even a critic like Koonce chiefly concerned with isolating ironic effects admits that Defoe portrayed 'a woman with a powerful, unmotivated sense of manifest destiny which she is in the act of reconciling with an equally 'powerful, if conveniently underdeveloped, sense of morality' ('Moll's Muddle', p. 380). M. E. Novak, the most extensive defender of Defoe as an ironist, seems to have modified his position somewhat by concluding a recent consideration of the 'complexities' of the book with the admission that Moll may indeed embody a sort of vital contradiction: 'And if she can be both the ideal convert and the wayward servant-whore-thief at the same time, she shares with the Kwakiutl shaman the very natural ability to exist in a number of states at the same time.' (See 'Defoe's 'Indifferent Monitor': the Complexities of *Moll Flanders*', *Eighteenth-Century Studies*, 3 (1970), 365.)

century England. Therefore, if Moll is to be free and really to live in those streets she must, it seems, embody or enact a contradiction which is more than merely lifelike inconsistency.

In truth, the narrative (Moll, if you will, or Defoe) seems aware of that separation and contradiction and strains noticeably towards a rudimentary kind of naturalism. The 'editor' claims in the preface that Moll's language has been changed and made fit to be seen and read, that some parts have been omitted, others shortened. Such a claim invites readers to imagine forbidden details, to flesh out the almost austere and rapid sequence that the book really is. But the preface also claims thereby that Moll is the creature of her environment, that her language and point of view coincide with the circumstances she has passed through. An editor is required to separate Moll from her life, to create a Moll who can speak about her life without being what her life implies.

Moll herself begins her story by speculating in her opening paragraphs about what would have become of her under different social circumstances, in a more rational and humane society. There she would have been placed in an orphanage and not 'brought into a Course of Life, which was not only scandalous in itself, but which in its ordinary Course, tended to the swift Destruction both of Soul and Body' (8). Moll's theory has little connection with the plain facts of her narrative, for what she experiences by being born in Newgate and passing through various hands until she reaches her 'nurse' in Colchester is quickly summarized in several paragraphs and has nothing essentially to do with her subsequent career as a criminal. The facts are that she could as easily have come to her criminal career through any number of alternative sets of circumstances which are not related to the lack of state provisions for orphans and deserted children. Real eighteenth-century criminals were indeed products of vicious circumstances and partly produced by state indifference to child welfare. But Moll, unlike Bob Singleton and Colonel Jack, is not really served badly by the social circumstances surrounding her childhood.

She has sufficient dramatic sense, however, to arrange the opening pages of her narrative in sequences which favour calamity, or often dwell first and foremost upon the melodramatic possibilities of a situation. When her nurse dies, Moll

lingers over her childish terrors and the cruel taunts of her
nurse's daughter, who withholds her 'fortune' of twenty-two
shillings: 'Now was I a poor Gentlewoman indeed, and I was
just that very Night to be turn'd into the wide World; for the
Daughter remov'd all the Goods, and I had not so much as a
Lodging to go to, or a bit of Bread to Eat' (17). It is only after
this scene has been properly elaborated that we are told much
more briefly[6] that compassionate neighbours inform the
mayoress who had previously taken a fancy to little Moll and
she is taken into her household. She becomes, in effect, an
upper-servant in that house, raised on a par with the daughters.
Not only circumstances but nature, too, joins in all this generosity, as Moll tells us in her summary of her education as a young
lady in a gentle house in Colchester: 'By this Means I had . . .
all the Advantages of Education that I could have had, if I had
been as much a Gentlewoman as they were, with whom I
liv'd, and in some things, I had the Advantage of my Ladies,
tho' they were my Superiors; but they were all the Gifts of
Nature, and which all their Fortunes could not furnish' (18).

It is, of course, true that Moll begins as an isolated infant
waif. Normally, we would expect that early isolation such as
Moll provides for herself would produce insecurity and dependence in adolescence and maturity. But the book cares very
little for plausibility of that narrowly personal sort. Moll tries,
in a sense, to look both ways in describing her childhood as part
of the chain of circumstances which made her what she became. But both the incidents from her childhood that she places
before us are as much illustrations of her independence and
somehow instinctive sense of strong isolation as they are
examples of social determinism. The first of these is a half recollection of being left in Colchester by gipsies when she was a
little more than three years old, or perhaps, Moll adds significantly, of her leaving them: 'I have a Notion in my Head, that I
left them there, (that is, that I hid myself and wou'd not go any
further with them)' (9). The natural limitations of recollection
require that such precocious independence remain uncertain.
Not so the second childhood incident, which is actually the
main anecdote that Moll has for us about her early years. Plying

---

[6] In Starr's edition, the deliverance occupies four lines, the calamitous circumstances about twenty-five. See pp. 16–17.

her needle, little Moll declares to her nurse that she will never go into service and will live on her own, supporting herself by her spinning and thereby becoming a 'gentlewoman'. Little Moll innocently supposes that gentle-folk live by their own exertions, that they are independent wage-earners. The reality of gentility is quite the opposite: 'all I understood by being a Gentlewoman, was to be able to Work for myself, and get enough to keep me without that terrible Bug-bear *going to Service*, whereas they meant to live Great, Rich, and High, and I know not what' (13). Moll's fantasy is of authentic independence through labour, an apparently rare possibility for very young children who were engaged in spinning yarn for the manufacture of woollens.[7] What Moll will have to learn to do in the course of her narrative is to relinquish this middle-class dream of honest and self-sufficient survival.

In reality, the dream would be quickly dispelled; a worker like Moll, owning nothing but her own ability to work, is a prisoner of the compulsive cycles of the free market. Moll is given this fantasy by the narrative to demonstrate her membership in a category beyond class and real social experience. Her desire to be nothing but her own woman marks her for us readers as an instinctively free spirit, one not bound by inner compulsions like Robinson Crusoe nor committed like Bob Singleton to his own free-floating nullity but aggressively eager to be independent of circumstances from the very start. The problem is that Moll will have to exchange this ideology of personal freedom for the praxis of independence: movement, secrecy, capital accumulation, and constant manipulation of others by constant withholding of the self. It must seem as if in making this exchange, Moll retains her desire for original freedom, a blameless and intact selfhood which is existentially prior to the various false selves forced upon her by social circumstances. The narrative as we read it is a detailed recording of the many forms of social survival, techniques as liberating for the reader as the spectacular survivals of Crusoe and Singleton.

[7] As Starr notes in his edition, Defoe in his *Tour* mentions Colchester and other places where by spinning yarn 'the very children after four or five years of age, could every one earn their own bread'. But later in the same volume, Defoe revises that by pointing out that he never saw young children working the looms 'except at Colchester in Essex'. (See *A Tour through the Whole Island of Great Britain* (Everyman edition), I. 62, 266.)

But Moll's initial fantasy is crucial in this regard, for it establishes her as a victim who learns to act in self-defence; it posits
the pre-social innocence required to face socially imposed
necessity with a full ruthlessness which the reader is invited to
accept because of the clear moral antithesis involved.[8] That is,
Moll's 'character' as an event in which we participate is the
giving up of the ideology of freedom for the praxis of independence. We participate joyfully in that praxis not simply for
its own sweet sake but because we respond to the ideology of
personal freedom which supports it and for the loss of which it is
the only just recompense.

Moll is taken up into the middle classes by her adolescence in
the Mayor's house at Colchester, but she remains outside the
middle-class values which that house exemplifies in its residents
largely by virtue of her preliminary rooting in freedom. When
she is courted and seduced by the 'elder brother' of the house,
she is committed to a version of the freedom she expressed in her
childish wish for self-sufficiency. For in that seduction she is
still a victim of nature, that is, of the sense of power provided by
her own natural accomplishments and beauty, the mature
equivalents of her childish independence. But like that fantasy,
Moll's self-confidence is bound for failure by social realities: her
education and her natural parts combine to make her an untenable rival for the genuine daughters of the house. Just as
circumstances (the death of her nurse) intervene to make her
childish independence lapse rather than fail, so here circumstances (the seduction by the elder brother) intervene to divert
Moll from actually trying to rise by sheer natural abilities into the
middle-class world of her employers. She begins not only as the
victim of 'nature' but as the sole embodiment of it in the context of the socially established moral cynicism of the household.

This is not to say that the incident is melodrama, that it consists of a simple heroic opposition between nature and society,
innocent Moll versus a corrupt and knowing world. Moll does

[8] The irony of the situation co-operates with little Moll's innocence. The woman
she thinks is a 'gentlewoman' is, in her nurse's words, 'a Person of ill Fame, and has
had two or three Bastards' (14). The irony is at society's expense, for the only
model of independence it displays to innocent eyes involves dependent crime of
some sort. Moll will in time master that irony by becoming another sort of person
of ill fame, a triumphantly secret thief and 'whore' whose independence will be
genuine.

invoke socio-historical conditions and her own ignorance as the specific causes of her seduction: 'knowing nothing of the Wickedness of the times, I had not one Thought of my own Safety, or of my Vertue about me' (22). Her seducer, in the same vein, is 'a gay Gentleman that knew the Town as well as the Country' (19) and who engineers the seduction by a number of carefully executed stratagems. Moreover, Moll has to claim that her seduction was her original disaster, the source or seed of her ultimate moral degeneration into swindler and criminal. As we read, we are conscious of the whole episode as something rather different, something which happens as much from Moll's sense of freedom as from ignorance, and something which is the real beginning of her strength rather than merely the first surrender to circumstances.

The episode illustrates the characteristic double view of the book towards its incidents. Moll is essentially an active intelligence which transforms itself to meet the needs of experience, but she is also necessarily first a passive entity to whom things happen. The book is aggressively committed like all Defoe's narratives to 'variety', to movement of the self through many circumstances and changes. But since those necessary changes must come from the outside, Moll throughout waits for things to happen to her; like Crusoe and Singleton and the others, she depends upon a guaranteed world of whirling circumstances.[9] Even as a thief, for example, she avoids aggressive crimes like house-breaking and counterfeiting. Rather, she walks the streets and waits for the profitable opportunities that will offer themselves. Moll responds to events and dominates them, but she cannot be said to initiate them. What she must have of a primary and assertive nature is a residual self somewhere beneath the various social selves, that authentic self we have already observed in the process of being frustrated and submerged because of the nature of the social world. In meeting

[9] Note, for example, the following sequence after Moll has been abandoned by her Bath lover: 'I found no encouraging Prospect; I waited, I liv'd regularly, and with as much frugality as became my Circumstances, but nothing offer'd; nothing presented, and the main Stock wasted apace; what to do I knew not, the Terror of approaching Poverty lay hard upon my Spirits: I had some Money, but where to place it I knew not, nor would the Interest of it maintain me, at least not in *London*.'
'At length a new Scene open'd. . . .' (129)

hostile circumstances she negates that self, but that negation becomes an affirmation in the process. Some Hegelian terms are, I think, appropriate and illuminating here, for Moll's relationship as self to the 'other' of experience is manifestly a dialectical one. In order to 'become herself', Moll has to confront the negativity of the other. The two initial terms, the assertive self and the negating other, produce a third term wherein 'the first term [self] is found again, only richer and more determinate, together with the second term [other], whose determination has been added to the first determination. The third term [self involved in other] turns back to the first term by negating the second one, by negating therefore the negation and limitation of the first term. It releases the content of the first term, by removing from it that whereby it was incomplete, limited and destined to be negated, or that whereby it was itself negative.'[10]

The seduction operates, to translate these terms into the concrete events of the novel, as a rite of passage into the world of sexual and social exploitation that is nothing less than the actual and operative world of the story. But that world is thereby defined as an environment that must be faced and mastered rather than as a set of circumstances that determines the self. The initiate, in this case, remains apart from the world into which she is introduced; the seduction is there precisely to illustrate the necessity of a new knowledge of self as both in and out of the circumstances of its world. The seduction (the second term, the other) releases the self from the negative determination and limitation which define it by itself. Let us call that negativity spontaneous desire.

Young Moll is in this sequence clearly possessed by her own spontaneous desire for what she calls the 'person' of her seducer and for the gold he gives her. She describes herself as 'taken up Onely with Pride of my Beauty, and of being belov'd by such a Gentleman; as for the Gold I spent whole Hours in looking upon it; I told the Guineas over and over a thousand times a Day' (26). She enacts the compulsive ignorance of self when it naïvely desires the other, since it depends totally upon the other for its fulfilment. In the seduction, Moll is obliterated by the

[10] Henri Lefebvre, *Dialectical Materialism*, trans. John Sturrock (London, 1968, first published 1938), p. 34.

experience: 'My Colour came, and went, at the Sight of the Purse, and with the fire of his Proposal together; so that I could not say a Word, and he easily perceiv'd it; so putting the Purse into my Bosom, I made no more Resistance to him, but let him do just what he pleas'd; and as often as he pleas'd; and thus I finish'd my own Destruction at once' (28–9).

Old Moll's description of the events leading to the seduction reveal the qualities of mind and the self-positioning skill that she is to acquire later, a mind extraordinarily aware of contingencies and always ready to approach experience as a network of possibilities, and always therefore able to stand apart from mere spontaneous experience. Her summary of the situation begins as a moral warning to unwary young women but turns away from such banalities and into the first extended exemplification in the narrative of the amoral analysis of action that defines the style and self of the mature Moll:

Thus I gave up myself to a readiness of being ruined without the least concern, and am a fair *Memento* to all young Women, whose Vanity prevails over their Vertue: Nothing was ever so stupid on both Sides, had I acted as became me, and resisted as Vertue and Honour requir'd, this Gentleman had either Desisted his Attacks, finding no room to expect the Accomplishment of his Design, or had made fair, and honourable Proposals of Marriage; in which Case, whoever had blam'd him, no Body could have blam'd me. In short, if he had known me, and how easy the Trifle he aim'd at, was to be had, he would have troubled his Head no farther, but have given me four or five Guineas, and have lain with me the next time he had come at me; and if I had known his Thoughts, and how hard he thought I would be to be gain'd, I might have made my own Terms with him; and if I had not Capitulated for an immediate Marriage, I might for a Maintenance till Marriage, and might have had what I would; for he was already Rich to Excess, besides what he had in Expectation. (25–6)

Moll is saying without any equivocation that the purpose of a knowledge of self and of the other, moral or psychological, is self-protection, or, better, self-reservation. Spontaneous desire simply reaches out for the object of desire, thinking that it can appropriate the other directly. The seduction is the first step in the dialectic process which converts spontaneous desire into capable self-possession. The analytical Moll who describes the seduction is the third term that results from the collision of self and other, the calculating self able to operate within the other, seeing the old spontaneous part of itself as merely obeying the determination of the other. The other, too, is now viewed in its negative fullness, as itself bound by its own need to be simply the other. The elder brother's shrewdness is superficial, determined by his own sexual duplicity. He fails to realize Moll's innocence and judges her as if she were as self-interested as he is.

G. A. Starr has observed that 'Moll's world is one in which things are not good or evil but characteristically good *and yet* evil', and that the imaginative secret of the book is thus a 'double vision' which 'extends from the structure of individual sentences and paragraphs to the ethos of the book as a whole'.[11] Such an analysis is excellent but static in its implications, taking the moralistic surface of the book as its ultimate content. If we look beyond the categories of good and evil and consider the energy that Moll communicates in her expansive career to us as onlookers, we see that there is a third term beyond the double vision that Starr speaks of which exploits the moralistic antithesis of good and evil. In this opening sequence, we are being prepared for a career in which Moll will repeatedly perform her dialectic with the world and emerge with a self intact or, rather, fortified and expanded.

Her seducer's post-coital advice is that she marry his eager younger brother. Moll's reluctance is part of her still intact ideology of naïve freedom; she cannot 'think of being a Whore to one Brother, and a Wife to the other' (31). That is, Moll is not yet ready to do what she will do repeatedly throughout the book—reside comfortably within contradiction, play several inconsistent roles at the same time in order to survive. The elder brother's rhetoric, as Moll presents it, is a series of summarizing clauses, extenuating circumstances: 'he entreated me to consider seriously of it, assur'd me that it was the only way to Preserve our mutual Affection, that in this Station we might love as Friends, with the utmost Passion, and with a love of Relation untainted, free from our just Reproaches, and free from other Peoples Suspicions; that he should ever acknowledge his happiness owing to me; that he would be Debtor to me as long as he liv'd, and would be paying that Debt as long as he had

[11] *Moll Flanders*, Introduction, pp. xx–xxii.

Breath' (56). Moll accompanies his soothing casuistry with her melodramatic alternative to the marriage: 'turn'd out to the wide World, a meer cast off Whore, *for it was no less*, and perhaps expos'd as such; with little to provide for myself; with no Friend, no Acquaintance in the whole World, *out of that Town*' (56). But action in this context is made possible by a third possibility, neither the imposed and specious compromise of loveless marriage nor the imposed extravagance of solitary ruin but the clear perception of the necessity of self-preservation: 'I began to see a Danger that I was in, which I had not consider'd of before, and that was of being drop'd by both of them, and left alone in the World to shift for myself' (57). From the Hegelian analogy, we can say that this small shift in emphasis is the assertion of a self which locates itself within the compulsions of the other and remains simultaneously outside those compulsions, aware of itself as determined and thereby freeing itself. In choosing marriage with Robin the younger brother, Moll begins, in a small way to be sure, to choose herself rather than the other.

What is obtrusive about this sequence, both before and after the actual seduction, is its minute observation of circumstances, relationships, possibilities, contingencies. In this, the book reveals its almost obsessive interest in the amplification of those possibilities which precede action. What distinguishes *Moll Flanders* from mere criminal biography of the period and what makes the book a novel in the full modern sense of the term is its tendency towards extended meditation on the nature of action rather than the mere description of action itself. Moll seems to develop and emerge as a character in so far as she is constantly preparing for future action even as she indulges in action itself. She is most fully herself when she keeps something of herself (or her substance, frequently and literally her capital) aside and ready for future possibilities. Of course, the perfection of such techniques involves the drastic revision of what we ordinarily think of as personality; it involves dramatic isolation of those self-conscious aspects of personality which turn it into a role, a way of pure and deliberate acting rather than that mixture of the irresistible and the arranged that we think of as self-consciousness.

This opening sequence is very much a preliminary. Moll's

self-assertion is still tentative and held in the context of naïve spontaneity. It is only after her quickly summarized five-year marriage to Robin that Moll claims maturity. Courted by various suitors, she refuses to become involved: 'The Case was alter'd with me, I had Money in my Pocket, and had nothing to say to them: I had been trick'd once by *that Cheat call'd* LOVE, but the Game was over; I was resolv'd now to be Married, or Nothing, and to be well Married, or not at all' (60).

Even that claim looks premature in terms of what actually happens to her. Moll seems to be concerned still with spontaneous desire. After all, there she is in London now, a merry widow in lodgings presided over by a draper whose sister is 'one of the Madest, Gayest things alive' (59). Moll declares openly that she 'lov'd the Company indeed of Men of Mirth and Wit, Men of Gallantry and Figure, and was often entertain'd with such' (60). Because of that unsound inclination, she marries unwisely, her husband a draper but one who aspires to gentility, an 'amphibious Creature, this *Land-water-thing*, call'd, *a Gentleman-Tradesman*' (60). But her transition from the naïve spontaneity of the seduction is clearly in process, as she describes herself aware of her circumstances, able to manœuvre with skill but unsure of her own best interest: 'I was catch'd in the very Snare, which *as I might say*, I laid for my self; *I say laid for myself*, for I was not Trepan'd I confess, but I betray'd my self' (60). That confession, by virtue of its peculiar insistence and repetition, is an assertion of selfhood and independence, especially in Moll's immediate context of a humiliating seduction and a forced marriage.

But the incident records the emergence of Moll's new and mature self in more subtle ways as well. She is now, noticeably, a secret self within the events of the narrative itself, as much outside her behaviour in her actions as she is in her retrospective narration of them. We become fully aware around this point in our career as readers of the book that Moll's greatest concern as a narrator is to establish her separate consciousness as an actor in the events of her life. Thus, she here observes that she observed then as a widow on the make that 'the brightest Men came upon the dullest Errand, *that is to say*, the Dullest, as to what I aim'd at' (60). Moll's control within her narrative is a matter of separateness as actor, a sense of apartness much more consistent than either Crusoe's or Singleton's. Unlike them, moreover, she has already mastered the art of indirect discourse and action, as indeed she is forced to by the much more sophisticated society in which she moves. For example, Moll tells us that she liked men of wit and spirit; that is, she is sexually attracted to men who are socially versatile and thereby, by her own implication and emphasis, sexually potent. That is the meaning of Moll's explanation of her preference for a man 'that was something of a Gentleman too; that when my Husband had a mind to carry me to the Court, or to the Play, he might become a Sword, and look as like a Gentleman, as another Man; and not be one that had the mark of his Apron-strings upon his Coat, or the mark of his Hat upon his Periwig; that should look as if he was set on to his Sword, when his Sword was put on to him, and that carried his Trade in his Countenance' (60). The sword is a badge of aristocratic sexuality, a device which accompanies and underlines the sexuality implicit in the kind of social versatility Moll here admires. But, alas, such men are naturally disinclined for the married security Moll also desires. Moll presents herself to these gay pseudo-gentlemen as someone of like mind, but she is also of another mind. She wants, that is, to combine sexuality and social versatility with the stability (sexual and social) of marriage. Her curious reticence to say just that, her coy paradox that makes their single-minded liveliness into 'dullness', is of a piece with her complicated and disguised desires.

In marrying her 'Gentleman-Tradesman', Moll is doing much more than miscalculating and obeying the social and psychological probabilities of her situation. On the level of structure that character exists to further, she is setting out on the first of many excursions into the social contradiction and inconsistency that the book reveals and tries to master. Moll is herself a contradictory mixture, half waif and child cottage spinner, half middle-class young lady. As a widow of limited substance, she is, like her new husband, involved in aspiring and aggressive social movement. Indeed, the highlight of their marriage, the only incident from it that Moll relates, is their impersonation of nobility during an extravagant jaunt to Oxford. That hilarious trip is the concrete if exaggerated expression of what their marriage represents: social versatility and aspiration. All this underlines the real and recurring structure and function of the book: to enact a self which can move freely through social circumstances, revealing at once their superficiality and their desirability, providing the satisfactions of free social movement by a solid and established self whose consciousness is somehow based beyond social circumstances even while cunningly and joyously moving through them. As everyone knows, *Moll Flanders* is about eighteenth-century social and economic realities, but it is also about the superior reality of a self which moves through them, mastering them with a powerful dialectic rhythm and never succumbing to their full implications as cumulatively limiting realities.

To be sure, the book may be said to reveal and dramatize the difficulty of such an accommodation of reality to the desires of the self. The draper is soon bankrupt and decamps for France, leaving Moll in the position of having 'a Husband, and no Husband' (64). This latter is one of Moll's favourite constructions. She tells us that her Bath lover 'had a Wife' and that 'he had no Wife, that is to say she was as no Wife to him' (109, 120). Her banker's clerk tells her, in the same way, 'I have a Wife and no Wife' (134). Moll is herself at Bath 'a Woman of Fortune, tho' I was a Woman without a Fortune' (106).[12] Such a construction points not to ambiguity but to contradiction, a total disparity between social appearance and personal reality which is the pervasive condition the narrative dramatizes. Earlier, Moll had been unable to consider being both whore and wife. Now she has learned a strategy to meet contradiction with disguise. The evasive action she learned as a courted widow is now intensified and literalized. She retires to the Mint under the first of many aliases, Mrs. Flanders. There, to borrow her construction, she is a debtor and no debtor.

The Mint, like Newgate later in the story, is distilled social compulsion, a place which exemplifies the inexorability of social determinants. Yet here is Moll, friendless, as she tells us, and in retreat from her husband's creditors, a debtor finding safety in debtors' prison, audaciously converting circumstances into a version of freedom. Her disdain for her fellows in the Mint reveals the quality of her strength; her superiority to

---

[12] Starr notes the recurrence of the construction and the paradoxes that accompany it (pp. 367–8 n.).

them lies, again, in her separation from the facts and her real residence in her self:

> But it is none of my Talent to preach; these Men were too wicked, even for me; there was something horrid and absurd in their way of Sinning, for it was all a Force even upon themselves; they did not only act against Conscience, but against Nature; they put a Rape upon their Temper to drown the Reflections, which their Circumstances continually gave them; and nothing was more easie than to see how Sighs would interrupt their Songs, and paleness, and anguish sit upon their Brows, in spight of the forc'd Smiles they put on; nay, sometimes it would break out at their very Mouths, when they had parted with their Money for a lewd Treat, or a wicked Embrace. . . . (65)

Clearly, what Moll finds contemptible in these men is their lack of control and consistency. Like all of Defoe's characters, she learns to be more horrified by disorder than by evil. We can add that as characters in fiction they are justified in equating disorder and evil, for disorder precludes the order that constitutes being and freedom for a character. The delusive idea of freedom implicit in the dissipations of Moll's degenerate associates in the Mint is escape from circumstances by pleasure, a temporary solipsism that Moll despises as ineffective. She realizes here and in her subsequent actions what Georg Simmel insisted upon, that 'freedom is not solipsistic existence but sociological action', and that it is a continuing struggle to escape the domination of particular relationships with others and with institutions.[13] In fact, her career begins to fit the rest of Simmel's analysis of freedom: 'But it no less consists in a power relation to others, in the possibility of making oneself count within a given relationship, in the obligation or submission of others, in which alone it finds its value and application.'[14]

Indeed, Moll emerges from the Mint as an expert female tactician, now fully accomplished and without even the small illusions she cherished before. She helps a friend trick a reluctant suitor into marriage and from that experience resolves to engineer her own survival. Once again, this involves further

[13] *The Sociology of Georg Simmel*, trans. and ed. Kurt H. Wolff (New York, 1964), p. 121.
[14] Simmel, p. 122.

disguise and even, in Moll's own terms, outright transformation: 'I resolv'd therefore, as to the State of my present Circumstances; that it was absolutely Necessary to change my Station,
and make a new Appearance in some other Place where I was
not known, and even to pass by another Name if I found
Occasion' (76). But she goes further than this. On the advice of
the friend she has helped, she resolves to take the offensive, to
become a man by adopting the aggressively fraudulent tactics of
the male world: 'as we had observ'd, *as above*, how the Men
made no scruple to set themselves out as Persons meriting a
Woman of Fortune, when they had really no Fortune of their
own; it was but just to deal with them in their own way, and if
it was possible, to Deceive the Deceiver' (77).

But the book is nicely delicate in such crucial matters. Moll
never becomes, even later in her worst moments as a thief, a
nakedly aggressive character. She retains her theoretical innocence as a character by a series of quasi-legal protective
measures and self-reservations. Through a careful series of suggestions, her suitor is led to believe that she is wealthy, and her
insistence on her poverty in that context becomes a way of convincing him that she is wealthy. She is, to return to her own
construction, a cheat and no cheat:

Besides, tho' I had jested with him, as he suppos'd it, so often
about my poverty, yet, when he found it to be true, he had fore-
closed all manner of objection, seeing whether he was in jest or in
earnest, he had declar'd he took me without any regard to my
Portion, and whether I was in jest or in earnest, I had declar'd my
self to be very Poor, so that *in a word*, I had him fast both ways;
and tho' he might say afterwards he was cheated, yet he could never
say that I had cheated him. (80)

It needs to be emphasized that Moll in this sequence, and
indeed from the date of her first widowhood in London,
operates with female accomplices. Moll's career is, on the surface, a series of relationships with men, but those relationships
are usually subordinate to a powerful and instrumental alliance
with a female conspirator. Her career culminates in a relationship with a woman: the 'governess' who helps her become a
master-thief.[15] Defoe's characters, famous for their individuality,

[15] See below, pp. 119–20.

tend to acquire allies at moments of action, characters who help them to act and absorb at the same time most of the blame for action. Moll here marries her Virginia planter and enters the visible social structure of marriage, but the real alliance is with the invisible league of self-conscious women, an informal but powerful organization. Women thus 'organized' are, like pirates and traveller-merchants, a society within society, an authentic group manipulating the inauthentic relationships ordinary society offers.

Moll passes directly (in terms of narrative space, a few paragraphs) into another relationship with a woman, this time her mother-in-law/mother in Virginia. The trip itself, by the way, is of no interest to the narrative, summarized in a paragraph in spite of its dreadful storms and encounter with a pirate. What matters for Moll is the powerful alliance with her mother-in-law in the face of complex circumstances, the real dangers that the narrative is interested in. Faced with another contradiction, the greatest one yet, that she is once again a wife and no wife, married to her brother, Moll passes quickly from the rhetoric of desolation to the tactical joys of analysis and self-preservation. Viewed as a character in the normal affective sense, her calm in this crisis is monstrous as well as implausible. But in terms of her real function as an indestructible personal energy centre, her control is appropriate and actually winning. She waits for her mother's 'Rhapsodies' (96) to subside and, 'When these things were a little over with her we fell into a close Debate about what should be first done before we gave an account of the matter to my Husband' (96). What the women fear and seek to neutralize is the practical power and emotional incompetence of Moll's husband/brother: 'we could neither of us see our way thro' it, nor see how it could be safe to open such a Scene to him; it was impossible to make any judgment, or give any guess at what Temper he would receive it in, or what Measures he would take upon it; and if he should have so little Government of himself, as to make it publick, we easily foresaw that it would be the ruin of the whole Family, and expose my Mother and me to the last degree' (96).

So two women, Moll and her mother, share a secret, a characteristic situation in the novel. It can be said that in Defoe's narratives in general the secret is the source of personal authenticity, what sets a character apart from his society, guarantees and sustains that apartness, and in short makes him a character. Criminals like Captain Avery and Moll in her criminal phase are thus always attractive figures in an individualistic culture. Their secret criminality, it can be argued, is primarily a means towards a dramatic apartness and consequently undeniable authenticity rather than a significant act *per se*. The interest and complexity of *Moll Flanders* lie not only in the varieties of apartness, criminal and legal, that it enacts but also in its ability to locate Moll both within and without society, to keep her moving through society and within herself at approximately the same time. To put it another way, the book's greatest achievement in relation to Defoe's narratives is to make her apartness a social necessity and personal reality rather than a fantasy of escape. For Moll's exact secret here in Virginia with her husband/brother is that she is disqualified from social participation and at the same time threatened by a powerful world of legal forms and institutions: 'and if at last he should take the Advantage the Law would give him, he might put me away with disdain, and leave me to Sue for the little Portion that I had, and perhaps wast it all in the Suit, and then be a Beggar; the Children would be ruin'd too, having no legal Claim to any of his Effects; and thus I should see him perhaps in the Arms of another Wife in a few Months, and be my self the most miserable Creature alive' (96–7). The sequence of disasters—legal, financial, personal—reveals the instinctive priorities of Moll's being. It is not, as some have been quick to assume, that she despises the personal, but rather that she enacts in her character and career the fact that the personal depends upon the legal and the financial for its existence. Moll's ultimate secret is not really her incest but her knowledge of that sequence, her knowledge that the individual sustains himself by consciousness of social forms and thereby negates their negation and affirms a new kind of self.

This process of dialectical transformation of disastrous social circumstances into personal affirmation and freedom is actually what occurs. Moll's revelation to her husband/brother is a model of steely control, made all the more formidable by contrast with his near collapse: 'I observ'd he became Pensive and Melancholly; and in a Word, as I thought a little Distemper'd in his Head; I endeavour'd to talk him into Temper, and to Reason him into a kind of Scheme for our Government in the Affair, and sometimes he would be well, and talk with some Courage about it' (103). But he attempts suicide twice, and Moll finds herself changed by these circumstances: 'My pity for him now began to revive that Affection, which at first I really had for him' (104). His despair changes 'into a long ling'ring Consumption' (104) and Moll finds herself 'restless too, and uneasie; I hanker'd after coming to *England*, and nothing would satisfie me without it' (104). The pattern is clear: Moll submits to circumstance and admits her incest, although her admission is carefully planned and her relationship to the incest is made into an objective one. That negation negates itself in her husband/brother's illness, and Moll is fortified and propelled to England in a new and richer version of herself. The narrative is at pains to be specific about this combination of circumstances and inner desire which transforms Moll: 'and so *my own Fate pushing me on*, the way was made clear for me, and *my Mother concurring*, I obtain'd a very good Cargo for my coming to *England*' (104). That precise alignment of desire and circumstance is what all Defoe's characters strive for, and as such it may be said to mark the end of a division in Moll's career. In returning to London, Moll embarks on a new stage of her life, one in which she is to repeat the relationships she has had so far as mistress and wife but with a new consciousness and a refined skill in the art of survival.[16]

[16] Douglas Brooks has seen the structure of the book in these repetitions. He has argued that the book has a bipartite structure consisting of Moll's unconscious psychological recapitulations of her initial sexual and marital adventures in her life of crime. Brooks says that Moll's incest is an unconscious re-enactment of the imaginary incest she committed while married to Robin and dreamt of his elder brother, her initial seducer. Moll punishes her brother/husband the way the elder brother punished her, making him commit incest. Then, to atone for that she returns to England and sleeps chastely (for a time) with her Bath lover. Brooks shrewdly discovers, in short, a psychological structure in the events of the book which provides a pathological coherence for the character of Moll considered as a 'personality'. (See '*Moll Flanders*: An Interpretation', *Essays in Criticism*, 19 (1969), 46–59.)
    Arthur Sherbo has dismissed this and other structural readings of the book by calling all repetitions in Defoe's novels at times a sign of the poverty of his imagination and occasionally an index to his fascination with certain basic and recurring situations. (See *Studies in the Eighteenth-Century English Novel*, East Lansing, Michigan, 1969, p. 157.) Sherbo's impatience with fanciful readings is understandable, but a reading like Brooks's is persuasive. The solution, I think, lies in reminding

The quality of that consciousness is evident in the way Moll positions herself, having learned the secret of active placement of the self where it can respond to circumstances in a profitable manner. If we listen to Moll's explanations, she seems still to be caught up in spontaneous desire. Bath, she explains, 'is a Place of Gallantry enough; Expensive, and full of Snares; I went thither indeed in the view of taking any thing that might offer' (106). But she also explains that she is still caught in contradiction, 'being now, *as it were*, a Woman of Fortune, tho' I was a Woman without a Fortune' (106). She is, in fact, waiting (or lying in wait) for opportunity to offer, trusting in a world of bountiful circumstances which the agile self can master and turn to self-advantage: 'I expected something, or other might happen in my way, that might mend my Circumstances as had been my Case before' (106). There is a progression at work here. Moll has gone from innocent maiden to gay and partially designing widow, and then to calculating bigamist with her husband/brother after her gentleman-tradesman has run away. There has been a fairly precise increase in each connection of Moll's power in relation to the institution of marriage, that is, her action has acquired increasing sociological meaning. Her personal power is exercised both within the various relationships and in relation to the institution of marriage. And in dominating marriage itself, Moll exercises power over society. She takes the office of mistress and in the process of her narrative converts that initial sexual irregularity (with the elder brother) which makes her totally vulnerable into a liberating and totally dominant position in a parallel relationship with her Bath lover.

That dominance in the context of that pattern is behind the curious relationship she has with her Bath lover, a courtship in which her victory is a matter of almost total reserve. She allows him (again by means of a female accomplice, her landlady) to propose assistance and then refuses it. He offers again: 'How-

---

ourselves that Moll the literary character does not properly have the unlimited psychological depth she would have if she were an analysand on a couch. But, on the other hand, to say with Sherbo that the novel is merely its episodic surface is to ignore the imaginative unity we feel as we read. The answer lies, as this chapter is concerned to show, in a unity whose structure lies on the social and existential surface of selfhood rather than in the psychological depths of personality.

ever, it was not long before he attack'd me again, and told me he found that I was backward to trust him with the Secret of my Circumstances, *which he was sorry for*; assuring me that he enquir'd into it with no design to satisfie his own Curiosity, but meerly to assist me, if there was any occasion' (110). The code is clear enough. If Moll reveals herself and asks for 'assistance', she becomes a dependent mistress. So Moll holds out, 'secretly very glad', but refusing to ask. She accepts money, however, but in a ritualized way which preserves her independence and makes him the sexual aggressor. He asks her to bring him all her money and then to fetch his money box:

He took the Drawer, and taking my Hand, made me put it in, and take a whole handful; I was backward at that, but he held my Hand hard in his Hand, and put it into the Drawer, and made me take out as many Guineas almost as I could well take up at once.

When I had done so, he made me put them into my Lap, and took my little Drawer, and pour'd out all my own Money among his, and bad me get me gone, and carry it all Home into my own Chamber. (112)

In spite of the overt sexual suggestions of this gift and its manner, their relationship remains chaste, and that chastity is in context a sign of Moll's power over her lover, since her reserve extracts these elaborate means of self-display from him. At his suggestion, they perform extensive feats of sexual abstinence: 'I frequently lay with him, and he with me, and altho' all the familiarities between Man and Wife were common to us, yet he never once offered to go any farther, and he valued himself much upon it' (115–16). Her lover offers this service as an earnest of his real affection, as something that he supposes will please her and enhance him in her eyes. Like the strange ceremony with the money, it is a ritualized act of service which Moll presents in order to expose its coercive and self-serving nature.

Their chastity ends when Moll allows him 'to discharge him of his Engagement for one Night and no more' (116). Moll's confessed wickedness renders this bizarre affair all the more impressive as an expression of her power, since she says she mastered her own spontaneous desire for him up to this point in order to achieve perfect mastery of her lover and the situations he has devised. Psychologically, I think, the incident makes little sense, unless we care to invoke a suddenly complicated reciprocal of desire and repression as the secret of Moll's personality. What we have in her is not an analysand but a character in a narrative context performing certain acts. Those acts in the particular context created by the narrative (a woman of no fortune, technically a bigamist, depending upon a married man for her survival) are an extraordinary assertion of control, a transformation (comic and joyous) of the office of mistress and of the sociological reality of male dominance in such a relationship. The concrete truth of the narrative and the pleasure it seeks to give us as readers lie in such a formulation, somewhat different from the facts of mere personality.

From the beginning of her story, of course, Moll has offered other interpretations of these and other facts of her career. These comments form a kind of moralistic superstructure, sometimes plausible and parallel to the other structure I am concerned with, sometimes not. Here, for example, Moll laments her weakness, her surrender to her Bath lover, but defends it as the result of circumstances and irresistible inclination: 'It is true, *and I have confess'd it before*, that from the first hour I began to converse with him, I resolv'd to let him lye with me, if he offer'd it; but it was because I wanted his help and assistance, and I knew no other way of securing him than that: But when we were that Night together, and, as I have said, had gone such a length, I found my Weakness, the Inclination was not to be resisted, but I was oblig'd to yield up all even before he ask'd it' (119). That happens to be, if we check Moll's cross reference, not quite the case. She recorded a very careful set of tactics to extract submission only on her terms; in her chronology, she declares that she would have submitted to him only after he had acknowledged her moral superiority and helped establish her financial independence. Her narrative as we read it says something different from her occasional moralistic summaries. The latter stress dependence upon compulsive circumstances; the narrative proper enacts purposeful action. It is the pattern we noticed at the beginning of this chapter and the characteristic pattern of Defoe's narratives: free action in the context of compelling circumstances.

As its selection of events makes obvious, the narrative exists to give us the pleasure of watching Moll cope with desperate circumstances. Her subsequent six years 'in this happy but unhappy Condition' (120) with her Bath lover are summarized in a sentence. We pass directly to Moll's latest predicament when her lover repents the connection, and we are given side by side an account of her own repentance and her successful lies to get a last £50 out of him. After a page or so of moral summarizing and conventional extenuations (a woman is weak and helpless, if only she had met a good husband rather than a married man, etc.), Moll reveals her actual posture under the theory of repentance—commitment to the techniques of survival and a hope that circumstances will provide an opening. It is, we can see as we read, an actuality which elicits a style of quite unusual directness, freed from the normal qualifications and parentheses that the depiction of complicated action usually involves: 'But all this was nothing; I found no encouraging Prospect; I waited, I liv'd regularly, and with as much frugality as became my Circumstances, but nothing offer'd; nothing presented, and the main Stock wasted apace' (129).

As Moll sinks deeper into what she herself in that bleak stylistic moment describes as circumstance, she edges towards the ultimate circumstances that will drive her to crime. But she also rises further in her readiness for action, her skill and agility in the game of survival growing noticeably with each encounter. Her last set of actions before turning criminal involves her most complicated tactics so far and her most flagrant violation of institutions. She progresses, that is, from merely theoretical bigamy to actual bigamy. Both marriages, moreover, are contracted under the falsest and most clearly self-seeking circumstances Moll has yet invoked. She now actively engages in impersonation rather than defensive disguise. With the banker's clerk who impresses her deeply, she tells us, with his honesty, she passes for 'a Woman of Fortune' and 'a very modest sober Body' (138) and ventures one of her most aggressive theoretical statements: 'which whether true or not in the Main, yet you may see how necessary it is, for all Women who expect any thing in the World, to preserve the Character of their Virtue, even when perhaps they may have sacrific'd the Thing itself' (138).

Her simultaneous campaign in Lancashire as a rich widow is also aggressively fraudulent. There, her assets are exaggerated by a female accomplice and she marries handsome Jemy, who thinks she has £15,000 and passes himself off as the possessor of great wealth in Ireland. When they discover their mutual deception, they part amicably, Moll recognizing in Jemy some-one who is exactly like herself engaged in blameless self-preservation. She excuses him as an amateur, 'a Gentleman, unfortunate and low, but had liv'd well' (151), and a victim of his accomplice's greed and poor planning. Indeed, her romp with Jemy is full of the highest spirits in the book and Moll's narrative convinces us that he succeeds in reviving her spon-taneous desire. The real Moll under all those protective social selves declares herself touched, deeply distressed at losing her Jemy. And yet when she returns to London, 'tho' with the utmost reluctance on my side' (159), she is still capable of remarkable discretion: 'I gave him a Direction how to write to me, tho' still I reserv'd the grand Secret, and never broke my Resolution, which was not to let him ever know my true Name, who I was, or where to be found' (159). That 'grand Secret' (even to us, her intimates, that remains a secret) is a sign of her now fully developed reserve, a reserve which resists even her extravagant desire for Jemy.

In the context of the book, Moll's reserve in the face of her first unqualified desire since her initial seduction by the elder brother is an expression of the power she has acquired by her experiences. We expect fictional characters to 'grow' and mature. Strictly speaking, Moll's power is not primarily a matter of personal growth or development, although we find ourselves drawn to such terms. What we experience as readers is actually a series of parallel incidents which form a pattern of transformations quite apart from any structure of personality. Like Crusoe, Moll converts the self-destructiveness of natural impulse into profitable self-assertion. If we look closely at her various relationships since the initial seduction, they are pre-sented as devoid of any but the most generalized sexuality. That sexual distance follows from the trauma or lesson of Moll's

seduction, as she herself explains it to us. What she now does is
the result of the dialectical movement of the narrative implicit
in that schema of relationships: from disastrous sexuality to
profitable sexual involvement to a synthesis of sexuality and
profit. By experiencing generalized sexuality in the context of
various relationships for survival, Moll negates the initial
negation and destructiveness of sexuality. She converts the
opposition between sexual desire and survival into a synthesis
which leads to social advancement. The affair with Jemy,
intense as it is, can now exist simultaneously with her negotiations with the bank clerk: 'I had taken care all this while to
preserve a Correspondence with my honest Friend at the Bank,
or rather he took care to Correspond with me, for he wrote to
me once a Week' (160). Moll has encouraged her banker to
divorce his whorish wife; she told him as she left for Lancashire
'that as soon as he had su'd out a Divorce from his first Wife, if
he would send me an Account of it, I would come up to
*London*, and that then we would talk seriously of the Matter'
(141). And now, pregnant by Jemy, she arrives in London to
hear that the divorce suit prospers only slowly. Her reaction is
alert to the exact advantages for her of that delay: 'for tho' I
was in no condition to have had him yet, not being so foolish to
marry him when I knew my self to be with Child by another
Man, as some I know have ventur'd to do; yet I was not willing
to lose him, and in a word, resolv'd to have him if he continu'd
in the same mind, as soon as I was up again' (160). The kind of
elastic energy displayed in a sequence like this and exemplified
in passages like this one is more a matter of structural heroics
than it is of psychological plausibility. The pattern the narrative
follows in order to arrive at a moment like this obeys the repeti-
tive schema of myth rather than the incremental details we
associate with the novel. Or, to put the matter the best way,
Moll pretends to be a novelistic character who is subject to compulsions of development within the conditions of her environment, so that her story may deliver the pattern of an indestructible and elastic self which reduces apparently formless incidents
to a pattern of survival.

At this point, Moll enters into two relationships to secure herself. She marries her bank clerk in time, but first she has to have
her baby. To accomplish that she makes contact with the

sinister midwife and criminal queen whom Moll comes to call her governess. This connection is the culmination of Moll's alliances with various females throughout the book, and it is the most effective and important of them, for various reasons. Her governess enables her to have her child secretly and marry her banker, and when he dies five years later, she becomes Moll's instructor and protector in crime. In exercising both these key functions, the governess welcomes Moll definitively into the female sub-culture whose outlines the book has traced thus far. The governess presides over a secret lying-in hospital; later she will be a receiver of stolen goods on a large scale. These are institutions within institutions, illegal operations which mimic and thereby undercut the legitimate operations of society. Until now, Moll has done this kind of undercutting on her own and in less than formal fashion. For the first time in her book, Moll becomes, in her associations with the governess, a part of that society within a society, or rather, she feels that she is a part of it and tells us that she derives strength from it. Moreover, as the following passage shows, she is perfected in the language and *mores* of that sub-culture, in the recognition of the necessity of secrecy in words and actions. Moll's understanding landlady, a tacit member of the society, introduces the midwife to Moll with hints of her special predicament:

I Really did not understand her, but my Mother Midnight began very seriously to explain what she meant, as soon as she was gone: Madam, *says she*, you seem not to understand what your Landlady means, and when you do understand it, you need not let her know at all that you do so.

She means that you are under some Circumstances that may render your Lying-Inn difficult to you, and that you are not willing to be expos'd; I need say no more, but to tell you, that if you think fit to communicate so much of your Case to me, *if it be so*, as is necessary; for I do not desire to pry into those things, I perhaps may be in a Condition to assist you, and to make you perfectly easie, and remove all your dull Thoughts upon that Subject.

Every word this Creature said was a Cordial to me, and put new Life and new Spirit into my very Heart; my Blood began to circulate immediately, and I was quite another Body; I eat my Victuals again, and grew better presently after it: She said a great deal more to the same purpose, and then having press'd me to be free with

her, and promis'd in the solemnest manner to be secret, she stop'd
a little, as if waiting to see what Impression it made on me, and what
I would say. (162)

Moll's claim that she 'Really did not understand' her landlady is strange and unlikely, given her history of close dealing.
As usual, inconsistency and personal contradiction are functional and structural indicators. That inconsistency is a sign of
the transition which is taking place as Moll slides into a community for the first time in her narrative, a group whose main
representative, the governess, will absorb a good part of the
blame attached to what Moll will subsequently do as a member
of it. For Moll sees to it that she remains apart in some sense
even from this society within a society that she now formally
joins. She and her narrative both exploit this micro-society even
as they depend upon it for colour and continuity. The narrative,
like Moll in the passage above, draws life from its subversive
anti-social energies. After a marvellously itemized display of the
various lying-in plans that the governess offers, we are treated to
a wide-eyed tour of the secret workings of her operation: "'tis
scarce credible what Practice she had, as well Abroad as at
Home, and yet all upon the private Account, or in plain
*English*, the whoring Account' (169). Moll tells us that in four
months 'she had no less than Twelve Ladies of Pleasure brought
to Bed within Doors, and I think she had Two and Thirty, or
thereabouts, under her Conduct without Doors, whereof one, as
nice as she was with me, was Lodg'd with my old Landlady at
St. Jones's' (169). These are the familiar sensational pleasures of
criminal fiction: a vast network of crime operating secretly
under our noses is a pleasure to contemplate and feeds at once
our curiosity and our righteousness. *Moll Flanders* is hardly
above such conventional pandering. In fact, Moll's criminal
career imitates and parallels that transparent strategy of
criminal fiction. She will, in time, become a famous criminal
and her life will turn into the sensational verification of a near-
legendary career. At the same time, Moll will claim that her
life was first a mere desperate response to circumstances, and
then a negative and shocking example of how a life of crime
hardens the criminal and destroys his humanity. Her claim not
to understand her landlady when she is first introduced to her
governess is a mark of that necessary renewal of her innocence

which precedes her criminal career and attempts to make her a victim as well as a hardened practitioner.

But overt crime raises more clearly and forcefully than any other sequence in the book the issue of the nature and function of literary personality. Moll spends five years and only about one-quarter of her book as a criminal[17] (she is never by any fair definition a whore, rather the occasional mistress of a baronet), and yet that part of the book is the one most readers claim to remember, or the part which seems to colour their descriptions of Moll, that 'aging whore', as a recent reviewer described her.[18] One can easily suggest reasons for this state of affairs. Crime is attractive narrative material; in an individualistic society especially, it can be satiric and liberating, shocking and moral. Like many other popular criminals of the day and after, Moll clearly provided and continues to provide those satisfactions. All these are the effects of Moll's narrative. The causes lie within the pattern or structure of separation that the book is most about. What makes Moll more than just another counterfeit lady or Mother Ross and renders her criminality the most liberating aspect of that vigorous and indomitable intelligence most readers remember is that crime is the perfect culmination of Moll's career, the series of actions and circumstances that allows Defoe's narrative to do best what it has all along tried to achieve. Crime is simply the ultimate test for the self because it requires at one and the same time utter dependence upon circumstances and absolute freedom from them. Crime in the universe created by Defoe's narratives demands for its beginning complete helplessness, and also demands complete competence in the difficult techniques of crime.[19] Crime permits the clearest separation from society and grants the criminal membership in a subversive and coherent counter-society. And yet at the very same time in the world of mimetic narrative such as Moll's, it makes her the victim of circumstances, places her

---

[17] In Starr's edition, from page 190 to page 306, 136 pages out of 343.

[18] *Times Literary Supplement*, 4 April 1972.

[19] Many critics have pointed to desperation as indicative of Defoe's moral and social sensitivity, which it doubtless is. But few have gone on to remark on the strange connection between that helplessness and the total competence in crime his heroes display. Desperate people make poor criminals, or it can be argued that a realistic writer should recognize the likelihood that they will be less than masters of the criminal arts.

squarely for us as the result of her history as a woman, in a specific social reality. The 'character' of Moll as she begins her criminal career exists to enact that paradox rather than to present the psychological reality or the social quality of desperation. The quality of her criminal acts—the style in which she presents them and the way in which she commits them—is the clearest indication of that.

Obviously, Moll has a long history of power and guile when she arrives at the moment of 'desperation' that propels her into crime. Her last legal connection is her marriage with the bank clerk, and it ends when he displays what Moll contemptuously summarizes as the sort of weakness she would never be guilty of: 'if he had had Spirit and Courage to have look'd his Misfortunes in the Face, his Credit was so good, that as I told him, he would easily recover it; for to sink under Trouble is to double the Weight, and he that will Die in it shall Die in it' (189). A moment later, however, she remarks that she 'wanted that Spirit in Trouble which I told him was so necessary to him for bearing the burthen' (190). But Moll's narrative has told us better, for her late husband, we are informed, had merely lost money and had considerable 'Credit'. Moll, on the other hand, has lost all her 'credit', all her natural assets and earning capacity as a marriageable woman have been depleted by age: 'it was past the flourishing time with me when I might expect to be courted for a Mistress; that agreeable part had declin'd some time, and the Ruins only appear'd of what had been' (189). In the context in which we operate as readers, Moll has not lost her defining skills but only her external equipment.

Her external helplessness has to be total so that she will be forced to adapt her guile to her new situation. And towards that end, Moll's invocation of helplessness is indeed thorough and suitably intense: 'no Friend to comfort or advise me, I sat and cried and tormented my self Night and Day; wringing my Hands, and sometimes raving like a distracted Woman; and indeed I have often wonder'd it had not affected my Reason, for I had the Vapours to such a degree, that my Understanding was sometimes quite lost in Fancies and Imaginations' (190).

Now Moll is no novelist; she is only a successful and fulfilled self who attempts to render the desperation she claims she once

felt. So she can only tell us she was desperate, and in the process she objectifies her condition and despises it: 'like a distracted Woman'. She claims she went out and began her career
as a thief 'one Evening, when being brought, as I may say, to
the last Gasp, I think I may truly say I was Distracted and
Raving' (191). The caution and legal exactness of those phrases
as well as the over-all apologetic invocation of necessity do not
obscure the exact rendition of the moment. The moment of
detail, as we have noted before, is the self-assertive moment in
Defoe's narratives; the rendering of action as the precise
alignment of the self's alertness to the relationships around it
is the key moment in this sequence and in others in the book.
Here, as so often before, the self is magically confronted with
the means for survival; Moll wandering she 'knew not whither'
is like Crusoe suddenly shipwrecked. Crusoe is given tools, Moll
a shop at the exactly opportune moment:

I pass'd by an Apothecary's Shop in *Leadenhall-street*, where I saw
lye on a Stool just before the Counter a little Bundle wrapt in a
white Cloth; beyond it, stood a Maid Servant with her Back to it,
looking up towards the top of the Shop, where the Apothecary's
Apprentice, as I suppose, was standing up on the Counter, with his
Back also to the Door, and a Candle in his Hand, looking and
reaching up to the upper Shelf for something he wanted, so that
both were engag'd mighty earnestly, and no Body else in the
Shop. (191)

From careful and casuistical speculation about her lack of
moral position in one sense, Moll passes to exact physical
position and relationship to her environment. As we have seen
elsewhere, the sequence and the progress are nothing less than
the characteristic rhythm of Defoe's narratives. It can be
objected that Moll's clarity about the techniques of shop-lifting
and her melodramatic and extenuating vagueness about her
isolation are the results of her retrospective narration. Having
become a master thief and having thereby escaped her des-
pairing helplessness, she writes best about the moment of theft.
But it is one of the main points of this study that such an analysis
violates the experience of the book we receive as readers, that
when we invoke such a view of Moll we are operating as
critics and creating a synthetic (in both senses of the term)

version of her which is not operative in the moment of participation (or excited and assenting observation) that the book
aspires to induce in us as readers.[20] In composing this falsely
coherent literary personality on the model of actual personality, we are doing, in one sense, what all novels invite us to do.
But *Moll Flanders* and the rest of Defoe's narratives reveal by
their relative crudity that such an invitation is partly a trick to
make the assertions and simplifications of action itself acceptable. The real personality we construct after the fact of reading
enables us to have the unreal and therefore satisfying personality we experience in the act of reading.

To be sure, Moll continues in these opening sequences of her
criminal career to insist that she was driven by necessity and
even assisted in her execution by a mysterious local power, the
Devil who snatches her from repentance and hesitation by
whispering in her ear: 'I had an evil Counsellor within, and he
was continually prompting me to relieve my self by the worst
means' (193). But the exact inventories and precise rendering of
the techniques of shop-lifting exist in the narrative side by side
with Moll's apprehensions. After a paragraph listing the contents of the stolen parcel with such precision as 'a Suit of
Child-bed Linnen in it, very good and almost new, the Lace very
fine', Moll switches back to inner and inexpressible turmoil:
'All the while I was opening these things I was under such
dreadful Impressions of Fear, and in such Terror of Mind, tho'
I was perfectly safe, that I cannot express the manner of it'
(192). Moll as narrator is simply inadequate to the task of
rendering that inner struggle. So her narrative picks up speed
and momentum (her second crime involves details in motion,
not arrested as they were in the first opportunity in the shop),
and her second theft is described in twice as much detail. Moll
claims here to have been tempted to kill the child whose neck-
lace she steals, but that claim is clearly to counterbalance the

[20] D. W. Harding has suggested that the normal loose critical terms to describe
a reader's involvement in fiction such as identification and vicarious participation
are inexact. Harding proposes that for wish fulfilment we substitute 'wish-formula-
tion or the definition of desires'. Reading a novel is 'the social act of affirming with
the author a set of values'. I would add only that neither reader nor author may be
fully aware of those values and their implications and that the process of affirmation
and definition may be a complex one. (See 'Psychological Processes in the Reading
of Fiction', *British Journal of Aesthetics*, 2 (Apr. 1962), 144–6.)

practised ease and sudden satisfaction she now brings to crime. The real moral burden of the crime is, in fact, shifted to the child's parents, vain, self-seeking, and careless in allowing such a situation to develop.

The thoughts of this Booty put out all the thoughts of the first and the Reflections I had made wore quickly off; Poverty, as I have said, harden'd my Heart, and my own Necessities made me regardless of any thing: The last Affair left no great Concern upon me, for as I did the poor Child no harm, I only said to my self, I had given the Parents a just Reproof for their Negligence in leaving the poor little Lamb to come home by it self, and it would teach them to take more Care of it another time. (194)

Every reader of *Moll Flanders* recognizes that speed and momentum; the more reflective wonder whether they reveal Moll's moral shallowness (and in the process Defoe's moral irony at her expense) or her marvellous humanity. The real message and effect of the book precede that moralistic reflection. What the book actually presents is Moll's entry once again into a world of movement and opportunity in which she survives by observation of that movement and the taking of opportunity. Structurally, in other words, the crime sequence presents Moll's techniques of survival at their clearest and therefore at their most memorable. The disposition of the self in the face of the other that we have witnessed thus far in the novel becomes fully externalized here. Moll enters crime, or is forced into it, by circumstances. Her response to that compulsion resolves itself into a technique of stillness among movement all around her. The self acquires stability by moving into the flow of circumstances; the ongoing dialectic of self and other operates as Moll is forced by necessity to negate her own stillness (poverty in the world is lack of forward financial movement) and move into crime. But her apparent lack of aggressive movement in that world (a technique and disposition she has learned in other situations of the novel so far) transforms the world from a collection of compulsive circumstances into a field of opportunities and relationships. Moll's 'indirection' and discreet sensitivity to detail remove the negative and merely compulsive character of social circumstances. The new first term (self needing to move forward aggressively for survival) negates the negation of the second term (other, Moll's declining circumstances), and the conjunction produces a third term (self, now fully realized because balanced, moving forward while apparently still). To put it a slightly different way, Moll's qualitative modification of the merely quantitative force of circumstances allows her to survive; her observation of opportunity gives static and therefore useful pattern to what otherwise appears as the random and destructive dynamic of experience. Thus, the third crime she describes involves movement all around her; a thief closely pursued throws part of his booty at Moll's feet. The thief is caught and passes by Moll with his captors:

I STOOD stock still all this while till they came back, dragging the poor Fellow they had taken, and luging the things they had found, extremely well satisfied that they had recovered the Booty, and taken the Thief; and thus they pass'd by me, for I look'd only like one who stood up while the Crowd was gone. (195)

When the crowd leaves, Moll picks up the booty with a new serenity, 'with less Disturbance than I had done formerly, for these things I did not steal, but they were stolen to my Hand' (196). Moll becomes a thief and no-thief, marvellously in and out of circumstances, above (or beside) the mad flow of urban violence, transforming it by observant self-reservation into profit. Moll is thus reflecting what seems to be the actual quality of urban eighteenth-century life—isolation, helplessness, threatening movement—and enacting a magic solution to the problems such qualities raise for the autonomous self. Even her second and more blameworthy entrance into crime is hedged by the arrangement of events. It is not usually remembered that Moll tries honest quilting work after her initial outburst of crime for survival. She reports that she 'work'd very hard, and with this I began to live' (199). Her definitive entry into crime is now a matter of inner compulsion, of desire rather than circumstances: 'the diligent Devil who resolv'd I should continue in his Service, continually prompted me to go out and take a Walk, that is to say, to see if any thing would offer in the old Way' (199). It is an old trick. Moll has been driven by necessity and has acquired a taste for the forbidden. The mechanism of vice takes over and poverty is succeeded, as Moll

says later, by avarice as a driving passion, as a form of necessity.[21] In a way, she is not responsible; in another, she clearly is.
The sentence itself dramatizes this central contradiction. Moll
begins with the euphemism, the innocent surface quality of her
act. She is practised in the art of indirect discourse. The
clarifying clause after the 'that is to say' is a descent, frequent in
her style, to the facts of action. But note the passive voice
needed to describe such action. Moll's greatest clarity is when
she describes her own alertness by means of opportunistic
apartness, or active passivity.

In moments of real power such as Moll now begins to achieve,
Defoe's heroes acquire an associate, partly, as we have seen, to
absorb some of the guilty responsibility of power. Here as she
becomes a thief, Moll returns to her governess. At first, of
course, she pretends that her booty is her own wasting stock and
exercises her habitual discretion. Since she already knows in
detail about her governess's illegal activities (although the mid-
wifery has been terminated and she has turned pawnbroker),
Moll's caution is perhaps excessive. But Moll's reserve upon
entering into any relationship is her signature by this point in
the book. Her reserve is a sign of her power and confidence; her
criminal career marks her period of greatest reserve and,
obviously, of her greatest power. It is appropriate, then, that
Moll should exaggerate her discretion; at this point she has
more to hide than at any other place in the story. 'More to hide'
—the expression reveals a truth about the self in *Moll Flanders*
and Defoe's other narratives: their confessional mode is a sign
that selfhood is a matter of secrecy; the more the characters
have to 'reveal' (one can only reveal what was at some point
unknown to others), the more they may be said to exist. Crime
is an activity, at least in the way Moll practises it (and it is
interesting that Defoe wrote no novel about a highwayman),
which demands total secrecy and which thereby accumulates
large amounts of selfhood, perhaps something like the total
selfhood the novel aspires to portray.

[21] A few pages later (203), she reflects that 'as Poverty brought me into the Mire,
so Avarice kept me in, till there was no going back; as to the Arguments which my
Reason dictated for perswading me to lay down, Avarice stept in and said, go on,
go on; you have had very good luck, go on till you have gotten Four or Five
Hundred Pound, and then you shall leave off, and then you may live easie without
working at all.'

Moll's criminal career is a matter of many overt disguises. When she begins, she notes carefully that she was 'dressed', that is, looking like the prosperous matron she no longer was: 'I dress'd me, for I had still pretty good Cloaths' (191). Eventually she drops her initial disguise of declined prosperity and confides in her governess, although even then she carefully omits her initial thefts and presents herself as the innocent victim of circumstances from her latest crime in the alehouse where she walked away with a silver tankard. 'I told her the strangest thing in the World had befallen me, and that it had made a Thief of me, even without any design' (200). The governess advises her not to take the tankard back; she speaks out of what she thinks is her superior sophistication: 'You don't know those Sort of People Child, *says she*, they'll not only carry you to *Newgate*, but hang you too without any regard to the honesty of returning it' (200). Moll's reply is perhaps her most disingenuous moment: 'What must I do then? says I' (200). Moll engineers matters so that her governess thinks she is the dominant partner in their new relationship as thief and receiver of goods. She reserves a good part of herself from her governess, in a sense disguising herself from her partner in crime as well as from her victims. (This relationship is made quite literal later when Moll assumes male disguise and passes as such with her male confederate as well as with their victims.) When a few paragraphs later, the governess actually offers to teach her the trade of shop-lifting, Moll still protests that she has no skill. We know that Moll is equivocating; she has already demonstrated at least a tremendous aptitude for the craft. Her fear is actually of involvement, of losing her separateness by joining the guild of thieves, of being no longer Moll but *a* thief: 'I trembled at that Proposal for hitherto I had had no Confederates, nor any Acquaintance among that Tribe' (201).

After these complicated manœuvrings of the self into a relatively blameless and secure position, the narrative moves into an extended account of the exact techniques of crime. All of these are exhilarating displays of agility and skill by which Moll 'grew the greatest Artist of my time' (214). The occasional moralizing fades out as Moll exhausts the permutations of profitable disguise, dressing as a man, a beggar, passing as a fine lady who walks in St. James's Park and gambles near

Covent Garden, winning a lawsuit as a wealthy widow falsely accused of theft. Moll underlines that variety, insisting that it surpasses exact depiction: 'I Had sometimes taken the liberty to Play the same Game over again, which is not according to Practice, which however succeeded not amiss; but generally I took up new Figures, and contriv'd to appear in new Shapes every time I went abroad' (262).

The pleasure for us as onlookers is compounded of delight at the social aggression implicit in such disguises and the deeper and related satisfaction of watching Moll maintain herself intact apart from all those impersonations, mastering society and its forms without ever diminishing her power by self-revelation. We have the sense as we read that Moll recognizes the social subversion implicit in her disguises; she understands the immunities that attend certain social positions. Apprehended stealing a piece of plate, she pulls out her purse which has twenty guineas in it and proves to the magistrate that she intended not to steal but to buy some spoons. The magistrate takes this substance as proof that Moll is no thief, 'for indeed the sort of People who come upon those Designs that you have been Charg'd with, are seldom troubl'd with much Gold in their Pockets, as I see you are' (272). Moll's reply underlines the *naïveté* of such static assumptions and her own subversive sophistication: 'I Smil'd, and told his Worship, that then I ow'd something of his Favour to my Money' (272).

As this and other incidents reveal, her artistry lies, as she herself emphasizes, in her delicacy and extraordinary caution. As her experiences proceed, we are asked to admire her skill at disguise and escape rather than at crime itself. That is to say, once again the real feat and the genuine assertion of self lie in the relationship to circumstances, the freedom and apartness that Moll manages again and again. The work she finds most congenial is, therefore, the quasi-legal compounding of prohibited goods and sharing the bounty with Customs officers. She makes £50 in one deal; the rest of the time much less: 'but I was willing to act safe, and was still Cautious of running the great Risques which I found others did, and in which they Miscarried every Day' (211).

This contempt for careless confederates and victims which runs through her account is especially clear and important, for

Moll defines herself as a great thief in relation to them. Her powerful difference and impenetrable secrecy reach a climax in her liaison with the drunken gentleman who picks her up at Bartholomew Fair. Moll's contempt for him is specifically a scorn of his lack of self-control, his loss of identity and status in a moment of surrender to mere natural impulse.

This was an Adventure indeed unlook'd for, and perfectly undesign'd by me; tho' I was not so past the Merry part of Life, as to forget how to behave, when a Fop so blinded by his Appetite should not know an old Woman from a young: I did not indeed look so old as I was by ten or twelve Year; yet I was not a young Wench of Seventeen, and it was easie enough to be distinguish'd: There is nothing so absurd, so surfeiting, so ridiculous as a Man heated by Wine in his Head, and a wicked Gust in his inclination together; he is in the possession of two Devils at once, and can no more govern himself by his Reason than a Mill can Grind without Water; His Vice tramples upon all that was in him that had any good in it, if any such thing there was; nay, his very Sense is blinded by its own Rage, and he acts Absurdities even in his View; such is Drinking more, when he is Drunk already; picking up a common Woman, without regard to what she is, or who she is; whether Sound or rotten, Clean or Unclean; whether Ugly or Handsome, whether Old or Young, and so blinded, as not really to distinguish; such a Man is worse than Lunatick; prompted by his vicious corrupted Head he no more knows what he is doing, than this Wretch of mine knew when I pick'd his Pocket of his Watch and his Purse of Gold. (226)

In the context created by the narrative, the Baronet (as he turns out to be) is despicable because he is a 'poor unguarded Wretch' (226); he provides an opportunity that Moll has not been look-ing for. He is totally outside the complex world that Moll moves in; nothing at all is needed to trick him. In his condition, he destroys himself by revealing the worst part of himself. His openness is precisely the opposite of Moll's defining secrecy, and the drunken baronet is the object of such unusual and extended denunciation because he is Moll's significantly exact anti-type, sensually diffuse, dependent for status upon given rather than earned sexual and social roles, and divided from his rational instinct for self-preservation by his outrageously spontaneous desires. He cannot, Moll's word is exactly to her point, 'distinguish', he cannot handle the multiple dangers always implicit in reality. Those dangers and the necessary extreme and incessant caution for surviving them are the real and, at this point, the explicit concern of the narrative. Moll admits this in her most relevant piece of moralizing a little later, at the end of her crime sequence. Shortly before she is arrested, she tells us that the survey of her career we have just read should warn us that the world is full of exquisite thieves like her and to beware. But her warning hardly removes our admiration for her, and the force of the narrative as gathered by what she calls our 'Senses and Judgment' tells us that we must imitate her caution and reserve if we are to survive a world full of Molls:

... every Branch of my Story, if duly consider'd, may be useful to honest People, and afford a due Caution to People of some sort, or other to Guard against the like Surprizes, and to have their Eyes about them when they have to do with Strangers of any kind, for 'tis very seldom that some Snare or other is not in their way. The Moral indeed of all my History is left to be gather'd by the Senses and Judgment of the Reader; I am not Qualified to preach to them, let the Experience of one Creature compleatly Wicked, and compleatly Miserable be a Storehouse of useful warning to those that read. (268)

However, Moll's narrative is interested only in promoting Moll, no matter what she herself may say to the contrary. Her arrest is accordingly a finely rendered and inevitable affair, the result of her lapse from perfect vigilance. After her narrowest escape,[22] she grows slightly over-confident: 'not at all made Cautious by my former Danger as I us'd to be' (272). Her arrest is abrupt and arbitrary, and her awareness of legal niceties almost saves her. But she is victimized by two relentlessly savage servant-girls who have caught her in the precise moment of theft: 'the Justice was enclin'd to have releas'd me; but the sawcy Jade that stop'd me, affirming that I was going out with the Goods, but that she stop'd me and pull'd me back as I was upon the Threshold, the Justice upon that point committed me' (273). Moll's arrest is, in short, the inevitable victory of unpredictable circumstances, so randomly and variously destructive that no one can hope to hold them off for ever. We are made to feel

---

[22] That is, the time when she saves herself by pulling out twenty guineas in front of the magistrate. See above, p. 130.

that Moll is defeated by a stupid and unfortunate concatenation of circumstance rather than by any failure of nerve or in execution on her part.

Moll's greatest test and perhaps the most interesting sequence in the book is the Newgate episode. It records Moll's greatest defeat and as a result her greatest triumph. Throughout the crime sequence, Moll has mentioned Newgate as the dread alternative to crime, and when she is actually confronted with it, she writes her most impassioned paragraph:

. . . and I was carried to *Newgate*; that horrid Place! my very Blood chills at the mention of its Name; the Place, where so many of my Comrades had been lock'd up, and from whence they went to the fatal Tree; the Place where my Mother suffered so deeply, where I was brought into the World, and from whence I expected no Redemption, but by an infamous Death: To conclude, the Place that had so long expected me, and which with so much Art and Success I had so long avoided. (273)

Such a paragraph raises once more the question of literary personality and our perception of it as readers. Moll's fear of Newgate is perfectly plausible if somewhat melodramatically rendered. One can easily talk about its sources at the deepest levels of behaviour: infantile trauma co-operates with and intensifies adult experience. But such a pathology is invoked at this moment by Moll's rhetoric rather than sustained by the action. We are asked as readers to imagine only here at this particular moment that Moll is confronted with the reality of Newgate. With such limitations, this moment is a means towards a structural end rather than an end in itself, or, less invidiously, this emotional moment establishes a personal depth to Moll's fears which is parallel to the structural depth of the experience of Newgate in relation to her other experiences in the book. Moll's fear is an indicator and an intensifier of the central structural opposition of the book, which emerges here at its clearest. Newgate is simply pure compulsive circumstances, a place where the self is so restricted and oppressed by the other that it loses all independence and becomes habituated to an environment which embodies personal destruction. It is not only that Newgate is 'an Emblem of Hell itself' (274), a filthy and degrading place, but that its inhabitants are changed from

themselves into part of it, that they are, most horrible implication of all, brought to accept death: 'it would be worth the
Observation of any Prisoner, who shall hereafter fall into the
same Misfortune and come to that dreadful Place of *Newgate*;
how Time, Necessity, and Conversing with the Wretches that
are there Familiarizes the Place to them; how at last they become reconcil'd to that which at first was the greatest Dread
upon their Spirits in the World, and are as imprudently Chear-
ful and Merry in their Misery, as they were when out of it'
(276).

Moll's defeat lies in her unprecedented transformation by
these oppressive circumstances into something which she does
not choose to be: 'I was become a meer *Newgate-Bird* . . . so
thoro' a Degeneracy had possess'd me, that I was no more the
same thing that I had been, than if I had never been otherwise
than what I was now' (279). Such a clear and coldly abstract
emphasis on metamorphosis and a kind of thorough amnesia of
the self does not serve probability; the radical break with the
past may be said to be a deliberate violation of the psychological continuity this episode originally invoked for its power
and meaning. The extravagance and inconsistency, I submit,
are neither offensive nor ineffective because we have as readers
all along been involved in an imaginative world where the
main issue is the struggle between the self and the oppressive
other. Moll is, in a sense different from the normal psychological categories, correctly afraid that Newgate will bring her
back to her helpless infancy. In the context of the book, Newgate is much more than a personal obsession from Moll's past.
The prison is a concrete embodiment of social restriction, unlike anything Moll has so far had to deal with in its effective
concreteness, its real and effective exemplification of the control that society aspires to exercise over the self. Yet even Newgate can hardly be said to be graphically rendered. Think of
Dickens's prisons and confining houses and Defoe's Newgate is
barely presented as a real place. Defoe's austere style and
almost abstract imagination are interested primarily in relationships rather than images. What matters about Newgate is not
its concrete existence as a wretched habitation but its power to
suppress and transform the self. Newgate is primarily, therefore,
irresistible social fact, the distilled compulsion that Moll

escaped by instinct and luck as a child in Colchester and which now gathers its forces for one great assault on her extraordinary freedom. Newgate violates the dialectic we have seen operating in the narrative by resisting the energies of the self to surround and possess experience from a point outside it. Newgate is a pure interior that allows no external viewpoint, a locale whose physical laws preclude the self from the mental relationship to environment by which it defines itself.

Of course, if Newgate did not exist in just this oppressive form, it would be necessary to invent it. Moll's shocked analysis of its dehumanizing thoroughness and then her account of her own defeat by its atmosphere act as proof of the heroic necessity of her struggles throughout the book to avoid social determinants. Newgate proves that resistance such as Moll has managed is required for the self to exist.

Moll's recovery is a matter of re-establishing contact with the world outside the prison, of re-entering relationships in which she can exercise her being in all its craft and power. First, she begins to recover by finding that her Lancashire highwayman-husband has been brought to Newgate. Her response is grief and sorrow, but the effect of her emotions is to separate herself from her degraded companions and from fatally unconscious serenity. 'I quitted my Company, and retir'd as much as that dreadful Place suffers any Body to retire' (280). Moreover, she grieves because she has been the cause of Jemy's taking to the road, 'the occasion originally of his Mischief' (280). Guilt restores Moll to herself: 'the first Reflections I made upon the horrid detestable Life I had liv'd, began to return upon me, and as these things return'd my abhorrence of the Place I was in, and of the way of living in it, return'd also; in a word, I was perfectly chang'd, and become another Body' (281). As Moll notes, she has felt guilty before. Her first reflections upon entering Newgate included extensive repentance, but that was the result of fear in the face of impending retribution for a mis-spent life. The guilt that restores Moll (a short time afterwards) to herself and to action is the guilt that accompanies power; she remembers what she was and did. In between lamentations, she boasts, in a way, of Jemy's prowess as a highwayman; he has become as much a legendary figure as she: '*Hind*, or *Whitney*, or the *Golden Farmer* were Fools to him' (281). Throughout these paragraphs, Moll's language is precise on this issue of self-consciousness. Beneath the conventional language of repentance, we can easily read the language of self-assertion: 'In short, I began to think, and to think is one real Advance from Hell to Heaven; all that Hellish harden'd state and temper of Soul, which I have said so much of before, is but a deprivation of Thought; he that is restor'd to his Power of thinking, is restor'd to himself' (281). The sincerity of Moll's repentance need not be debated; it is an effective means for restoring her consciousness, for underlining the gravity of her situation. It provides the perspective (the view from outside) that is otherwise fatally lacking in Newgate. Moll is herself aware of the taint of instrumentality that surrounds her repentance and returns to her earlier disparagement of her guilt as founded merely on fear: 'yet even this was nothing but fright, at what was to come; there was not a Word of sincere Repentance in it all' (282). But in bringing Jemy on stage, her narrative has already marked the beginnings of her transformation back to the old Moll in unmistakable terms.

The account of her trial and condemnation takes place within the new context provided by these signs of a reawakened consciousness. Moll continues, she tells us, to be racked by fear, but she makes a point of maintaining her privacy now. She lies awake and cries out fearfully, 'Lord have mercy upon me, and the like' (283). The impatient summarizing implicit in that last phrase tells us a great deal about Moll's gathering strength even in what are supposed to be her worst moments. Her reticence, reserve, and increasing clarity as her condemnation grows nearer and surer are enforced by the contrasting behaviour of her governess and by the force of Moll's placement of herself in the narrative. She says less and less and others talk more and more as the moment of condemnation approaches. First Jemy and now the governess provide relational assurance for Moll. She is now more and more her old self because she can exist in relation to them, that is, apart from and together with them.

For an example of the apartness, we can look at the way the governess's lamentations take up much of the account for a page or so. Moll's description of the scene conveys her narrative's impatience with the weakness and self-disclosure of public grief: 'she cry'd and took on, like a distracted Body, wringing her

Hands, and crying out that she was undone, that she believ'd there was a Curse from Heaven upon her, that she should be damn'd, that she had been the Destruction of all her Friends, that she had brought such a one, and such a one, and such one to the Gallows' (283). Moll makes no such hysterical speeches; she carefully tells her governess that she is not to blame: 'I would not hearken to you, therefore you have not been to blame, it is I only have ruin'd myself, I have brought myself to this Misery' (284).

And at her trial she reports that her crying had exhausted her and made her sleep, so she 'had more Courage . . . than indeed I thought possible for me to have' (284). Moll speaks well in her defence but is convicted anyway. When the sentence is announced next day, it is her governess who has the extreme reaction, Moll remains numb and quiet. Her condition is terrible but inexpressible, summed up in a brief paragraph: 'It is rather to be thought of, than express'd what was now my Condition; I had nothing before me but present Death; and as I had no Friends to assist me, or to stir for me, I expected nothing but to find my Name in the Dead Warrant, which was to come down for the Execution the *Friday* afterward, of five more and myself' (286). Contrast this calm summary and its deliberate reticence with the longer paragraph describing the reactions of Moll's governess:

> My poor Governess was utterly Disconsolate, and she that was my Comforter before, wanted Comfort now herself, and sometimes Mourning, sometimes Raging, was as much out of herself (as to all outward Appearance) as any mad Woman in *Bedlam*: Nor was she only Disconsolate as to me, but she was struck with Horror at the Sense of her own wicked Life, and began to look back upon it with a Taste quite different from mine; for she was Penitent to the highest Degree for her Sins, as well as Sorrowful for the Misfortune. (286)

Moll never loses control in this public fashion; her despair as she describes it is a private and internal matter. Her transformation back to consciousness, we recall, was the result of her secret relationship with Jemy, not, as is the case with the governess, a response to the brutal stimulus of condemnation. Moll can hardly deny, of course, that condemnation affected her. She swoons several times, but only in private or with her minister friend.[23] But the resulting emotion, she tells us more than once, is well beyond her powers of evocation, secret therefore by virtue of its inexpressibility: 'The Word Eternity represented itself with all its incomprehensible Additions, and I had such extended Notions of it, that I know not how to express them' (287). And again, 'I relate this in the very manner in which things then appear'd to me, as far as I am able; but infinitely short of the lively impressions which they made on my Soul at that time; indeed those Impressions are not to be explain'd by words, or if they are, I am not Mistress of Words enough to express them' (287–8). When Moll is brought to proper repentance by a solicitous clergyman, she reports that she 'was cover'd with Shame and Tears for things past, and yet had at the same time a secret surprizing Joy at the Prospect of being a true Penitent, and obtaining the Comfort of a Penitent' (289). That is a spiritual banality in itself, but in the book's own continuity and frame of reference that conventional secret joy is linked with Moll's powerful and defining apartness.

Finally, when Moll learns of the reprieve she describes the 'dismal groaning and crying . . . from the Condemn'd Hole' and the 'confus'd Clamour in the House' (291) from the other prisoners. For herself, she remains 'Dumb and Silent, overcome with the Sense of it, and not able to express what I had in my Heart; for the Passions on such Occasions as these, are certainly so agitated as not to be able presently to regulate their own Motions' (291–2). Moll's silence is enforced on the one hand by the psychological shape of the moment, on the other it is an assertion of freedom, a refusal to become part of the shapeless clamour of Newgate around her. Emotions such as these, she herself notes in a characteristic manner, are not able to be regulated. Moll consistently avoids emotions which cannot be managed, which bring no profit to the self and indeed wear it out. Once again, an utterly conventional emotional moment has meaning in the narrative as part of a structure to which it contributes rather than on its own terms.

Three things are evident from the Newgate episode. First,

---

[23] Moll explains that the clergyman came to her apartment, 'for I had obtain'd the Favour by the help of Money, nothing being to be done in that Place without it, not to be kept in the Condemn'd Hole, as they call it, among the rest of the Prisoners, who were to die, but to have a little dirty Chamber to my self' (290).

Moll's progress is not simply from fear to moral stupidity to repentance. Such a bald moral summary neglects the actual strategies of the narrative, the implications of Moll's language (a mixture of the jargon of repentance and the familiar analytical summarizing that is her means of self-assertion), and the context of her career. Moll's progress is from total helplessness to relative freedom, from the supine indifference Newgate imposes to the secret sense of self and self-importance that Moll gathers for herself from what she observes around her. Secondly, that progress is a matter of re-entering relationships, with Jemy and with her governess. The self can only be aware of itself as such when it sees itself operating upon others, and Moll's narrative revives her by granting her responsibility of a sort for Jemy's career and responsibility for her governess's frantic spasms of repentance. With those relationships in hand, Moll is secret and powerful once more. Jemy does not see her; she sees him and will eventually move powerfully to rescue him from prison and reward him with a better life. Moll remains reserved and calm on the outside as her governess has those fits of guilt; her privacy is a form of power, a refusal to expose herself at her weakest.

The third implication of the Newgate sequence is the result of the first two. The entire episode is the clearest example in the story of the way *Moll Flanders* enacts the novelistic solution for the problem of individualist consciousness. The relative freedom that Moll achieves by virtue of her narrative arrangements (both in disposition of events and in distribution of language) in the face of the ultimate compulsions of prison and death represents in dramatic terms a solution to the problems of survival in a market society. To put it less dogmatically and more generally, the freedom given Moll by the secrecy and apartness which the narrative is everywhere at pains to enact argues that Defoe's great achievement in this book was to communicate something important in the structure of eighteenth-century feeling. *Moll Flanders* is especially a part of the century's expanding literature of privacy; from real journals to fictional memoirs of private life, the problem that writers of the period face again and again is the alignment of the self and the world. As far as I am concerned, that problem is in some ultimate sense the result of the economic and social conditions summed up in the term market society, where each man's apartness is the condition which creates and animates society and each man's apartness is simultaneously affirmed and negated. But that can hardly be demonstrated. What can be asserted is that *Moll Flanders* is clearly an effort to tell a story in which the private self by means of the various strategies I have discussed preserves itself without falsifying the destructive truth of public experience. The imaginative centre of *Moll Flanders* lies in its ratification of the possibility of private survival and even autonomy. The social and historical truth in literature, Lucien Goldmann wrote, lies not in any reflection of specific social circumstances but in 'the fact that the *structures* of the universe of the work are homologues of the mental *structures* of certain social groups or in intelligible relation with them'.[24]

Whether or not one accepts that connection between the book and history, the last sequence in the book completes the defeat of Newgate and the total transformation of the non-being into which Moll sank briefly under its influence. Moll emerges stronger than ever, capable again of disguise and manipulative movement through social realities, essentially untouched by the repentance she claims. Moll is reprieved and set for transportation, but before she allows herself to leave Newgate in her narrative, she inserts with some violence to the external structure of her story an account of how she managed to bring her Lancashire husband, Jemy, with her. That rescue and their establishment as prosperous planters in Maryland are a coda to the story, a demonstration that the self can survive intact the worst of disasters, the near annihilation of Newgate and all that it represents. Both the necessity for that demonstration and the uneasy fit between such a trick and the penitential surface of the narrative appear in Moll's apology for telling this part of her story:

It may perhaps be thought Trifling to enter here into a Relation of all the little incidents which attended me in this interval of my Circumstances; I mean between the final order for my Transportation, and the time of my going on board the Ship, and I am too near the End of my Story, to allow room for it, but something relating to me, *and my Lancashire Husband*, I must not omit. (295)

What she offers is a sequence resembling her earlier transactions: disguise, secret observation of Jemy, and then self-revelation and self-assertion within that relationship. She informs Jemy that her case is worse than his and proceeds quite incredibly to tell him a self-justifying version of her career: 'I told him so much of my Story as I thought was convenient, bringing it at last to my being reduc'd to great Poverty, and representing myself as fallen into some Company that led me to relieve my Distresses by a way that I had been utterly unacquainted with' (298). Finally and most aggressively, she gains still more power by revealing a secret—that she had saved him from capture at Brickhill by diverting his pursuers. By concealing and revealing herself simultaneously to advantage, Moll gains power over Jemy. She rescues him from his indifferent stupor and puts them on course for what she ecstatically describes as a place 'where we should look back on all our past Disasters with infinite Satisfaction, when we should consider that our Enemies should entirely forget us, and that we should live as new People in a new World, no Body having any thing to say to us, or we to them' (304). Such bliss is exactly what Moll's desires would shape: total escape from the responsibilities of past action, secret contemplation of the past from a new identity which guarantees a new and total kind of privacy. Moll's manipulative energies coincide at this point as never before with her spontaneous desire, or, better, her spontaneous desire exactly equals the pleasures of powerful apartness.

The trip and the preparations for it partake of this new synthesis. Moll organizes her capital with a new openness and gusto, arranges by judicious bribery for comfortable transportation for them both apart from the other mere convicted felons, and most important, conceals part of her story from Jemy. Her explanation of this strange but, in the light of her career, quite consistent reserve is as follows: 'I Gave him an Account of my Stock as faithfully, that is to say of what I had taken to carry with me, for I was resolv'd what ever should happen, to keep what I had left with my Governess in Reserve; that in case I should die, what I had with me was enough to give him, and that which was left in my Governess Hands would be her own, which she had well deserv'd of me indeed' (311). Moll is still involved, in short, in preserving her relationships with both people. This is a familiar situation; when she first met Jemy she was negotiating with her bank clerk. More consistently than that, Moll has kept parallel male and female relationships going on in her career, but this is the most explicit rendering of the necessity of such a situation.

On the trip itself Moll is equally explicit about her powers, moving with new confidence straight through the contradictions of her position. It is the quintessential moment of Moll's career. In that moment she performs her dialectic operation on experience at its clearest: she is a transported felon, but within those externally compulsive and limiting circumstances the real Moll resides and controls, having negated the negation of her position by means of the products she has acquired in the course of the circumstances that led up to her transportation. The circumstances of her transportation (her life of duplicity and outright crime) are transformed into a product, a possession (her stock) which turns transportation into a new, overtly exultant liberation:

> . . . but I who had between seven and eight Hundred Pounds in Bank when this Disaster befel me, and who had one of the faithfulest Friends in the World to manage it for me . . . had still Three Hundred Pounds left in her Hand, which I reserv'd, as above, besides some very valuable things, as particularly two gold Watches, some small Peices [*sic*] of Plate, and some Rings; all stolen Goods; the Plate, Rings and Watches were put up in my Chest with the Money, and with this Fortune, and in the Sixty first Year of my Age, I launch'd out into a new World, as I may call it, in the Condition (as to what appear'd) only of a poor nak'd Convict, order'd to be Transported in respite from the Gallows; my Cloaths were poor and mean, but not ragged or dirty, and none knew in the whole Ship that I had any thing of value about me. (312)

The catalogue of goods enforces and indeed guarantees the transformation. And Moll in turn transforms her highwayman-husband, who comes on board humiliated by his circumstances. She describes his revival through her control and confidence and in the process analyses and undercuts his kind of personality. He is 'so reviv'd with the Account I gave him of the Reception we were like to have in the Ship, that he was quite another Man, and new vigour and Courage appear'd in his very Countenance; so true is it, that the greatest of Spirits, when overwhelm'd by their Afflictions, are subject to the greatest

Dejections, and are the most apt to Despair and give themselves up' (315). So much for 'the greatest of Spirits'. Moll implies her own superiority in the analysis, her own superior power as a covert and indirect force. She does the same thing at length when they reach Virginia. She handles arrangements, chooses and supplies their plantation, and tells us openly that Jemy cannot be left alone; he is a prisoner of his history and his circumstances as she is the master of hers: 'he was bred a Gentleman, and by Consequence was not only unacquainted, but indolent, and when we did Settle, would much rather go out into the Woods with his Gun, which they call there Hunting, and which is the ordinary Work of the *Indians*, and which they do as Servants; I say he would much rather do that, than attend the natural Business of his Plantation' (328).

In managing Jemy and establishing their plantation, Moll is resolving the contradiction between desire and survival that her story began with. She has Jemy and her plantation; having Jemy is part of her means of having that security, and arranging her security is a way of making Jemy love her the more. So too, in finding her son, Moll continues that kind of resolution between desire and survival. For the first time, Moll allows herself to feel deep maternal affection. She sees her son (from her marriage to her husband/brother) and she asks the mothers among us to imagine her turmoil: 'let any Mother of Children that reads this, consider it, and but think with what anguish of Mind I restrain'd myself; what yearnings of Soul I had in me to embrace him, and weep over him; and how I thought all my Entrails turn'd within me, that my very Bowels mov'd, and I knew not what to do' (322). This seems strange from a woman who has left a trail of abandoned children (nine who have lived, including this one). The grotesque psychological inconsistency marks the structural consistency which determines Moll's 'character'. She is now in a position to mediate between spontaneous desire and survival, and maternal urges can be safely admitted. And not only admitted but added to the power of the self, compatible with its growing security and safely expanding possessions. Moll thus learns immediately after her great emotional crisis at seeing her grown son that her mother-in-law/mother has left her an estate in trust with her grandson. Her new problem is to take possession of her son and her estate without revealing her secret to her husband, in short, to have a secret and no secret, to become public without losing her private status. Moll discourses at length on the 'natural' necessity of revealing a secret, 'a Secret of Moment should always have a Confident, a bosom Friend, to whom we may Communicate the Joy of it, or the Grief of it, be it which it will' (325).

We know from Moll's career that she has resisted this natural tendency with some rigour, that she has existed in a real way by being secret. But now 'nature' (what I have called spontaneous desire) can safely be released, since it is in Moll's new state quite compatible with the strength and security of the self. In ironic fact, Moll's new natural commitment is the result of her most 'unnatural' commitment, the incestuous union with her brother. But in order to realize the natural maternal affections (crucially accompanied by considerable material advantage), Moll has to repress the equally natural but potentially disadvantageous need to share her secret with her husband. The resolution, as always in the book, is a new relationship: Moll writes to her old husband/brother, but the letter is read by her son. The two of them become an affectionate pair of conspirators. To be sure, Moll enters into the alliance with her son only slowly, and only eventually after the death of her son's father revealing that she has a new husband. And even then, she pretends she has just married him. To the absolute end, Moll survives by being secret. When there are no more secrets and she can even tell her last secret to that innocent gentleman, her husband, the story ends.

Especially with a tangled conclusion like this one, a career like Moll's has little to do with psychological or historical probability. Her resilience and infinite resourcefulness are far removed from any reasonable theory of personality or any possible set of normal social expectations. Her attractiveness stems from her function: to assert and enact the possibility of survival and prosperity in the face of impossibly limiting and even destructive circumstances. We respond as readers to her story because she enacts the delightful autonomy of the self without seeming to violate the equally autonomous facts of nature and society. She is an instrument for our delight in human survival, and towards that end she has to be more than human.

# V

## *Colonel Jack* : The Self Enters History

Nota: man is the intelligence of his soil,
The sovereign ghost.

. . . . . . .

Nota: his soil is man's intelligence.
That's better.
Wallace Stevens, 'The Comedian
as the Letter C'.

### I

DEFOE'S narratives are thick with ideas, arguments, contro-
versies, even polemics, and critics are often tempted to perform
their services by extrapolating and systematizing those ideas
and telling readers that the narratives are about this or that.
Such conclusions are usually intimidating, since the experience
involved in reading the narratives seems to exclude that kind
of coherence.[1] But mere readers have a defence. For one thing,
commentators have to rely heavily on specialized learning to
interpret Defoe's narratives: his political and economic
journalism, the ideological context, the literary and historical
circumstances. Such matters are obviously important, and form
part of our understanding of the structure of the works. But
Defoe's narratives may be said to exploit ideas much more than
they resolve them or even articulate them fairly. Indeed, ideas
in the experience we have of reading the stories are simply
part of the resources of the self, always important as instruments
for clarification or definition or presentation of the self rather
than for any particular moral, spiritual, social, or historical
content they may have. As I read the novels, the self in Defoe's
narratives presents itself as existentially prior to any particular

---

[1] Starr's description of the dramatically rich confusions of *Colonel Jack* is excellent:
'Rather than offering a consistent hierarchy of values, with mercantile morality or
natural law or divine law or genteel honor at its summit, *Colonel Jack* pits these
codes against each other, dramatically but inconclusively.' (See *Defoe and Casuistry*,
p. 87.)

idea and is never totally contained by an idea at any given moment. In Defoe's narratives, one can follow Sartre's observation that the artist 'radically distinguishes things from thought'.[2] Defoe's heroes in the process of narrative detach themselves from the static world of discursive thought and become that special and dynamic event I have called literary personality. In Sartre's words again, those narratives arrange that 'Being sparkle as Being, with its opacity and its coefficient of adversity, by the indefinite spontaneity of Existence'.[3]

The situation is nowhere more apparent than in *Colonel Jack*. On the one hand, the story can be read (i.e. explained) as a narrative treatise on the idea of natural goodness, Colonel Jack serving as Defoe's Émile and the novel itself recording the normally tough-minded Defoe's infection by the fashionable sentimentalism of the moment, perhaps influenced in that direction by the production the month before the book appeared of Steele's *The Conscious Lovers*.[4] Those are interesting speculations. But if we find ourselves more interested in the fact of the narrative than in speculation about Defoe, we have to admit that what we perceive and remember as readers is a variety of scene and situation which quite overwhelms the ideas isolated by historical critics. I wish to argue here in this chapter that what matters to us as participants and onlookers of narrative is that central energy we call Colonel Jack using those ideas among other devices to serve our delight by surviving and prospering under the most unlikely circumstances, indeed, in the face of those impossible circumstances with which Defoe's heroes are routinely faced.

That energy or will to power is what animates all Defoe's heroes, but here it is demonstrably more diverse in its accomplishments than anywhere else. *Colonel Jack*, James Sutherland has noted, is an amalgam of all the narrative arrangements displayed in Defoe's previous books.[5] Each of those we have

---

[2] *What is Literature?*, trans. Bernard Frechtman (New York, 1965), p. 108.

[3] *What is Literature?*, p. 108.

[4] M. E. Novak calls Colonel Jack 'Defoe's Émile, the natural man living in society. He follows the laws of nature which dictate self-interest and takes from society only what he needs to stay alive.' (See *Defoe and the Nature of Man*, p. 75.) Samuel Monk points out that the book was published a month or so after Steele's play was produced. (See Monk's Introduction to *Colonel Jack* (Oxford English Novels, 1965), p. xiv. All further references in the text are to this edition.)

[5] *Daniel Defoe: a Critical Study* (Cambridge, Mass., 1971), p. 198.

looked at so far may be seen as an attempt to localize the energy of the self in a particular narrative convention, and in fact to accommodate the self to the limitations implicit in each of them or in their attendant circumstances. Moll, Crusoe, and Singleton are dissolved by their narratives into their various conventional roles, and the selves we perceive exist in a dialectical relationship with those roles: the characters are first subjugated and then liberated by their transformation of the particular reality involved in impersonating a thief, a castaway, or a pirate-adventurer. We have seen repeatedly that separation or secret consciousness is the key source of that power which Defoe's characters exercise, what marks them as ultimate masters of experience from the mere slaves of it all around them. Like them, Colonel Jack has a number of conventional, pseudo-historical roles to inhabit, but unlike them, he is formally separate from the start, granted a secret and socially guaranteed apartness by his gentle birth. That initial and quite absolute technicality allows Jack his great variety, and of course that variety contributes further to his apartness. As his wonderful sub-title declares, Jack plays so many roles that he remains essentially apart from them all, identified in our minds with none of them.[6]

His style is immediate evidence of that preliminary apartness. It is a prose style rather different from those employed by Defoe's other narrators, but its difference lies in its extension and full possession of the characteristics of the retrospective narrator. Overall, that style is much given to neat summarizing, enacting Jack's self-consciousness in its noticeable tendency to outline cause and effect, to dwell in orderly fashion upon the meaning of a moment, to construct authentic parallelisms and to avoid those informative but digressive tendencies that characterize narrators like Moll and Singleton. If we put the

---

[6] From the critical perspective of the well-made novel, that variety can be seen as mere diffuseness. Defoe may have begun the book as an exercise in conventional rogue narrative and then switched to what W. H. McBurney calls a 'Novel of Doctrine'. McBurney suggests that Defoe sensed a profitable new direction his story could take. In order to dramatize Jack's development and further that direction, he had Jack rearrange his childhood in the second part of the novel and remember himself as more ignorant and innocent than he was. (See '*Colonel Jacque*: Defoe's Definition of the Complete English Gentleman', *SEL*, 2 (1962), 321–36.) Jack's revised version of his childhood can also be explained in the context of the narrative at that point as part of Jack's necessary self-dramatization.

opening sentence of *Colonel Jack* next to the openings of Crusoe, Singleton, and Moll, it is recollected tranquillity itself. They speak out of the whirlwind of their exciting careers, Jack is nothing if not calm:

> Seeing my Life has been such a Checquer Work of Nature, and that I am able now to look back upon it from a safer Distance, than is ordinarily the Fate of the Clan to which I once belong'd; I think my History may find a place in the World, as well as some, who I see are every Day read with pleasure, tho' they have in them nothing so Diverting, or Instructing, as I believe mine will appear to be.[7]

The coherence in that sentence is appropriate for a gentleman-adventurer, planter, soldier, and trader and catches the tone we expect of such a man: two parallel clauses (with slight syntactic variations), the second expressing Jack's firm grasp of his exact historical claim to singularity, introduce his confidently understated presentation, concluding with an ironic acknowledgement of rival books which dismisses them in the process. Jack offers us cause and effect instead of slightly bewildered sequence such as we have most of the time from the other narrators. In place of the evangelical convictions Crusoe depends upon to define that new consciousness out of which he tells his story, Jack offers the secular wisdom of history and society understood by participation, generalization about such matters informed by experience. In place of the pious moralizings that Moll drags out after the fact to justify her story and to contradict the praxis she embodies, Jack offers us wonder tinged with irony, openly promises us from his first sentence a genteel mixture of diversion and instruction which invites us to be sceptical about the moral content of the latter.

But the apartness Jack requires is primarily a matter of direct revelation. He is told at an early age by the woman who cares for him that his father directed that he be told he was a gentleman, 'and this he said was all the Education he would desire of her for me, for he did not doubt, he said, but that sometime or other the very hint would inspire me with Thoughts suitable to my Birth, and that I would certainly act like a Gentleman, if I believed myself to be so' (3). There seems to be

---

[7] Starr notes that the prose style is 'rich in figures of balance' and that 'a yoking together of opposites permeates the whole story'. (See *Defoe and Casuistry*, p. 83.)

a subversive implication in that to the effect that social class is a matter of personal belief rather than actual property, but it is really a perfectly orthodox bit of the classless ideology of the middle classes: the best people are those who believe themselves to be best. The myth is psychological rather than genetic, the hint of superiority must be given. But the narrative handles this piece of commonplace bourgeois exhortation by ignoring those implications of self-creation and treating gentility as if it were a transmittable spiritual substance, something which somehow operates on Jack to make him feel better and different and certainly thus apart from his material circumstances. That treatment is crucial to the mechanism of the narrative. In being bound by the necessity of his genetic inheritance (even though in the name of probability it requires the trigger of the nurse's information), Jack is effectively free by not being free. The genetic compulsion (which is actually an ironic and accidental psycho-social fact) allows Jack to have a self which is formally prior to the facts of his experience.

Eighteenth-century England made limited provision for a *carrière ouverte aux talents*, so all of Defoe's success–adventure stories are presented as wonderful exceptions to a fairly rigorous implicit social and natural necessity. All Defoe's heroes we have seen so far are criminals or sinners in one sense or another, exceptions to a norm who apologize as they go about their singular careers. Colonel Jack's mysterious gentle origins allow him to illustrate natural and social necessities even as he violates them extravagantly. In place of the residual natural self that Crusoe, Moll, and Singleton begin with and return to, Jack claims a powerful social identity as his ultimate personal substance.

One famous result of that gentility seems to be his 'goodness', his instinctive revulsion at cruelty and excessive violence. But the point even as we read about Jack's precocious tenderness is surely that he is thereby naturally apart from the mechanical violence of his associates and turned towards survival on a socially higher and more sophisticated level than they are. Surrounded as it is in the narrative by extraordinary luck and prudent calculation, Jack's goodness leads him towards accumulation and the authentic survival implicit in that activity. The narrative, in short, enacts the instrumentality of goodness, revealing it as part of Jack's praxis of survival and social expansion, but all the while exploiting the fiction that Jack's goodness is part of a genetic compulsion.

The other and opposite result of Jack's gentility is his easy parisitism. What separates Jack from his environment and his associates is at the same time the source of his exploitative relationship with them. More than any other of Defoe's heroes, he is served by others who somehow recognize or discover his worthiness. His career is to a considerable extent the result of a series of surrogates and benefactors who exist to further his movements. Doubles are a characteristic feature of Defoe's narratives; there are more of them in *Colonel Jack* than anywhere else and their function is here at its clearest. Reality must be served; the recurring problem Defoe's narratives try to solve is to mediate somehow between those opposed worlds of desire (summed up in terms like survival and self-assertion) and circumstances (the world of natural and social facts and the determinants they carry). From the beginning, Jack is almost magically surrounded by others who obey in their lives the laws of circumstances that he manages to evade. In other words, Jack's world and the people in it change and respond, while he may be said to participate and observe, managing to remain essentially and improbably still in the middle of the convincing movement of others.

One can discern in the narrative as a whole a pattern of development from dependence upon these surrogates and benefactors to self-containment. Just as we hear nothing of his goodness after his childhood, Jack in time becomes his own surrogate; he is capable, as are none of Defoe's other tricky heroes, to live separate lives by himself, to be several people at the same time. The narrative insists that he is always, whatever happens and whatever he does, still Colonel Jack, even though he never quite finds the life style or situation which will allow secure and public self-presentation as Colonel Jack, gentleman. His goodness and his parasitism dissolve eventually when he has no further need of others, but his narrative continues to arrange situations for him in which he is something other in public than the private reality we know about. His narrative continues, we can say, to honour well past the point of probability the definition of the self in terms of its secret opposition to the other.

Roland Barthes has suggested that realistic narrative is dominated by metonymic discourse and constitutes a series of discrete statements or particular events which combine elements of a system without ever overtly revealing that system.[8] Thus, an event in *Colonel Jack* acts as if it were simply a message, fairly exact information about an act. But the individual messages are combinative acts within a code, using elements of the code to communicate and perpetuate it. Broadly speaking, the code consists of the dynamic antithesis between the self and its environments, and the larger and unutterable message that constitutes the book is the vivifying dominance of the self in that antithesis.

Given this apparent movement we can observe in the narrative from dependence to independence, it is tempting to follow Professor Monk and call *Colonel Jack* an adumbration of the *Bildungsroman*.[9] But the more accurate thing to notice is that Jack's progress in the narrative is not a development or a maturation but rather a matter of movement which perpetuates the message of the book and records the continuing and indeed expanding power of the self. Jack seems to develop, and he certainly grows older and richer and more powerful in the course of his story. But what he actually does underneath the progressive diversity and irregularity of his career is to assert himself at the expense of the other over and over again, to resist development and the submission to fact that is implicit in it.

If we look at the text, Jack is presented fully formed. When he is recognized as fine-looking under his urchin's rags by passers-by in the street, he tells us that he 'lay'd up all these things in my Heart' (8), that is, that he has a meditative centre quite apart from the natural circumstances of the moment. At the same time Jack is precociously conscious that his social role as a street boy is just that, a role: 'I pass'd among my Comrades for a bold resolute Boy, and one that durst fight any thing; but I had a different Opinion of my self, and therefore shun'd Fighting as much as I could' (7). His mates, on the other hand, are complementary opposites, illustrating

---

[8] *Elements of Semiology*, trans. Annette Lavers and Colin Smith (London, 1967), p. 60. The insight, Barthes notes, is borrowed from Roman Jakobson.

[9] *Colonel Jack*, Introduction, p. xvi.

the extremes of unconscious behaviour. 'Captain' Jack is 'an
original Rogue, for he would do the foulest and most villainous
Things, even by his own Inclination; he had no Taste or Sense
of being Honest, no, not, I say, to his Brother Rogues; which
is what other Thieves make a point of Honour of; I mean that
of being Honest to one another' (6). 'Major' Jack is 'a merry,
facetious pleasant Boy' with 'native Principles of Gallantry in
him, without any thing of the brutal or terrible Part that the
Captain had; and in a Word, he wanted nothing but Honesty
to have made him an an excellent Man' (6). It does not
matter that Major Jack has 'some thing of a Gentleman in
him' (6) and has learned to read and write and to speak well,
just as Colonel Jack has. It is Colonel Jack's narrative and he
can use the same facts to reach different conclusions about
himself. More than the rest of Defoe's narrators, he grants
only himself the complications and powers of self-consciousness.
What is curious but inevitable is that we readers accept that
unlikely singularity as one of the key fictions behind the fiction.
To return to the linguistic analogy from Barthes's semiology,
the over-all code is implicit in the various messages. Jack
exists as a street urchin in a world of pure social compulsion,
where those around him act only as they must. In describing
them for us and in placing himself in their world, Jack partakes
of a self-consciousness denied to everyone else, even though his
rendition of that world insists that he is partially subject to it.

Jack's initial career as a street urchin and thief is the longest
in the book (about a third of the narrative) and naturally sets
the pattern for subsequent adventures. It is a pattern which in
organizing the adventure demonstrates just how the narrative
is really concerned to rescue the self from the limitations and
determinations of experience, even while the self is granted
experience in the fullest and most varied sense. Here Jack is
preserved from the degrading actualities of being a real thief
and urchin and turned into a crypto-trickster figure, a magically
privileged hero. By its various strategies, the narrative records
Jack's transformation from street urchin to a person of substance, although that substance remains temporarily secret
and in reserve. Such a temporary reserve is typical of the
narrative as a whole, serving as a transition device. Typically,
Jack acquires something new, whether substantial like money

or spiritual like the desire to learn or the knowledge that he has courage, and he uses that new acquisition as the base of his next adventure. Jack accumulates personalities and identities in this manner without ever losing the secret consciousness of superiority with which he began. Indeed, that consciousness provides the form and the exact means of acquiring new identities. The self, in effect, becomes richer and richer in experience without altering or losing its rooted and defining need to be powerfully apart from experience.

Although appropriately crude and grossly substantial, Jack's first adventures in accumulation are only superficially criminal. Jack's innate goodness provides him, he tells us, with a crucial reserve towards these acts and their benefits which preserves him equally from criminal habituation and real responsibility. Although presumably involved in many crimes, he tells us specifically about six, each one somewhat different from the others and each one providing him with a different kind of separateness. His first two adventures make him a totally passive accomplice of Robin, 'one of the most exquisite Divers, or Pick-pockets in the Town' (17).[10] Here in his first two crimes, Jack is given his share of the proceeds for being a decoy and merely carrying the stolen wallets. The bulk of the first scene involves Jack's predicament over the disposal of the four guineas and fourteen shillings which are his share of the

---

[10] Robin's expertness at picking pockets is as carefully described as Moll's perfection in the art of shop-lifting. *Colonel Jack* continues the exciting enumeration of the techniques of illicit survival, techniques which in their very exactness mitigate the blame we might attach to them. Victims, as in *Moll Flanders*, are careless and irresponsible, failing to compete properly in a world which implicitly admires skill and precision and rewards them as virtues. Jack continues to marvel at the dexterity of his accomplices: 'How he did to Whip away such a Bagg of Money from any Man that was Awake, and in his senses; I cannot tell' (44). And again, before the third crime, Jack watches men in front of the Exchange and marvels equally at their carelessness: 'This Careless way of Men putting their Pocket-books into a Coat-pocket, which is so easily Div'd into, by the least Boy that has been us'd to the Trade, can never be too much blam'd; the Gentlemen are in great Hurries, their Heads and Thoughts entirely taken up, and it is impossible they should be Guarded enough against such little Hawks Eyed Creatures, as we were' (45). Jack himself performs exquisitely this time: 'Now, 'tis mine, said I, to my self, and crossing the Alley, I brush'd smoothly but closely by the Man, with my Hand down flat to my own Side, and taking hold of it by the Corner that appear'd; the Book came so light into my Hand, it was impossible the Gentleman should feel the least motion, or any body else see me take it away' (46).

loot. That sequence has been justly admired as a rendition of the psychological dynamics of urban paranoia and the fear and exaltation that accompany it. But the function of the psychological exactness that Defoe's narratives can occasionally encompass is to allow his narrators to free themselves from the implications of experience. Jack's difficulties with this stolen money exorcise the blame attached to it, as his innocent fear and his pathetic although temporary loss of the money in the hollow tree obviously earn him the money. Guilt and goodness are instrumental for acquisition. Jack's innocence, as he himself notes, preserves him from the implications of such a violent ritual of appropriation:

> It would tire the Reader should I dwell on all the little Boyish Tricks that I play'd in the Extacy of my Joy, and Satisfaction, when I had found my Money; so I break off here:   Joy is as Extravagant as Grief, and since I have been a Man, I have often thought, that had such a Thing befallen a Man, so to have lost all he had, and not have a bit of bread to Eat, and then so strangely to find it again, after having given it so effectually over, *I say*, had it been so with a Man it might have hazarded his using some Violence upon himself. (26)

Defoe's heroes characteristically pull up short of the uncontrollable implications of experience. They thereby underline the functional and self-preserving nature of their personalities. Jack's grief and joy, he emphasizes for us, are possible only because they have his innocence as a context. The narrative sees to it that such psychological turbulence is a means towards a desirable end at this point; that fact of turbulence is deliberately and pointedly restricted by the facts of Jack's youth. And that kind of turbulent fact does not appear again.

Jack's third crime involves actual pilfering, as he himself now performs skilfully. The wallet he steals contains a mass of securities, cheques, and diamonds that are of no value to him and his present accomplice, Will. Together, they engineer an elaborate transaction to return the wallet for a reward without suffering any reprisals. This is the second such transaction Jack has been involved in. The first time (his second crime) he is confronted with non-negotiable wealth Jack is filled with guilt and thinks 'that it was a sad thing indeed to take a Man's Bills away for so much Money, and not have any

Advantage by it neither; for I concluded that the Gentleman, who own'd the Bills must loose all the Money, and it was strange he [Jack's accomplice] should keep the Bills and make a Gentleman loose so much Money for nothing' (29). Here again, Jack wonders about his 'strange kind of unin-structed Conscience' which makes 'no scruple of getting any thing in this manner from any Body, yet I could not bear destroying their Bills, and Papers, which were things that would do them a great deal of hurt, and do me no good' (55). Obviously, Jack's goodness is transparently a matter of an intelligent sense of order and utility. What appals him is the waste of energy involved in such a transaction, and Jack's emerging skill involves cancelling that waste. He not only works to convert that wasted crime to profit but also, and more significantly, to transform the necessarily limited acquisition inherent in such crimes into the potentially expansive accumu-lation made possible by the quasi-legal transaction of stolen securities. These transactions involve extensive negotiations with the legitimate world of business. They enable Jack to employ his talent of innocence (in this case of appearing innocent, which is thereby dramatized as the reality of inno-cence) and to refine almost out of existence the guilt he has incurred. The negotiations enable him, finally, to acquire a benefactor, an older man who grants him social stability and the promise of social advancement. Jack's criminal career is thus quickly turned into a refined and quasi-legal activity, relatively innocent and truly substantial.

In the first of these deals, Jack learns from his active accom-plice, Robin, that a thirty-pound reward has been offered for the stolen bills. Jack presents himself at the custom house, and the narrative is at great pains to contrast an innocent and passive Jack with a larger world of aggressive movement: 'While I stood there, one thrust me this way, and another thrust me that way, and the Man that sat behind began to look at me; at last he call'd out to me; what does that Boy do there, get you gone Sirrah, are you one of the Rogues that stole the Gentleman's Letter Case a *Monday last?*' (31) Such an opposition furthers Jack's purpose: he can be casually accused of the crime because he appears in such a context to be the last one who could have done it. The clerk feels no reluctance in front of such a waif to tell a nearby gentleman that the victim of the robbery will honour his word not to prosecute those who return his bills. Jack then confides in the clerk, hiding his part in the robbery but telling part of the truth, indeed the essential part: 'it was gotten into the Hands of a Boy, that would have burnt it, if it had not been for me' (33). As Jack puts it, the clerk 'carry'd' him to Tower Street and 'order'd' him to come there that night with the wallet. Such verbs are neutral enough in eighteenth-century usage, but they are least indicate that the clerk has taken over for Jack, the first of his benefactors to be won over by his innocence. When the robbed gentleman attempts that night to deduct from the reward the £12. 10s. bill that has already been cashed by the thieves, the clerk acts as Jack's champion and he gets the full twenty-five pounds reward.

The encounter is in bare dialogue for the most part, a dialogue which emphasizes for us as readers the dramatic heightening of Jack's innocence that is primary. What Jack tells the gentlemen are the facts of his life so far, facts which we have already gathered in their full narrative rendition. We thereby perceive those facts as part of Jack's nearly dramatic and almost studied performance. It is not that Jack is lying; it is rather that we have been given that information without the tears and pathos that they excite in the gentleman from the exchange. We therefore read the sequence as something close to contrivance but not quite. 'They ask'd me a great many Questions more, to which I answer'd in my Childish way as well as I could, but so as pleas'd them well enough' (38). That combination of genuine innocence and effective contrivance is the ideal state for Colonel Jack. It earns him not only his reward but a bank account with his benefactor, the clerk, who rescues Jack from the immediate danger of carrying such a large sum with him.[11] That account will be Jack's deliverance in a later and more serious situation, enabling him to convert incriminating loot into solid property.

In the second of these transactions, all the negotiations are performed by Will. Such variation is necessary not just to

---

[11] Although we cannot be certain about purchasing power, we do well to remember just how substantial these sums were in the early eighteenth century, when £50–£100 a year was a decent income for a skilled journeyman or a small shopkeeper. (See Ian Watt, *The Rise of the Novel*, p. 41.)

provide diversity but also because Jack is by now older and has lost his external innocent helplessness, no longer in rags but clothed at Will's insistence in a greatcoat. Will performs deliberately what young Jack has done instinctively in the previous situation. This transaction involves overt duplicity, so Jack stands aside and collects half of eighty pounds without involving himself directly in the fraud. Jack again performs but in another sense, for Will represents him as an inexperienced and reluctant thief who stole the pocket-book but was the victim of the irresistibly tempting carelessness of the owner: "'tis very strange Gentlemen should put Pocket-Books which have such things in them into those loose Pockets, and in so careless a manner', says the cunning Will, and the gentlemen nod in agreement (54). By itself, such a detail and many others do not mitigate any blame we might attach to Jack's criminal life. We are nowhere asked explicitly by the narrative's voice to consider Jack the victim of social circumstances or of personal necessity and to excuse him. Jack is saved by the narrative process itself rather than by any theory of behaviour or society the narrative can articulate. In both of these trans-actions, the narrative sees to it that Jack is performing, acting out a role to which he is not wholly committed and which, it is constantly implied, does not contain his whole personality. In both cases, Jack is made to stand aside while the others provide for him, bargain on his behalf, and create roles for him to which he only partially conforms. To the custom-house gentleman, he is an innocent waif and deserves his reward. To the robbed jeweller and his associates, he is an inexperienced thief who has shown them their carelessness and deserves his reward. That essential evasion of full participation in the acts of his life is something Jack accomplishes partly by the mechanics of retrospective narration, which ensures that the acts we ex-perience are both in the historical past and in the present tense required to read them. But the evasion which consistently reserves a part of Jack from the contamination of total partici-pation is mainly the result of those two features of the narrative which have emerged so far: Jack's muted and quasi-involuntary performance in roles others select for him, and the recurring and pervasive fiction of the latent goodness occupying the space behind these performances.

By himself, moreover, there seems to be little that Jack can do in this first part of his story. He notes that he was now rich, but 'so rich that I knew not what to do with my Money, or with myself' (55). He explains that, except for an occasional two or three pence for food, he spent almost nothing, and so 'in a whole Year I had not quite Spent the 15 Shillings, which I had sav'd of the Custom House Gentleman's Money, and I had the 4 Guineas, which was of the first Booty before that, still in my Pocket, I mean the Money that I let fall into the Tree' (55). Such frugality (which seems to violate the probabilities we might invoke for a hitherto poor youth now rich) and such exact accounting are new qualities for one of Defoe's criminal heroes. Singleton and Moll accumulate in a much vaguer fashion, and Moll's frugality is exercised in her dwindling state as she slides toward necessity. Jack seems to collect money the way he collects experiences; he accumulates it without letting it change him right away. The narrative, in fact, records three separate processes of accumulation. Jack gives us an exact accounting of his mounting assets, an exact description of his criminal experiences, and a running account of the moments of moral self-consciousness which accumulate as well. In time, Jack will accumulate enough of all three to propel him into a new stage of his career in Virginia, where he will be able to put them to use.

Jack is consistently careful throughout these criminal enterprises to draw a line between picking pockets or snatching purses and outright assault and battery. His companion in crime defines that difference by growing into 'a Man' and falling 'into quite another Vein of Wickedness, getting acquainted with a wretched Gang of Fellows, that turn'd their Hands to every Thing that was vile' (59). In other words, Will does two things that Jack never quite does: he develops a self directly out of his social and physical circumstances (encouraged by his physical strength and by his successes as a pickpocket) and he joins a group. It is out of those two errors that Will leads Jack into his last criminal act, stressing those two considerations as he persuades him: 'I always said you were a lucky Boy, Col. *Jack*, *says he*, but come you are grown almost a Man now, and you shall not be always at play at Push-pin, I am got into better Business I assure you, and you shall come

into it too, I'll bring you into a brave Gang *Jack, says he,*
where you shall see we shall be all Gentlemen' (59). In the
crimes that follow, Jack's is preceded by two violent assaults
committed by Will and another, full of the standard violence
of highwaymen: '*Sir, your Money?*' says Will, and when he is
resisted, knocks his victim down and 'told him with an Oath,
that he would Cut his Throat' (63). Jack is again at pains to
impress us with his hesitation and effective separation from
the criminal community he seems to be a member of now. His
crime is an almost gentle and certainly muted robbery of two
poor women which pointedly avoids the normal bombast:
'don't be frighted Sweetheart, *said I*, to the Maid, a little of
that Money in the bottom of your Pocket will make all easie,
and I'll do you no harm' (64).

This incident is the high point of Jack's goodness, his most
explicit and effective sensitive reaction, since it leads him for
the first time to plan restitution (rather conveniently the loot
amounts to 27*s.* 6*d.*). It occurs at the moment when Jack's
narrative has presented us with the full range of criminal
experience, from picking pockets to assault and battery. Given
that fullness, there is nowhere for Jack to go now except into
the confining repetition implicit in being a thief and only a
thief. Goodness is a means of ensuring the variety that is the
narrative value his book is most interested in. Moreover, this is
also the moment that Jack can escape the implications of his
experience, because he has also accumulated the proceeds of
that experience. Jack's bank account with the custom-house
clerk is the financial certification of the social and moral apartness that preserves him from being just another street criminal
like Will and the others. That account, like his goodness, now
makes it possible for him to be apart from the rush of circumstances that crowd around him thicker and faster than ever
before in the book.

Will and some others wound a man (who later dies) and
take 100 pounds in plate. Will is caught, but not before he
manages to hide the booty in Jack's lodgings. The incident
summarizes our perspective on Jack: he is implicated but
innocent, involved because of his position and his past (not
entirely against his will) but not quite an aggressive participant.
The problem, as always, is extrication, to slide away from the

effects of experience without denying experience. Jack tells us
all this in great detail which enforces complexity and then
records his meditations and movements:

> I Thank'd him [an old friend who has warned him], and went
> away, but in the greatest perplexity Imaginable; and now not
> knowing what to do with my self, or with the little ill-gotten Wealth
> which I had; I went musing, and alone into the Fields towards
> *Stepney*, my usual Walk; and there began to consider what to do,
> and as this Creature had left his Prize in my Garret, I began to
> think, that if he should be taken and should Confess and send the
> Officers to Search there for the Goods, and they should find them, I
> should be undone, and should be taken up for a Confederate;
> whereas, I knew nothing of the matter, and had no Hand in it.
> (71–2)

In the context of the narrative, this paragraph is superfluous.
The function of such redundancy is not information but action.
What we read is Jack separating himself by soliloquy and the
consciousness implied in it. The summary is an act of definition
of the situation and thereby of release from it. Guilty enough
if we look at the events of his narrative, Jack is made relatively guiltless by his isolated consciousness, strolling alone
and meditating, put upon by vicious, greedy, and foolhardy
associates. A phrase like 'this Creature' for Will, heretofore his
guide and mentor in crime, reveals the shift in our view of his
circumstances as Jack is transformed from participant to
victim.

Soon after, Jack meets Will and pawns the stolen plate for
him. Troubled by uneasy dreams that night, he learns the next
morning that Will has been arrested and he falls into solitary
despair: 'my very Joints trembl'd, and I was ready to sink into
the Ground, and all that Evening, and that Night following, I
was in the uttermost Consternation; my Head run upon nothing
but *Newgate*, and the Gallows, and being Hang'd; which I said
I deserv'd, if it were for nothing but taking that two and twenty
Shillings from the poor old Nurse' (75). We have seen repeatedly that Defoe's heroes are at their best when desperate
and alone. In the structure of survival which actually defies
psychological probabilities, emotional turbulence is invariably
accompanied by exact accounting, both moral and economic.

External danger enhances the internal competence of the self, which begins to provide for itself, focusing clearly on survival even as it perceives the amorphous alternative of destruction. Jack simultaneously repents his only real crime—robbing the old woman—and determines to secure his other booty, earned by skill and daring from careless and rich merchants and hoarded carefully: 'I had got together as you will perceive by the past Account, above Sixty Pounds, for I spent nothing' (75). He quickly invents a strategy to deposit that sum with his banker, the custom-house clerk. And, as so often in Defoe's narratives, the very circumstances that lead to despair provide tools for survival: 'there was a Suit of Cloths at one of our Houses of Rendezvous, which was left there for any of the Gang to put on upon particular Occasions, as a Disguise' (75). Those tools, moreover, are exactly rendered, those details serving as a significant opposite to the shapeless dangers that Jack faces—confiscation of his accumulated booty and imprisonment, annihilation in short. Just as Crusoe's equipment exactly catalogued saves him for us and from the shapeless horrors of the island, Jack's livery saves him from the loss of self in the same extraordinarily precise way: 'This was a Green Livery, Lac'd with Pink Colour'd Galloon, and lin'd with the same; an Edg'd Hat, a pair of Boots, and a Whip, I went and Dress'd my self up in this Livery, and went to my Gentleman, to his House in *Tower-street*; and there I found him in Health, and Well, just the same honest Gentleman, as ever' (75). The liberating joy implicit in that exactness marks this as one of the clearest examples in Defoe's narratives of the function of detail, that occasional and always purposive feature of them. Detail is what the self employs against the confusions and uncertainties of circumstance. Jack wears specific clothing to play a specific role in a real street, his invention supplying a fictitious biography to go with the livery and to account for the sixty pounds he brings with him—wages and an inheritance from one Sir Jonathan Loxham of Somersetshire.

This is the beginning of the recurring pattern of the book. Jack acquires and exercises power and freedom from circumstances by exact impersonation, by assuming multiple identities. Indeed, we are now in a position to look back and remark that the entire opening sequence of Jack's boyhood and adolescence is one long impersonation, Jack playing at being an urchin illiterate, possessed for us as readers from the very beginning of a self-conscious and powerful separation from the exciting and colourful but degrading circumstances he describes. The radical secret of *Colonel Jack* is that its hero is impersonating throughout, playing at even the most sordid and threatening reality he lives in, always the master of experience because he is somehow existentially prior to it. *Colonel Jack* illustrates what all Defoe's narratives attempt to resolve: the central myth of consciousness that the self is free and prior to experience must be reconciled with the facts of existence which decree that the self is the mere result of experience.

Jack's subsequent movements are in the service of that resolution. In the events which follow, he establishes himself as more and more innocent, both legally and morally: he is arrested falsely and he defends himself with great skill and is discharged, the warrant being for 'Captain' Jack; he finds the old nurse he had robbed and returns her money, rewarding her with an extra crown for forgiving her robbers. And yet when Captain Jack, a true and unrepentant thief, asks him to run away with him to Scotland, Jack goes, playing at being a fugitive, as he himself admits: 'I speak of myself, as in the same Circumstances of Danger, with Brother *Jack*, but it was only thus, I was in as much Fear as he, but not in quite as much Danger' (83). When they actually leave, in fact, Jack is without sin or crime, a companion rather than a participant in criminal retreat. Captain Jack is the aggressor in all this, stealing a horse for them to ride on and picking pockets for travel expenses. When Colonel Jack resolves to become honest in Edinburgh, learning to read and write and working for a Customs officer, Captain Jack wanders roguishly around Scotland and Ireland, returning at last as a foot-soldier when our other Jack needs him. It is thus Captain Jack who gives Colonel Jack the opportunity to join the army, his Customs officer employer having been ruined for malfeasance. It is Captain Jack who engineers their desertion from the army, and it is thus again Captain Jack who leads the Colonel to Virginia and a new and crucial phase in his career towards overt gentility. Captain Jack, all this action tells us, is in experience, acting boldly and being acted upon in turn. He does what

Colonel Jack cannot do and still remain the hero of the narrative. He is still another *alter ego*, creating opportunities for movement and absorbing the shocks, the blame, and especially the limitations that would affect Jack in the course of movement.

The desertion, for example, should flow from Colonel Jack's sense of proportion and ambition. By his own reckoning at this point, he has almost £100 drawing interest in London; not for him therefore to go 'a poor Musquetier into *Flanders*, to be knock'd on the Head at the Tune of Three and Six-pence a Week' (105) when he might buy a commission with his savings. But it is left for Captain Jack to propose desertion, allowing his 'brother' to protest and then to present himself as the victim of what he himself calls 'Circumstances' (105) and the pawn of his 'cunning Rogue', Captain Jack. The latter lures Colonel Jack away by talking to him, leading him to where a confederate is lodged, urging the moment and proposing instant action. Colonel Jack is made to hesitate, asserting prudence and self-possession to Captain Jack's impulsiveness.

The narrative needs Captain Jack. Characters like him make the assertions that spin the mechanism of the plot. We read adventure stories to participate in those specific and thrilling responses to experience which are quicker and truer than our own slow and ambivalent reactions. But *Colonel Jack* is, like the rest of Defoe's narratives, domesticated adventure in which attention is paid to the generalized movement of the self through experience as a category of being as well as to the specific jolts of separate experiences. Captain Jack will be hanged ultimately, and it is no more than just and pleasing that he should be. Unless you separate yourself from experience as Defoe's narrators do, it will kill you every time. Colonel Jack will survive and indeed prosper, going on past the confines of his unfinished story to complete (as the title-page says so deliciously) 'a Life of Wonders'. The colonel is like his readers, like us, in his story and kept safely out of it by his own self-conscious reservation. That reservation is enacted quite literally for us in a scene such as the one where Captain Jack urges him to join the desertion:

And when would you go away, *says I?*
This Minute, *says he*, no time to be lost; 'tis a fine Moonshining Night.

I have none of my Baggage, *says I*, let me go back and fetch my Linnen, and other things.

Your Linnen is not much, I suppose, *says he*, and we shall easily get more in *England* the old Way. (106)

Remember, our Jack has been contemplating desertion and has told us readers, to whom he never lies, that it is what he wants and needs to do at that moment. His reluctance is pure acting, emphasized as artifice by the dialogue and made even purer by Jack's line about going back for his baggage. The passage is, on the one hand, an expression of Jack's reluctance and fear in the face of what he wants to do. But given what we know about Jack and his material and ideological resources, that psychological dimension is very much a critical after-thought. What the narrative depicts as we read is the self at its most cunning and indirect, denying the very thing, it wants most to do. We know as no one else in the narrative does that Jack has his resources (his true 'Baggage') in his pocket, a bill from his secret banker in London. Captain Jack goes off truly un-provided, ready to forage, but Colonel Jack has a secret personality and the hidden material resources to certify it. He is, in effect, playing at being an adventurer, ready at the moment of necessity to produce himself (or part of himself) and survive or triumph. Just as we readers may be said to do, he evades the uncertainties of experience in the narrative by virtue of his accumulation from the past. We can extract ourselves from adventures and savour them safely by withdrawing to the identity we brought to the narrative. Part of our pleasure as onlookers of fiction comes from our solitary superiority in terms of a coherent and reliable past. Before the book was, we were. Colonel Jack begins with a reliable past, his gentle birth and secret sense of self and superiority, and continues as his narrative proceeds to accumulate an identity which serves him as cover and safe retreat.

This reserve sets him apart, of course, from a mere adventurer like his 'brother', Captain Jack. When they are shanghaied shortly after deserting from the army, they find themselves on their way to be sold as servants in Virginia. In the middle of adversity, while Captain Jack storms violently and ineffectually, Colonel Jack guarantees his survival by offering to pay the ship's captain twenty pounds apiece for their return. He produces his bill 'for 94 £ from the Gentleman of the Custom-House, and who to my infinite Satisfaction, he knew as soon as he saw the Bill; he was astonish'd at this, and lifting up his Hands, by what Witchcraft, *says he*, were you brought hither!' (115). Significantly, that strategy does not quite work. The captain claims that the winds prevent him from taking them back.[12] The result is not vulgar liberation, the freedom that Defoe's narratives abhor as the vacuum that precludes meaningful social movement. Instead, Colonel Jack shows us the complicated business of survival. The negotiation with the captain of the ship is the main feature of the voyage, with Jack playing a role, flourishing his bill, outmanœuvring the captain, who hopes to get the bill from him at journey's end. Jack uses his bill to accommodate himself to his new circumstances; he survives by making proposals which modify forced transportation into an opportunity for self-assertion. Jack amazes the captain by producing his bill, and instead of a rendition of suffering in the steerage, the narrative delivers another example of Jack's ability to transform desperate circumstances into opportunities for surprising self-display and power over others. Thus, when he reaches Virginia and the captain offers to take him and his bill back to England, Jack explains that he has 'grown indifferent' to that kind of proposal and has decided to serve his five years and avail himself of the 'Courtisie of the Country, *as they call'd it*; that is a certain Quantity of Land to Cultivate and Plant for myself; so that now I was like to be brought up to something, by which I might live without that wretched thing, call'd stealing; which my very Soul abhorr'd, and which I had given over, as I have said ever since that wicked time, that I robb'd the poor Widow of *Kentish* Town' (117).

In the context of his relationship with the ship's captain, that pious resolution is part of his triumph over him and the circumstances he represents. Pretending to negotiate for one kind of freedom, Jack informs us that he has simultaneously arranged another kind of freedom by weighing his past and his possible future. We are glad to see that Jack is honest and

---

[12] Jack notes that the Captain was telling the truth, as he learned later when he 'came to understand Sea Affairs better' (114). Such details modify whatever melodrama there is in the situation.

ambitious, but that goodness pleases most because it is founded
on the secret internal superiority of the self to its circumstances.
As ever, Jack's virtuous ambitions operate on us as signs of his
powerful apartness, manifestations of an agile will to power
which is really quite separate from moral categories. Each
reiteration at key moments like this one of Jack's desire to
improve himself constitutes a joyful trick upon necessity, a
stylish plucking of the flower of safety from the omnipresent
nettles of danger. Jack is consistently forced by necessity and
circumstances to do things which seem destructive but which
he converts by secret analysis into productive opportunities.
It is the trick, as we have seen, that all Defoe's heroes aspire to
master, and among them Jack's performance is the most skilled
and frequent.

Having arrived in America, Jack now begins to move much
faster, acquiring a series of roles in the rest of the book which
marks him as the most versatile of all of Defoe's narrators. But
even though he now graduates to legitimacy as overseer,
planter in his own right, and finally to traveller-adventurer-
soldier, he still enacts for us the liberating secrecy and apartness
from experience which mark his initial career as a criminal.
He still remains a private man playing profitably at being
a public man. He never neglects his primary function as a
character, to embody the self-generated private reality that is
beyond the final determination of social or public experience.

Take, for example, his initial elevation from servant to
overseer. He is sold to a rich planter and happens to hear a
speech delivered by his master to a newly arrived transported
felon: 'a young Fellow not above 17 or 18 Years of Age, and
his Warrant mention'd that he was, tho' a young Man, yet an
old Offender . . . an incorrigible Pick-pocket' (120). Jack is
astounded by the parallels in their careers, for the boy has been
transported 'for Picking a Merchant's Pocket-Book, or Letter
Case out of his Pocket, in which was Bills of *Exchange*, for a very
great Sum of Money' (120). Jack takes this and his master's
pious discourse to the boy quite to heart: 'I thought all my
Master said was spoken to me, and sometimes it came into my
Head, that sure my Master was some extraordinary Man, and
that he knew all things that ever I had done in my Life' (121).
The point to stress here is that the resemblances between Jack

and this boy are only superficial. Jack has been neither incorrigible nor careless enough to try to cash large bills. Jack uses this newly arrived 'double' to acquire guilt and further useful abhorrence of his criminal past. But he reminds us as well by all this that he is entirely better and smarter than this ordinary and clumsy felon. He is made to feel guilty, and yet the narrative's implicit comparison of Jack's career with his double's rescues him in our eyes from any traces of real guilt and incompetence. And finally that attenuated guilt propels him forward.

Thus, when Jack is called in shortly after this incident to appear before his master, who has noticed his tears during the speech, he can afford to be guilty at the very moment when he is to be franchised, elevated to overseer by virtue of his performance as repentant unfortunate in the interview which follows. That conversation carefully records two things—guilt and naïve cunning in using that guilt for promotion. He enters 'like a Malefactor indeed, and thought I look'd like one just taken in the Fact, and carry'd before the Justice; and indeed when I came in, for I was carry'd into an Inner-Room, or Parlour in the House to him' (122). Feeling and looking guilty, he can safely adjust his story and present himself to his master as someone who was also wronged: 'Indeed Sir, I have been a wicked idle Boy, and was left Desolate in the World; but that Boy is a Thief, and condemn'd to be hang'd, I never was before a Court of Justice in my Life' (124). He produces his bill, that certification of his worthiness, and wins his master's favour, as he won the custom-house clerk's favour, by a performance which combines naïve guilt with mysterious proof of substance and ability. As before, we experience Jack's performance as a marvellous synthesis of action and submission. The real Jack eludes his present master, for the real Jack is somewhere behind that naïve, half-repentant, half-competent *persona* whom the master consents to help and to promote to overseer.

Jack's mastery of such crucial indirection is responsible for his next great leap up the ladder of power, from overseer to free man and planter. He proves tender-hearted as an overseer, and the Negroes under his command, he explains, grow disorderly and reports reach his master. When the master visits,

Jack arranges matters so that he will be accidentally confronted
with two slaves being punished. Jack observes carefully that the
master is himself personally merciful even while recognizing
the need of employing severe managers.[13] Jack's manœuvres
force his master to make a public declaration that Jack's
severity is excessive and to use precisely those moral reserva-
tions Jack has a few pages earlier applied to himself. Jack's
satisfaction shows that he understands the mechanics of public
opinion: he is now transformed in that sphere into 'A Cruel
Dog of an Overseer, *says one of the white Servants behind,* he would
have Whipp'd poor *Bullet-head,* (*so they call'd the* Negro, that was
to be Punish'd) to Death, if *his Honour* had not happen'd to come
To Day' (131). In the interview which follows (in dialogue),
Jack's master congratulates him: 'What you are charg'd with,
is just contrary to what appear'd to me just now, and therefore
you and I must come to a new understanding about it; for I
thought I was too cunning for you, and now I think you have
been too Cunning for me' (132). Exactly the word, even though
Jack never admits his deliberateness. He has, in effect, manipulated matters so that his master has certified his own conduct
up to now, transformed his master into his double. His subsequent plan is to exploit the merciful disposition he shares
with his master by turning it into a grand strategy for managing
the slaves with unprecedented efficiency, thereby establishing
himself as the real master. The master in the story is inevitably
the narrative self like Jack who understands the instrumentality
of everything, even his own best impulses. Jack's confidence is
in the moral dynamics which rule all others in the world and
outside which, by implication and extension, he stands. Thus,
he separates himself from the entire society around him, or
rather, acquiesces in that judgement when his master makes it:

*Mast.* But do you think such usage would do? would it make
any impression? you perswade your self it would; but you see 'tis
against the receiv'd Notion of the whole Country.
   *Jack.* There are it may be Publick and National Mistakes and
Errors in Conduct, and this is One. (135)

---

[13] Jack explains to his master that these slaves are guilty of drunken and violent
rebellion against authority, and therefore 'to be Whipp'd that Day, and the next
three Days, twice every Day' (131).

In carrying this out successfully, Jack is adapting his characteristic strategy in crisis as we have observed it. He pretends to be one thing in order to repudiate it to achieve his over-all goal of power. He performs (relunctantly, he assures those in power like the master and, earlier, the custom-house clerk) in roles in order to achieve power without its dreadful moral responsibilities. Urban crime and colonial oppression are recognizable as rather sensitive areas of eighteenth-century reality, embracing moral danger and personal power, containing in overt form the implicit relationship between personal power and moral surrender in bourgeois society. What Jack does is to move capably through those areas without ever touching the ground long enough to sink into the quicksand of moral reality. His intelligent grasp of the relationships of power as the workable reality of things enables him to avoid the defiling substance of the concrete historical facts. He works as a hero by extracting the relational quality of otherwise simple and substantial, and therefore morally dangerous, historical realities. Crime and colonial management are transformed by his narrative into problems of survival, power, and the separation from the initial reality that goes with them.

The text is ample evidence of this. It does not consist of the details which surround colonial management, the artefacts and utensils of production, the faces and numbers of slaves, the dress and manners of colonial life. Significantly, when such details are unavoidable, Jack puts them in footnotes: the term 'Great Master' is used and Jack explains at the bottom of the page that, 'So the *Negroes* call the Owner of the Plantation, or at least so they call'd him, because he was a great Man in the Country, having three or four large Plantations' (136 n.). What this sequence tends to be is a reproduction in dialogue form of Jack persuading his master that his strategy for slave management will work. When Jack mentions the customary cruelty of the slave-owners, it is not to give us information about that particular practice as such or to treat it as a moral experience or an emotional reality, but to expose it as fallacious and inefficient.

The sequence includes a long narrative within that dialogue wherein Jack recounts how he has gained the absolute devotion of his slaves. This narrative consists of Jack's manipulation of the slaves by arranging a drama of mercy for them in which he and his master appear as singular paragons. The entire account is punctuated by his master's approving questions and applause: 'Prethee go on I am pleas'd with it all, 'tis all a new Scene of *Negroe* Life to me, and very moving' (142). We are shown with an almost Chaucerian subtlety Jack manipulating by his tale and in his tale; it is his manipulation of reality, his arrangement of it into a productive and self-serving tableau that is before us and of primary importance to the narrative.

It is thus exactly appropriate that Jack wins his freedom from his master by virtue of these exploits. The slave management incident is the high point of his career, the moment when he co-ordinates perfectly the contradictions of his narrative, that is, when his 'goodness' operates most effectively as an external self-dramatization for the acquisition of status and power, when his dramatic abilities to use that goodness have their fullest opportunity, both in winning over the slaves and in winning his master by a second dramatization of the original staging.

II

After such a triumph of histrionic virtuosity for the self, the only thing the narrative can do is depict prosperity. But mere prosperity is novelistically dull and morally dangerous: the self stands still and accumulates automatically without the vivacious distance from reality that defines it. Jack's narrative pauses to acquire new motives for movement in repentance, education, and curiosity. If, as Lukács remarked, the novel is the expression of 'transcendental homelessness',[14] then heroes like Colonel Jack express an early version of that homelessness which turns it into restlessly joyful acquisition of experiences to make up for their inevitable lack of place and purpose. Having achieved stability, Jack rejects it as incomplete by acquiring through new repentance and new awareness of the world another version of himself which requires that he move on again. There may indeed lie somewhere in the root cause of the existence of narratives like *Colonel Jack* a sense of the void that has to be filled with movement. The tempo of Defoe's narratives is far indeed from the silence of ultimate despair,

[14] *The Theory of the Novel*, p. 41.

but the frantic vibration of the self they feature may be seen as a defence against the potential and threatening emptiness of the novelistic universe.

That threatening emptiness is implicit in the careful conversion of the events of Jack's narrative in this uniquely stable period of his life into opportunities for a kind of movement away from their external meaning. Jack tells us how he sees events that appear quite different in meaning and consequence to those around him. He expresses his growing elation as he approaches the actual gentility he was meant for, but he also notes an increasingly violent revulsion at his past life which makes him secretly glad that a cargo bought with his original savings is lost at sea. He acquires a tutor in one of his white slaves and reads a curriculum of history, ethics, and languages with him, but notes carefully that he preserves his mastery in this relationship in more ways than one: 'In short, I made him to me, what my Benefactor made me to him, and from him I gain'd a Fund of Knowledge, infinitely more valuable than the Rate of a Slave, which was what I paid for it' (158).

When the tutor repents his criminal past and delivers a penitential autobiography in which he is grateful for his punishment as a way out of sin and temptation, Jack says nothing, deliberately turning down the opportunity for conventional revelation and stressing his own singular silence: 'However, I took no notice of it [i.e. his own criminal past] to him, for he had quite other Notions of me, than I had of my self; nor did I, as is usual in such Cases, enter into any Confidence with him on my *own* Story' (167). Jack may seem cautious to the point of paranoia; a criminal past is the norm in this part of the colonial world. But an incident like this underlines for us the difference between the world of Defoe's narratives and the universe of the psychological novel that we have learned to live in since the nineteenth century. In a classic *Bildungsroman*, Jack's tutor might well be a crucial figure, older, wiser like a father, but sympathetic and sinful like a comrade. If Defoe's narrative was interested in rendering the psychological reality of such a situation, it would spend time exploring their relationship or at least exploring the reasons for its failure to develop. But Colonel Jack is only pausing for a plausible transition between adventures, using the

tutor and the consciousness he has to offer as a propellant to a
more complex stage of adventure. In that process, Jack can
only exploit, master, and remain apart from his tutor. That is
the only relationship his being allows, and it is the relationship
that is meant to please us as readers by granting us the power
and self-sufficiency it implies. In his few pages, the tutor
emerges as a surrogate, a figure who articulates for Jack the
repentance that Jack says he experienced at this time. Real
repentance, however, involves an alteration in some sense of
the personality and a rejection of the past, and Jack never
changes, never in any essential way[15] rejects his past and the
prosperous present which is its result. The tutor, clearly,
repents for Jack, taking on himself the weakness of repentance
at such length that Jack slips revealingly into certifying that
repentance, acknowledging from his position of power the
sincerity of his tutor. The following paragraph is remarkable
in the way it reminds us of Jack's superiority and in the way it
contrasts the tutor's conversion with Jack's steady participation
in himself and his history:

We talk'd frequently upon this Subject, and I found so much
Reason to believe he was a Sincere Convert, that I can speak of him
as no other, in all I have to say of him: However, I cannot say my
Thoughts were yet Ripen'd for an Opperation of that kind; I had
some uneasiness about my past Life, and I liv'd now, and had done
so before I knew him, a very regular Sober Life, always taken up in
my Business, and running into no Excesses; but as to commencing
Penitent, as this Man had done, I cannot say, I had any Convictions
upon me, sufficient to bring it on, nor had I a Fund of religious
Knowledge to support me in it; so it wore off again Gradually, as
such things generally do, where the first Impressions are not deep
enough. (171)

The tutor's repentance is such that it requires verification;
its extravagance renders it suspect and Jack's certification of
its sincerity is curiously tentative. An actor himself, Jack
always tends to assume that others are acting. That therefore
very singular sincerity becomes suspect in still another way; by
its totality it obliterates the tutor and makes him into a 'peni-

---

[15] Of course, he does modify his past, as McBurney points out, making himself
far less capable and more innocent than he was. (See '*Colonel Jacque:* Defoe's
Definition of the Complete English Gentleman', *SEL*, 2 (1962), 324.)

tent'. Jack cannot effect such radical external transformations, 'commence' another career, and become something entirely different from what he has been in the face of the probabilities of development within circumstances that his narrative is committed to. As the paragraph insists so clearly, Jack is involved in the continuing process of being himself, that is, of leading the regular life he led before he knew his tutor. The implication is clear. Repentance of that total kind is an excess; Jack leads a life which runs into 'no Excesses'. In Jack's narrative context, that means a life which does not relinquish the conquests of the self, which cannot turn into a penitent or any other final type.

A paragraph like this one in Jack's repentance sequence is an indicator of the characteristic indirection we have observed in the book. Jack's repentance is a necessary stage in his adventures, both a pause in the action and a source of plausible humanity in which Jack gathers motives and heightens desire for further movement. But the most important function of the sequence is to act as a recharging of the self, and those other conventional uses of the sequence provide a plausible cover for that activity.

Once the repentance (such as it is) has been established, the narrative can safely pass on as it does in the next paragraph to the realities of the new degree of consciousness that Jack has acquired along with his pseudo-repentance:

. . . and we had nothing of Levity between us, even when we were not concern'd in religious Discourses: He read History to me, and where Books were wanting, he gave me Ideas of those things which had not been Recorded by our modern Histories, or at least, that our Number of Books would not reach; by these things he rais'd an unquenchable Thirst in me, after seeing something that was doing in the World. . . .

Now, I look'd upon my self as one Buried alive, in a remote Part of the World, where I could see nothing at all, and hear but a little of what was seen, and that little, not till at least half a Year after it was done, and sometimes a Year or more; and in a Word, the old Reproach often came in my way; Namely, that even this was not yet, the Life of a Gentleman. (171-2)

On the face of it, that seems an odd definition of a gentleman, someone who is involved directly in major historical events.

The oddness and incoherence of the definition reveal the recurring ambition of Defoe's characters towards self-assertive movement. To continue to be himself, it follows that Colonel Jack has to lunge back into compulsion after achieving static and contemplative leisure in America. But there is a crucial difference between being born into compulsive circumstances and choosing to enter history. Jack's mode of behaviour necessarily changes from acting to imposture. Formerly, he has been at least partially contained by the realities around him, and his existence as a character has been the manipulation and conversion of that reality into power and freedom for himself. Now, Jack passes into history and society, which he presents to us as things almost entirely external to him and in which his main delights and achievements are secrecy and apartness for their own sakes rather than for any concrete goals such as money and power they may yield. In what follows, Colonel Jack enters history as a soldier in order to be in it but never a part of it; he remains, by virtue of his past and his function as a separate narrative intelligence, effectively outside the meanings of those events. As traveller, merchant, and amorist he moves through society and samples satisfactions and interesting disasters without ever committing himself, that is, without ever acquiring a concrete social identity or a particular and defining location in society. To be a privileged onlooker is, of course, a familiar eighteenth-century ambition, from the Horatian contemplation of nature and society practised so notably by Pope and Addison to Boswell's secret delight in social impersonation recorded in his journals. Colonel Jack's impersonations are more like Boswell's, although they reverse the social direction. The satisfactions implicit in them are not those of the Addisonian contemplative whose solitude is mainly rhetorical and whose conclusions are public and ceremonial, celebrating public order from private vantage. Colonel Jack's privilege as spectator certifies his apartness, celebrates it as such rather than the events that it allows him to view. We are asked over and over again in this third part of his career to watch Jack impersonate a personality he has himself created. The historical events and the social structure are interesting obstacles for Jack rather than things of interest for themselves. Society and history are problems for the self to solve rather than sources of contemplative satisfaction in social and political order.

That emphasis is implicit in Jack's initial resolve as he leaves for Europe 'with a secret Resolution, to see more of the World, if possible, and reallize those things to my Mind, which I had hitherto only entertain'd remote Ideas of, by the help of Books' (172). The word 'secret' gives the game away. Jack is out to tour history and society, but his criminal past prevents openness about that ambition. Moreover, that secrecy is also appropriate because Jack is out to prove history and society to himself, to certify their existence by experiencing them on his own terms, thereby converting them into possessions, and illegal possessions at that. The experiences which Jack will have constitute a language, a conventional and familiar set of propositions about experience in history and society. Jack's secrecy and self-possession constitute a personal version of those otherwise conventional acts. Jack's career is a unique combinative act which aspires by virtue of Jack's unique separateness to escape the narrative stereotypes out of which it is constructed. The analogy at hand is linguistic. Jack's career is like a speech act (a *parole* in the context of the *langue* which is his career considered as a series of conventional acts) which seeks to assert his personal reality, his idiolect which is apart from the system of available combinations even as it employs them. Jack's secrecy and his hidden past are his personal accent, his particular gesture and intonation which his readers can hear.

Thus, when Jack finally arrives in London,[16] he returns to that secrecy: 'I had nothing to do now, but entirely to conceal myself, from all that had any knowledge of me before, and this was the easiest thing in the World to do; for I was grown out of every Body's knowledge' (184). Concealment means residence within a social reality, and Jack tells us further that he 'passed' for a great merchant and planter. The curious point to emphasize is that Jack is partly just the thing he 'passes' for, yet he describes himself as an impostor, is pleased by (even mainly

[16] *En route*, Jack has a variety of adventures: captured by a French privateer near the Channel and ransomed, he then observes the wars in progress in Flanders. The narrative continues to supply the steady pleasures of enumeration (Jack lists the contents of captured ships) and escape (Jack tricks his French captor out of his ransom money).

concerned about) the impression he makes rather than the comfortable reality he in truth possesses to some extent.

> I was now at the height of my good Fortune; indeed I was in very good Circumstances, and being of a frugal Temper from the beginning, I Sav'd things together, as they came, and yet liv'd very well too; particularly I had the Reputation of a very considerable Merchant, and one that came over vastly Rich from *Virginia*, and as I frequently brought Supplies for my several Families and Plantations there, as they wrote to me for them, so I pass'd, *I say*, for a great Merchant. (185)

Thanks to what Jack calls his French 'exchange', he also passes for a foreigner, a Frenchman:

> ... and I was infinitely fond of having every Body take me for a *Frenchman*; and as I spoke *French* very well, having learn'd it by continuing so long among them; so I went constantly to the *French-Church* in *London*, and spoke *French* upon all occasions, as much as I could, and to compleat the appearance of it, I got me a *French* Servant to do my Business, I mean as to my Merchandise. (186)

All this elaborate privacy, it can be argued, is somewhat unnecessary at this point in Jack's career. His only legal offence years ago was desertion from the army. He has been shanghaied to Virginia, and his return is not the illegal entry of a transported felon. He simply assumes that secrecy of this total kind is necessary. The narrative result is to make ordinary life in London interesting, an adventure wherein Jack asserts his extraordinary powers of disguise and secret movement. To be sure, later on, after serving in the French army on the Continent and running away from a gaol in Paris, he has solid reasons for his secrecy. But typically, Jack converts that relative necessity into absolute melodrama: 'I was now in *London*, but was oblig'd to be very retir'd, and change my Name, letting no Body in the Nation know who I was, except my Merchant' (232). It is that hyper-dramatization of legal necessity that constitutes Jack's victory over reality, that is, makes his situation into an opportunity for an unprecedented assertion of self in the creation of various selves. He resolves to stay and live on his Virginia income (a substantial £400–£600 a year), 'to settle somewhere in *England*, where I might know every Body, and no Body know me' (233). He chooses Canterbury,

where he improves upon his earlier impersonation of a Frenchman by passing as both a Frenchman and an Englishman:
'call'd my self an *English* Man, among the *French*; and a *French*
Man among the *English*; and on that Score, was the more
perfectly concealed, going by the Name of Monsieur *Charnot*,
with the *French*, was call'd Mr. *Charnock* among the *English*'
(234). Jack, then, is utterly private while leading a life (indeed,
'lives') which is by his own definition 'public'. At the point of
returning to Virginia, he considers that 'I could not prevail
with my self to live a private Life' (233). Residence in Canterbury is the perfect transformation of life into private power
over public experience. Jack is there what Defoe aspired to be as
Harley's spy in Scotland, all things to all men:

> Here, indeed, I liv'd perfectly *Incog.* I made no particular
> Acquaintance, so as to be intimate, and yet I knew every Body,
> and every Body knew me; I discours'd in Common, talk'd *French*
> with the *Walloons;* and *English* with the *English*; and living retir'd
> and sober, was well enough receiv'd by all Sorts; but as I meddled
> with no Bodies business, so no Body meddl'd with mine; I thought
> I liv'd pretty well. (234)

Such extraordinary self-reserve seems best understood as a
form of social innocence. Jack is in the world but decidedly
not of it. That innocence is paralleled in his amorous and
marital adventures. Jack begins them by establishing his
utter innocence, or, better, his total externality to the world of
sex and matrimony. He explains how he comes to meet a
certain lady by virtue of his public position as a gentleman
lodger and that their acquaintance is the result of social
necessity: 'This Lady put herself so often in my way, that I
could not in good Manners forbear taking Notice of her, and
giving her the Ceremony of my Hat' (186). She visits the house
where he lodges, 'and it was generally contriv'd, that I should
be introduced when she came' (186). In reality, he explains, he
has never sought women for any use; the present connection
thus follows directly from his social impersonation rather than
from any pressing or particular desire:

> I was a meer Boy in the Affair of Love, and knew the least of
> what belong'd to a Woman, of any Man in *Europe* of my Age; the
> thought of a Wife, much less of a Mistress, had never so much as

taken the least hold of my Head, and I had been till now as perfectly unacquainted with the Sex, and as unconcern'd about them, as I was when I was ten Year old, and lay in a Heap of Ashes at the *Glass-House*. (186)

Indeed, his 'desire' in what follows is excited by the lady's cunning indifference to him and her supreme possession of a reserve which is the social equivalent of Jack's privacy: 'She attack'd me without ceasing, with the fineness of her Conduct, and with Arts which were impossible to be ineffectual' (187). She draws Jack by what he carefully describes as her 'Witch-Craft' (187), by pretending indifference in so masterly a fashion that 'it was almost impossible not to be deceiv'd by it' (187). But since Jack is somewhere outside the social position he seems to occupy, she is the one who is effectively tricked: 'but the Cheat was really on my Side; for she was unhappily told, that I was vastly Rich, a great Merchant, and that she would live like a Queen' (187). What Jack omits is that he inhabits that role perfectly and invites us to enjoy his skill: 'She came to the House where I Lodg'd, as usual, and we were often together, Supp'd together, Play'd at Cards together, Danc'd together; for in *France* I accomplish'd myself with every thing that was needful, to make me what I believ'd myself to be even from a Boy, I mean a Gentleman' (191). Caught, then, in social and even personal necessity, Jack is nevertheless in a kind of control by virtue of his own social impersonation which supervises the events and which is in fact their ultimate cause.

Jack's admiring description of the lady's strategies reveals his own accomplishments in duplicity. Like a connoisseur, he notes that she 'was a meer Posture Mistress in Love, and could put herself into what Shapes she pleas'd' (190), a 'Camelion' who switches to an indifference so perfect 'that it did not in the least look like Art, but if it was a Representation of Nature only, it was so like Nature itself, that no body living can be able to distinguish' (190). Even their marriage is for Jack an exercise in extraordinary privacy: 'we gave the World the slip, and were privately Marry'd to avoid Ceremony, and the publick Inconveniency of a Wedding' (193). Finally, their divorce is the result not simply of his wife's extravagant manner of living but of her inability to maintain the duplicity that

Jack admires: 'she threw off the Mask of her Gravity, and good Conduct, that I had so long Fancy'd was her meer natural Disposition, and now having no more occasion for Disguises, she resolv'd to seem nothing but what really she was, a wild untam'd Colt, perfectly loose, and careless to conceal any part, no, not the worst of her Conduct' (193). Having no secrets, Jack's wife has no being; she is only what nature makes her. As moments like this make clear, Jack's narrative is built around the recurring proposition that openness is a surrender to nature and to society that involves a loss of self.

Jack's remedy is to become even more private, to cover his tracks by selling their household goods and pretending to disappear: 'I never let her know any thing of me, but that I was gone over to *France*' (197). He hires spies to watch her and becomes again the cunning Jack we know. She provides an antagonist, one already proved a worthy and stimulating opponent. Thus, when she attempts a reconciliation, hiding her subsequent extra-marital pregnancy, Jack gives one of those exuberant and clearly self-asserting paragraphs that are his particular signature as a character, a paragraph which incidentally analyses and corrects his opponent's defective strategies:

But I was too many for her here too, my Intelligence about her was too good, for her to Conceal such an Affair from me, unless she had gone away before she was visibly Big, and unless she had gone farther off too than she did, for I had an Account to a Tittle, of the time when, and Place where, and the Creature of which she was deliver'd, and then my Offers of taking her again were at an End, tho' she Wrote me several very Penitent Letters, acknowledging her Crime, and begging me to forgive her; but my Spirit was above all that now, nor cou'd I ever bear the Thoughts of her after that. (207)

Marital conflict has provided Jack in this episode with the antagonist he and his narrative need to keep them taut and alive. Jack is a classless hero fighting a reality with a distinctly social meaning. His wife is a mere member of the leisure class whom Jack masters by impersonation and the cunning privacy which that requires. He outwits not just her but her allies who employ the distinctively aggressive and brutal tactics of that leisure class: a gentleman who challenges him to a duel for refusing to pay a bill his ex-wife has drawn, a hired thug who wounds him, slitting his nose and ear. Later on in the narrative, his other marital misadventures lead him to the same kind of social antithesis. Jack wounds a French marquis in Paris who has cuckolded him with his second wife. This duel leads to a carefully detailed circuitous flight through Lorrain to Cologne and thence to The Hague and to London, and finally to Jack's most spectacular display of privacy in Canterbury. Even his third and best marriage leads ultimately to action which has distinct social resonances. He and his ship-captain's widow live happily for six years and have three children (in the space of three pages), but she takes to drink in the end because of her last lying-in. Jack is again cuckolded, this time by someone who is carefully identified as 'really a Gentleman' (241) and who makes his wife and her maid drunk and lies with them both. Jack waits for him alone in Stepney Fields, rejecting his impulse to challenge him to a duel, rejecting, in other words and in the central terms of the book, a public or social encounter and engineering a secret and private one. The gentleman refuses to draw his sword, and Jack canes him severely 'but forebore his Head, because I was resolv'd he should feel it' (243). The variation of the public form is significant. Jack is concerned not with public honour but with private justice, inflicting private pain rather than honourable death or insensibility. The rejection of the social form is complete when its instrument is smashed and its dignity reversed by an irreverent *coup de grâce*. Jack takes the gentleman's sword and breaks it 'before his Face, and left him on the Ground, giving him two or three Kicks on the Back-side, and bad him go and take the Law of me, if he thought fit' (243).

Once again, Jack retires, in various ways this time. He goes north to Lancaster and lives secluded. When his now penitent wife dies shortly afterwards, he resolves to marry again; but this fourth marriage involves an explicit rejection of the public and socially accepted meaning of marriage. He determines to make a match for purely private and severely functional reasons. In the context of Jack's career as a pseudo-member of society, that constitutes a total withdrawal from the game of social impersonation for participation in a world of unique personal assertion where Jack resolves to serve himself and suit his own private needs:

So I resolved, I would marry as anything offer'd, tho' it was mean, and the meaner the better; I concluded my next Wife should be only taken as an upper Servant, *that is to say*, a Nurse to my Children, and a House-keeper to my self, and let her be whore or honest Woman, *said I*, as she likes best, I am resolv'd I wont much concern my self about that . . . (245)

Nearly drawn out of privacy and the power and autonomy it grants by his marriages, Jack now marries to ensure it. This fourth and excellent prudential match is celebrated as an act of pure utility. For Jack's narrative is beyond moral revisionism, not really concerned to promote utility as a moral value or as *the* only authentic moral value in a hypocritical world. Rather, Jack's utilitarian marriage is in context a transformation of that already demonstrably dangerous institution which claims deceptively to provide and combine social status and libidinal pleasure. Marriage is turned into an instrument of privacy and powerful separation from society and from those transparent satisfactions which it offers to other less agile men. Jack's marital career is a meaningful sequence in which the narrator-hero purifies himself of the social and libidinal needs that marriage serves and in which he learns to make it purely an occasion for self-assertion on the most efficient and meaningful level.

At the end of his marital adventures, Jack's determination is preceded by what he himself calls near-madness: 'My Wife being now dead, I knew not what Course to take in the World, and I grew so disconsolate and discouraged, that I was next Door to being distempered, and sometimes indeed, I thought my self a little touch'd in my Head' (244). He then considers and resolves and determines. Characteristically, as we have seen, Defoe's heroes describe themselves as driven by circumstances to some kind of functional desperation which makes action possible. Jack claims his resolve is the result of that madness; he carefully disclaims responsibility for a radically liberating act: 'But I know not how it happen'd to me; I reason'd and talk'd to my self in this wild manner so long, that I brought my self to be seriously desperate, *that is*, to resolve upon another Marriage; with all the Suppositions of Unhappiness that could be imagined to fall out' (245). He goes on to describe a sequence of events in which he acts with such care and self-conscious deliberation about marriage that his 'desperation' is turned into part of the strategy for avoiding full responsibility for action. His desperation, as usual, accommodates itself to the opportunities which emerge only slowly in the natural flow of ordinary events:

> . . . at last, as he that seeks Mischief, shall certainly find it, so it was with me, there happen'd to be a young, or rather a middle aged Woman in the next Town, which was but half a Mile off, who usually was at my House, and among my Children every Day, when the Weather was tolerable; and tho' she came, but meerly as a Neighbour, and to see us, yet she was always helpful in directing, and ordering things for them, and mighty handy about them, as well before my Wife died as after.
>
> Her Father was one that I employed often to go to *Liverpool*, and sometimes to *Whitehaven*, and do Business for me; for having as it were settled myself in these Northern parts of *England*; I had order'd part of my Effects to be Shipp'd as Occasion of shipping offered to either of those two Towns, to which (the War continuing very sharp) it was safer coming as to Privateers, than about thro' the *Channel* to *London*. (245-6)

The famous circumstantiality so evident in these sentences is a means of negating the vertigo Jack experiences in the face of action. Those circumstances just happen to supply exactly what Jack needs; they provide the magic world of opportunity and indeed present themselves as a compelling situation rather than an arrangement supervised by the ordering self. The care that Jack lavishes on rendering them is part of that certification of circumstances, an attempt to present them as absolutely random and coincidental. Jack acquires his opportunity by going about his business, whose necessities come from outside, in this case, from history as well—'the War continuing very sharp'.

But once circumstances and desperation are set aside, the marriage can safely become a familiar exercise in secrecy and domination. The ceremony itself is the most perfectly clandestine of all his connections, performed by a Catholic priest who passes in the neighbourhood for a 'Doctor of Physick' but whose secrecy is encompassed by Jack's own: 'He knew that I understood his Profession, and that I had liv'd in Popish Countries, and in a Word, believ'd me a *Roman* too, for I was such Abroad' (248). His serviceable wife is acquired with a blunt proposal, to which Jack requires her instant compliance for no discernible reason. He makes her agree by giving her his last wife's clothes: '. . . look you there *Moggy, says I,* there's a Wedding Gown for you, give me your Hand now that you will have me to morrow Morning, and as to your Father, you know he is gone to *Liverpool* on my Business, but I will answer for it, he shall not be angry when he comes Home to call his Master Son-in-law, and I ask him no Portion' (247). Jack is asserting himself in this marriage, not only by its triumphant utility but by its re-enactment in such a clear fashion of the nearly gratuitous secrecy which constitutes his existence as a character.

Much the same pattern of emerging self-assertion is discernible in the military career which precedes and accompanies Jack's marital exploits. That career is, in Jack's own terms, the more satisfying part of his adventures in the world precisely because he is thereby committed to nothing except his own self-presentation. It is only when he is able to purchase a commission in the French army at Dunkirk that he is satisfied entirely: 'I was exceedingly pleas'd with my new Circumstances, and now I us'd to say to my self, I was come to what I was Born to, and that I had never till now liv'd the Life of a Gentleman' (207). But Jack's achievement begins in self-preservation rather than presentation. His immediate 'resolve' (a favourite word of his) is prompted by a context of what he presents as compelling danger—his ex-wife's outraged gentleman-creditor has hired thugs to ambush him. His military career begins, as action must in the world of Defoe's narratives, as a mixture of protective response and expansive self-assertion. It is simultaneously a retreat and an advance, a retreat grounded in the necessities of the moment which Jack stages a few paragraphs later as an advance into a liberating necessity.

His Irish regiment takes part in defeating 'the Famous Attack upon *Cremona*' (207) by the Germans, and Jack has 'the satisfaction of knowing, and that for the first time too, that I was not that cowardly low spirited Wretch' (208) that he has just finished being in London. Jack carefully derives that bravery from the dynamics of the moment, from the discovery of a quality he never knew he had until experience extracted it. Jack presents and discovers himself by giving in to experience, by continuing to move with it: '. . . Men never know them-

selves till they are tried, and Courage is acquir'd by time, and
Experience of things' (208). Moreover, Jack continues to be
brave in battle as the specific result of his experience rather
than through the assertion of an absolute and clearly possessed
courage. His men, he tells us, flatter him on his bravery at
Cremona, so that he 'fancy'd' himself such 'whether I was so or
not, and the Pride of it made me Bold, and Daring to the last
Degree on all Occasions' (208). All this clarity and honesty
about the source and nature of action are part of a continuous
deference to the dynamics of circumstances and their implication in Jack's achievements. In a way, Jack gains power by
knowing the limitations of power. He and his readers gain the
specifically novelistic power of seeing the crucial interplay of
experience and desire, of watching circumstances conspire
ultimately in their random way to make Jack into Colonel
Jack in the French army.

. . . some Body gave a particular Account to the Court of my being
Instrumental to the saving the City and the whole *Cremonese*, by my
extraordinary Defence of the *Po* Gate, and by my Managing that
Defence after the Lieutenant Colonel, who Commanded the Party
where I was Posted was kill'd; upon which, the King sent me a
publick Testimony of his accepting my Service, and sent me a
Breviat to be a Lieutenant Colonel, and the next Courier brought
me actually a Commission for Lieutenant Colonel in the Regiment
of ———. (208–9)

Indeed, Jack is careful to present himself as precisely the
minor figure he was in these great events, occasionally omitting
his own role in the fighting in order to summarize the events
of the campaign but then returning to his private manœuvres
in the context of those public events. He continues, for example,
to acquire money along with honours and experience and to
tell us in detail about those acquisitions. At one point in a
battle, he is captured by a German officer, but the Germans
are the victims of a counter-attack and the officer turns himself over to Jack to save himself in that reversal. Jack and some
'sixteen or seventeen' others are thus released, but Jack is the
only one to gain a captive officer who gives him twenty Pistols
in return for his exchange as a prisoner. At another point, he
commandeers a rich burgher's house in Alexandria in the duchy

of Milan and helps himself before retreating to '200 Pistols in Money and Plate, and other things of Value' (209). These private acts remind us, as Jack himself declares in the middle of his military summary, that he is 'not writing a Journal of the Wars, in which I had no long Share' (215).

In spite of the title of the book, Jack is only briefly a soldier: about fifteen pages is all he manages on the subject. Once Jack exploits this aspect of his career for the self-discovery and accumulation of experience and money it has to yield, he has, necessarily, to move on. We can only be interested in experience as a problem for the self, whether of assertion in it or extraction from it. We are interested in Jack's establishment as a soldier and his rise in the ranks. The narrative continues to please its implied readers by reaffirming the powerful apartness of its hero, by reminding us indirectly that Colonel Jack with his Irish regiment is a triumph of self-management and promotion for Jack the waif. Jack's little tricks of accumulation and his quick response to the main chance are the means of connecting the facts of history with the realities of private experience; his mode of operation, we are led to see, is essentially what it was when he slept in the ashes of the glasshouse. But having mastered history by private participation in it, the last and perhaps the most satisfying trick Jack can show us is his escape from it.

To be sure, history provides the circumstances for escape and the psychological climate which makes retreat from the wars a plausible thing. Jack is wounded and captured but still lucky and singular: 'I came off much better than abundance of Gentlemen, for in that bloody Battle we had above 400 Officers kill'd or wounded, whereof three were General Officers' (221). Jack finds that his 'secret Design to quit the War' (222) has to be kept hidden because 'it was counted so Dishonourable a Thing to quit, while the Army was in the Field, that I could not Dispense with it' (222). It is the most natural thing in the world for Jack to be so far above (or beneath) the values of the culture in which he lives that he describes these values with the puzzled objectivity of an anthropologist. The effect of such a tone is to present experience as more like a series of problems which can be analysed by the self than a sequence of events that were participated in. We perceive Jack waiting for circumstances rather than wholly in them, able to tell us at last that his problem is solved by 'an intervening accident [which] made that Part easie to me' (222).

That accident is nothing less than a shift in the European power struggle, the renewal of France's war with England and Holland. Jack's only concern, he tells us rather pointedly, is to exploit the French plan to send troops to Scotland with the Old Pretender. He feigns 'a great deal of Zeal for this Service' (222) and is introduced with great ceremony to the Chevalier himself. That meeting in Jack's summary reminds us that Colonel Jack is still the unconcerned and uninvolved self he was at the very beginning of his narrative, nearly autonomous in his desire for pure survival on his own terms. For here he returns explicitly to the subtle style of self-impersonation we have seen him use as a boy. Presented to the Chevalier as what indeed he has been ['an Officer in the *Irish* Brigade, and had serv'd in *Italy*, and consequently was an old Soldier' (223)], he sees himself as merely inhabiting that role, certainly now and, in a way, even then. Jack is bent upon release from the war and return to England, so much so that he fails to grasp the dangers he faces in going back there in this fashion. In short, his manipulation of history involves some submission to its dangers; his indifference to political ideology and drive towards pure self-satisfaction are partly purified of their subversive individualism by the narrative's invocation of history's compulsions, those likely disasters obscured by Jack's drive for self-satisfaction.

I had no particular attachment to his Person, or to his Cause, nor indeed did I much consider the Cause, of one Side or other, if I had, I should hardly have risqu'd not my Life only, but Effects too, which were all as I might say, from that Moment forfeited to the *English* Government, and was too evidently in their Power to confiscate at their Pleasure.

However having just receiv'd a Remittance from *London*, of 300*l*. Sterling, and sold my Company in the *Irish* Regiment for very near as much, I was not only insensibly drawn in, but was perfectly Voluntier in that dull Cause, and away I went with them at all hazards . . . (223)

Like all Defoe's narrators, Jack presents himself in the tangles of circumstance, a web here and elsewhere evoked by the controlled summarizing of events and their consequences. But that necessity is eventually converted into freedom by the same innocent desire to survive and to acquire that brought Jack into experience at the beginning of his narrative. Standing there before the Chevalier, Jack is really something other than the brave colonel of an Irish regiment. Engaged in a glamorous and chivalric cause, his motives and ultimate plans are still the self-conscious promotion of a self totally apart from that cause or indeed any cause.

The firm grasp of the self in its precise historical circumstances is a new achievement for Defoe's narrators and gives Jack and his narrative a new solidity. But that very specificity enhances the fruitful opposition between the self and its environment. Jack's ability to comprehend history and place himself in it makes history into something external and therefore manageable in some sense. Throughout his narrative, Jack's keen desire is to understand the exact historical circumstances around him, indeed to surround himself with those circumstances. He leaves prosperity as a Virginia planter to get back into history. Thus as a beggar boy, his effort is to find out what is going on around and beyond him, 'always upon the Inquiry, asking Questions of things done in Publick as well as in Private, particularly, I lov'd to talk with Seamen and Soldiers about the War', and 'I never forgot any thing they told me' (10). 'By this means, as young as I was, I was a kind of an Historian, and tho' I had read no Books, and never had any Books to read, yet I cou'd give a tollerable Account of what had been done, and of what was then a doing in the World, especially in those things that our own People were concern'd in' (11). This looks at that point in the narrative like plausible childish fascination with military exploits and is obviously an anticipation of Jack's adult achievements as a soldier. But Jack presents it also as an indicator of his aggressive and quite unique self-consciousness. It predicts not only his military career but the form of many of his subsequent exploits. Jack exists in a clear relationship with historical events in their actual existence: he is precisely involved in the contemporary realities of finance, military recruitment, indentured colonial servitude, slavery and colonial management, trade, international European rivalries, and recent English politics and civil war. Jack's achievement is to

participate in all this history without ever becoming either
the mere result or neutral recorder of historical events. For
him and thereby for us history is always eventually a means of
expansion and self-assertion. For the best example, his final
crisis is the result of quite specific historical events and is
solved in the context of other exact historical conditions. In
this closing sequence historical conditions provide both the
problem and its solution; Jack seems to be the prisoner of
historical circumstances, indeed history seems here to catch up
with him at last. But he escapes and prospers to new heights by
expertly exploiting other historical conditions and acquiring
the last and perhaps the most extravagant of his personalities.

When his fourth wife, the serviceable Moggy, dies, Jack
returns to Virginia and discovers after a time that his first wife
is among his indentured servants. Transformed by her experience and now full of repentance, she marries Jack again.
Their tranquil life is suddenly interrupted by the arrival in the
colony of transported Jacobites. Jack now tells us what he has not
mentioned in its proper place, that he was involved for a time
in the Jacobite adventure of 1715 along with the priest who
married him to Moggy. Jack fears that these new arrivals will
expose him and meditates on the folly of thinking that he could
escape the past:

> But an unseen Mine blew up all this apparent Tranquility at
> once, and tho' it did not remove my Affairs there from me, yet it
> effectually remov'd me from them, and sent me a wandring into
> the World again; a Condition full of Hazards, and always attended
> with Circumstances dangerous to Mankind, while he is left to choose
> his own Fortunes, and be guided by his own short sighted Measures.
> (264)

The incident and Jack's reaction to it are a perfect illustration
of the relationship between the real and the conventional
desires of the narrative, its super- and infra-structure in ugly
but exact terms. Jack and his narrative require movement,
energy, and variety. The tranquillity carved out by Jack is
interesting in the achievement but hardly in the possession. To
maintain the motion the narrative requires and to retain Jack's
hard-won domestic tranquillity as an achievement, circumstances are made responsible for the resumption of Jack's

career. But here the narrative is at its most transparent. Circumstances are, in effect, invented, as Jack tells us something from his past we did not know. Such insertions to justify action can be seen as evidence of Defoe's haste and relative incompetence as a narrator. But they are also evidence of the narrative's instinctive awareness of the energy that makes Jack a character and of the appropriateness of an end to his story in which he continues to be himself, moving and transforming.

Jack flees, feigning illness and a need to take the waters at Nevis and Antegoa. He sails away in a sixty-ton sloop loaded with a cargo of which we receive a joyously detailed accounting. His wife sends a commission to a friend in London to bargain for pardon, and all bets are covered. Word comes while they are trading that a general pardon for minor participants such as Jack has been issued by the king, but Jack is captured by the Spaniards. He escapes being sent to the Peruvian silver mines by virtue of his old agility at an impersonation which is only a slight variation on the truth:

> But I got better Quarter among them, than that too; which was, *as I have said*, much of it owing to my speaking *Spanish*, and to my telling them how I had fought in so many Occasions in the Quarrel of his *Catholick* Majesty, in *Italy*, and by great good Chance, I had the King of *France*'s Commission for Lieutenant Colonel, in the *Irish* Brigade in my Pocket, where it was mention'd, that the said Brigade was then serving in the Armies of *France*, under the Orders of his *Catholick* Majesty in *Italy*.
>
> I fail'd not to talk up the Gallantry and personal Bravery of his Catholick Majesty on all Occasions, and particularly in many Battles where by the Way, his Majesty had never been at all, and in some, where I had never been my self; but I found I talk'd to People who knew nothing of the Matter, and so any thing went down with them, if it did but praise the King of *Spain*, and talk big of the *Spanish* Cavalry, of which, God knows, there was not one Regiment in the Army, at least while I was there. (279)

Jack does more than talk. He becomes a hugely prosperous trader in Cuba, sailing to New England and New York to get European goods, which he then sells at enormous and completely illegal profit to the Spaniards. Technically, we can observe, such activity is treasonable behaviour for an Englishman—dealing with the enemy. But Jack is using history and its circumstances with greater dexterity than ever, turning adversity and captivity into unheard of profit and unparalleled public identity. He mystifies the New England merchants, inspiring legends without ever being contained by them: 'Well, it was the Cause of much Speculation among them, as I heard at second and third Hands; some said, he is certainly going to *Jamaica*; others said, he is going to Trade with the *Spaniards*; others, that he is going to the *South-Sea*, and turn half Merchant, half Pyrate on the Coast of *Chily* and *Peru*; some one thing, some another, as the *Men-Gossips* found their Imaginations directed' (292–3).

A second voyage meets with disaster, first pirates and then Spaniards who sight them and report Jack's ship as a privateer. But, again, the uses of adversity are sweet and spectacular as Jack goes into hiding, disguised as a Spaniard and living at the country retreat of his Spanish partners in trade. He becomes Don Ferdinand de Villa Moresa and enters with great enthusiasm into the splendours of merchant life in Spanish America, reporting in part: 'After the Goods were thus dispatch'd, it was equally Surprizing, to see how soon, and with what Exactness, the Merchants of *Mexico*, to whom these Cargoes were separately Consign'd, made the Return, and how it came all in Silver, or in Gold; so that their Ware-houses, in a few Months, were piled up, even to the Ceiling, with Chests of Pieces of Eight, and with Bars of Silver' (302). On the surface, Jack is full of wonder and admiration for the facts around him. We are in a position to see that Jack is himself the greatest wonder, completing a life of wonders and presiding over these splendours. He accomplishes that dominance by a familiar but still exquisite turn, an exercise in courtly generosity to his host and protector which is strikingly like his earlier acts of impersonation. Jack lists the contents of a bale of goods he has with him for just such contingencies, worth by his reckoning about two hundred pounds. In Jack's rendering his punctilious host is tricked into accepting this munificent present and returns in a polite passion which Jack interprets for us: 'I could easily see, he was exceedingly pleased; and told me, had he known the Particulars, he would never have suffer'd them to have gone, as he did, and at last used the very same Compliment, that the Governour at the *Havana* used, *viz.* that it was a Present, fit for a Viceroy of *Mexico*, rather than for him' (305). Jack's courtesy becomes in our reading of the stretch of his anecdotes an act of appropriation, a witty certification of his latest identity as Spanish merchant prince. As always, Jack lets us see that he stands just a bit to the side of all this; he carefully presents even this benign trick as a victory of courtly cunning, the result of his exact knowledge of the custom of the country. He caps the exchange by giving his benefactor's wife a present, insisting that it comes from his wife in Virginia: 'He was extreamly pleas'd with the nicety I us'd; and I saw him Present it to her accordingly, and could see at the opening of it, that she was extreamly pleas'd with the Present it self' (306).

Jack's great natural powers and the luck and resiliency which we are given to sense by the narrative will always materialize for him are the crucial difference between *Colonel Jack* and mere historical chronicle such as the lumpish *Memoirs of a Cavalier* (1720). The latter is a deadening historical narrative, quite as specific as *Colonel Jack* at its most specific, indeed full of actual historical personages and thick with convincing details of the actual religious wars on the Continent. What makes *Colonel Jack* a novel about a memorable central self is that its 'history', like Crusoe's island, Singleton's Africa and pirate oceans, and Moll's London, is turned from a dominating and hostile environment into a field for assertive personal action. As befits his social station, Colonel Jack transforms a larger and more generalized environment than any of his predecessors, history itself rather than any of the locales the others master. Jack needs his privileged background and inherent superiority, we discover at last, in order to take on such an extraordinarily complete world.

# VI

## *Roxana* : Nature, Knowledge, and Power

> In energetic minds, truth soon changes by domestication into
> power; and from directing in the dissemination and appraisal of
> the product, becomes influencive in the production.
>
> Coleridge, *Biographia Literaria*,
> Chapter XIII

ROXANA is at once the most conventional and the most
disturbing of Defoe's major narratives. It is clearly an attempt
to mine the popular vein of *chronique scandaleuse*, a 'secret
history' of low doings in high life such as Eliza Haywood and
others were turning out in great numbers during the 1720s.[1]
In conventional fashion, *Roxana* delivers an inside view of
private vices prevailing in public life, as the heroine moves
profitably and amorously up to the highest social circles. But
unlike the various persecuted maidens and insatiable cour-
tesans who tended to inhabit the genre, Roxana possesses an
imperious strength, efficiency, and self-reserve which have led
various commentators to speak of her with puzzled awe as
Defoe's only damned soul, a real sinner among his crew of
memorable but harmless rascals.[2] And of course Roxana is a

---

[1] The great exemplar in English was Mrs. Manley's infamous *Secret Memoirs and
Manners of several Persons of Quality, of Both Sexes from the New Atalantis* (1709), a
diffuse *roman-à-clef* which retailed a great variety of scandal about prominent
people. By the early 1720s, the prolific Eliza Haywood used the term 'secret
history' to apply to less diverse and more concentrated stories which made only a
conventional pretence to specific truth. Defoe's book seems to combine elements
of both, using some recognizable historical figures and a good deal of purely
fictional material.

[2] M. E. Novak argues strongly that Defoe presents Roxana as a palpably evil
character and her career as a satire upon 'a corrupt society'. (See 'Crime and
Punishment in Defoe's *Roxana*', *JEGP*, 45 (1966), 445–65.) Spiro Peterson describes
her career as a progress 'from a passive victim to a diabolic agent of evil', although
he softens that judgement by noting that Roxana's manipulation of eighteenth-
century marriage laws is within the 'legal modifications substantiated by the
courts of equity'. (See, 'The Matrimonial Theme of Defoe's *Roxana*', *PMLA*, 70
(1955), 175, 191.)
Most commentators, in short, have found Roxana an appalling person and

shockingly powerful and amoral character, but I would add that her power is nothing new in Defoe's narratives, here simply entirely visible for the first time. This new visibility is also entirely inevitable, the result of the conjunction of Defoe's imagination and this particular popular narrative pattern.

The secret history and the *chronique scandaleuse* are, obviously, self-conscious about social class. They draw their energy from a fascinated and envious condemnation of 'aristocratic' decadence; they characteristically present a world of upper-class violence and sensuality where women are the main victims of those urges, where values identified by the narratives as specifically masculine and assertive such as avarice, ambition, and lust defeat such specifically 'feminine' passive traits as submission, simplicity, honesty, and chastity. Such books locate the fate of their characters very precisely in their class situations; the lords and ladies in them are acting out the moral contradictions implicit in their social location. Innocent readers are invited to watch as such decadence and its thrilling results grow inevitably out of the social conditions of this stylized world: infinite leisure, sexual permissiveness and/or unlimited sexual opportunity, and unrestricted political and social combat. These same readers not only enjoy that exotic world of forbidden pleasures and achievements but are located by their

---

concluded with some justice that Defoe's purpose was to satirize her and the Restoration immorality she at times embodies. But perhaps more clearly here than in the other novels, certain difficulties arise which are the direct result of Defoe's apparent imaginative participation in his narratives. As William J. Howard has argued in an article on *Robinson Crusoe*, narrative seems to have become in Defoe's hands 'an artistic parallelism of the psycho-natural process within the artist, according to which the dichotomies within society have a kind of second subsistence in art, expressed in the tension between form and content—the form now manifested as a contemporary social myth, and the content as personal experience and personal judgment'. (See 'Truth Preserves Her Shape: An Unexplored Influence on Defoe's Prose Style', *PQ*, 47 (1968), 204.) There is without doubt satiric intent in *Roxana*, but the book exists as an example of failed satire and compellingly successful social myth. Thus, G. A. Starr admits that there are clear signs that Defoe regards Roxana as a 'damned soul', but notes that 'his imaginative oneness with her often seems virtually complete, and at such times we too may be drawn into a kind of complicity with her.' (See *Defoe and Casuistry*, p. 165.) In a similar fashion, John Henry Raleigh perceives in *Roxana* beneath the moralistic surface a 'deeper stratum of unity and meaning . . . indifferent to any claims save the force of life and love'. (See 'Style and Structure and Their Import in Defoe's *Roxana*', *Univ. of Kansas City Review*, 20 (1953), 133.)

relation as readers to such a world in the classless moralism needed to judge it. Such books always generate that moralism by implying that aristocratic society is bad precisely because it is artificial, based on unnatural power and freedom for the lucky few. 'Society' is invariably a compulsive machine which creates and destroys, providing a power for its members which leads inevitably to some kind of thrilling self-destruction.

Now the main force of Defoe's imagination is clearly to render the bourgeois individual's aggressive will to survive and to dominate, a will which is defined by its separation from society, a natural resisting impulse recognized in a context of unnatural compulsion, indeed realized as such in the dialectic of the self and society. Roxana is that same self-aggrandizing natural energy complex to be found at the centre of Defoe's other narratives. In this case, there is a great disparity between that force and the pattern provided by the commercial moment. All Defoe's main characters conform to some extent to the traditional literary type who inhabits their kind of narrative; they are partly contained by the stereotypes of traveller, merchant, thief, colonist, adventurer, and pirate. Roxana, like Moll before her, has her literary roots in a tradition of the assertive lower-class woman, the *picara*, the courtesan-whore, and the counterfeit-lady. But she invades in that guise a genre in which she has no secure conventional place, creating a narrative situation in which that consciousness tends to undercut the social compulsions the secret history requires and to convert moral melodrama into a comedy of the self which Defoe's narrative has, eventually, to retract by a desperate reversal.

There are, of course, aggressive female characters in secret histories, especially in the specifically scandalous *chronique scandaleuse*. But the classic female villain of the genre like Mrs. Manley's Duchess of Marlborough in *The New Atalantis* appropriates masculine vices such as self-assertion and self-possession; that appropriation makes those qualities worse in her than in men. Even Moll, we remember, is careful to maintain her female indirection. She acts to some profit as a transvestite thief and takes the offensive in various dealings with men, but she never reveals herself as a reverser of conventional roles. A crypto-feminist, she is content with disguise and manipulative cunning. Roxana adds feminist ideology to Moll's praxis. But instead of violently appropriating the masculine like Mrs. Manley's grotesque Zarah, she aspires to a new category and actually declares that her ultimate ambition lies in a powerful androgyny. When an eminent merchant proposes marriage, she refuses in the name of liberty: 'and seeing Liberty seem'd to be the Men's Property, I wou'd be a *Man-Woman*; for as I was born free, I wou'd die so'.[3] Roxana has a fully articulated ideology of freedom which grasps very clearly the central problem that she solves in her book, the loss of self attendant upon being merely a woman:

*Ay*, said I, *that is the Thing I complain of;* the Pretence of Affection, takes from a Woman every thing that can be call'd *herself*; she is to have no Interest; no Aim; no View; but all is the Interest, Aim, and View, of the Husband; she is to be the passive Creature you spoke of; *said I*; she is to lead a Life of perfect Indolence, and living by Faith (not in God, but) in her Husband, she sinks or swims, as he is either Fool or wise Man; unhappy or prosperous; and in the middle of what she thinks is her Happiness and Prosperity, she is ingulph'd in Misery and Beggary, which she had not the least Notice, Knowledge, or Suspicion of. (149)

Roxana is outside the ordinary secret history, in other words, by virtue of her individualist consciousness, her sense that she was 'born free', outside class and sex and their compulsions. To understand Defoe's *Roxana*, then, I think we must imagine that world of the secret history taken over by the kind of sensibility which can treat that compelling world as an initially threatening but potentially enriching environment, much like Crusoe's island, Singleton's Africa and pirate oceans, and Moll's and Jack's London and Virginia. For Roxana as for them an environment is ultimately a set of external problems to be analysed and solved rather than a set of involving and ineffable determinants. Roxana can, therefore, move through that world and survive, prospering as extravagantly as the blackest villain of any scandal chronicle. For most of her narrative, she remains essentially immune to the moral deterioration and loss of real freedom which are necessary parts of the moral dialectic

---

[3] *Roxana, The Fortunate Mistress*, ed. Jane Jack (Oxford English Novels, 1964), p. 171. All further references in the text are to this edition.

of the normal secret history, because she comes into her self-consciously social narrative from that classless world of pure assertive selfhood that Defoe's narratives imply. But in treating that aristocratic world as merely a field for individual opportunity, she emphasizes its artificiality and her naturalness at one and the same time and creates the most obtrusively powerful of Defoe's narrative selves. And thus the only one who has to be disavowed at the end.

This is significantly different from the 'naturalizing' that takes place in Defoe's other narratives in which various social-historical milieux are transformed into 'natural' environments in which the historical phenomena of class and society do not exist in either a final or a compelling form and in which socially aggressive movement is turned into mere necessary survival, a temporary and spontaneous rather than a permanent or deliberate social attitude. Moreover, Defoe's other heroes present themselves quite literally as natural or classless figures, either born outside normal class situations and social categories like Moll, Jack, and Singleton, or self-consciously rejecting a social situation for a natural one in the special case of Crusoe. Roxana is unique in her *déclassé* beginnings, lowered suddenly to the edge of survival from the social heights which are a part of the genre. Unlike the others, then, she returns to the unredeemed social world of the secret history, which must remain unnatural if it is to be mastered, must, that is, continually have its unnatural determinants revealed in order to allow Roxana's natural freedom to oppose them. The 'naturalization' of the environment in Defoe's other narratives becomes a relentless un-naturalizing of it in *Roxana*. Her efficiency and clarity of vision in that world become specifically subversive of its social realities, and, by extension, of all social realities. Defoe's other narratives tend to deny history and disguise the bourgeois self by that naturalizing which gives their protagonists an innocence and freedom they would not have if they survived in history and society truly rendered. *Roxana*, paradoxically, reveals the historical reality of the bourgeois self, its constituitive amorality, by denying the ability of a fully realized historical environment ever to contain it. The social implications of the popular format that we call the secret history (a simultaneous envy and aggression directed towards society) release in transparent form the aggressive nature of the narrative self. Roxana is a character by virtue of her refusal to be merely the conventional heroine (or villain) of the secret history; her character as an event consists largely of the continuous revision of that narrative stereotype she inhabits.

Normally, as we have seen, the self in Defoe's narratives is supposed to be acquired by the movements of an ongoing external necessity which generates individual freedom within it. In *Roxana* that necessity is quickly asserted and then is almost totally internalized, and Roxana is virtually self-propelling and ungenerated throughout her story. Unlike Defoe's other narrators, she has no preliminary childhood in adversity or a lower-class milieu to make her agile mind the plausible result of the pressures of actuality. Partly, of course, Roxana's upper-middle-class origins and the powerful self they would provide are given by the requirements of a secret history, which must be populated by the wealthy and the well-connected. But Roxana is from the first facts of her narrative and the ring of her style in the first few pages effectively outside the world of her autobiography by virtue of her analytic intelligence. All of Defoe's narrators are in some sense retrospectively outside the events they narrate, but Roxana's externality is extreme and significant in various ways.

She insists, for example, upon presenting a set of natural facts next to the socio-historical ones that constitute her beginnings. In telling us that her family were wealthy Huguenot refugees, she inserts her grasp of the moral complexity of what could have been told in simpler and almost heroic terms. Her father, she explains, was rich and independent, different from the majority of refugees 'who at that Time fled hither for Shelter, on Account of Conscience, or *something else*' (5). Her father tells her that many of the refugees who seek his help in England have come for economic advantage, to get a better price for their work. Such information has nothing to do with Roxana's story. It does, however, establish her for us as a supervising intelligence who distinguishes between natural facts (which tend to have an economic base) and the artificial simplifications of history: Huguenot refugees were victims of religious persecution is the historical illusion which Roxana qualifies with the reality of personal and economic motives which she has experienced. She is, in effect, thus introduced at once as an ironist who is aware of those two levels of reality: the public image and the private fact, or the social mask and the natural reality.

That ironic objectivity extends to the facts of her own beginnings, which she presents by daring us to question their accuracy: 'Being to give my own Character, I must be excus'd to give it as impartially as possible, and as if I was speaking of another-body; *and the Sequel will lead you to judge whether I flatter myself or no*' (6). The question is rhetorical, for Roxana's narrative is concerned to obviate our judgements and to show us as strictly as possible how truthful she has been. But the phrasing is revealing in its overt statement of externality—'as if I was speaking of another-body'. Unlike Defoe's other autobiographers, she can be exact about her origins and motives, clear and unashamed where the others tend to be apologetic and exploratory, pretending to look for hints of their subsequent selves in their early lives. Where the other narrators tend to begin with nullity or marginal social and personal identity, Roxana presents herself as a fully formed self from the beginning, an objective self in which she locates quite exactly her initial disaster and her subsequent prosperity. Such valid objectivity is only possible for a natural self which differentiates itself from the artificial historical facts in the act of reciting them. The more exact and analytic she is about her past the more authentic the narrative self becomes. In this summarizing paragraph of herself on the verge of her first marriage, Roxana maintains her ironic distance from that initial acquired self, refusing to speculate about the ultimate causes of that self but clearly suggesting here and elsewhere that she is the result of her surroundings:

I was (*speaking of myself as about Fourteen Years of Age*) tall, and very well made; sharp as a Hawk in Matters of common Knowledge; quick and smart in Discourse; apt to be Satyrical; full of Repartee, and a little too forward in Conversation; or, as we call it in *English*, BOLD, tho' perfectly Modest in my Behaviour. Being *French* Born, I danc'd, *as some say*, naturally, lov'd it extremely, and sung well also, and so well, that *as you will hear*, it was afterwards some Advantage to me: With all these Things, I wanted neither Wit, Beauty, or Money. In this Manner I set out into the World, having all the

Advantages that any Young Woman cou'd desire, to recommend me to others, and form a Prospect of happy Living to myself. (6–7)

The force of that italicized '*as some say*' is to reject natural explanation for dancing well and for everything else with which young Roxana is blessed. The point of this paragraph is that these achievements are social acquirements, and the purpose of this opening sequence in Roxana's story is to demonstrate that social acquirements are worthless as such. These gifts and predilections lead Roxana to her disastrous first marriage (indeed, her only technically legal one), and her obvious irony is that social determinants produce a self which cannot manage to survive. The story of Roxana's survival and prosperity lies in the acquisition, through economic necessity, of a natural perspective on social forms. Like all Defoe's heroes, Roxana does not change, although she has to pretend she does. The pretence is that the 'natural' self is discovered rather than acquired, an innate rather than a historical entity. She will claim to have been forced by necessity to discover a natural self with which she can direct her impressive but undirected social self. That initial dichotomy is the key antithesis the book depends upon and the one it continually enacts in various ways.

If we follow Roxana's directions and remember what she tells us about her dancing serving her later, we can see a clear instance of that new perspective and of the narrative's careful and quite coherent exposition of the appropriation of social forms by the natural self. Roxana meets her foolish first husband and is attracted to him through dancing: 'he danc'd well, which, *I think*, was the first thing that brought us together' (7). There is a whole complex of other reasons for the marriage, of course, but dancing is the quintessential artificial social activity among the others responsible for her marriage. Her husband is indeed a fool, as Roxana never tires of calling him, because he lives entirely in an artificial social world to which he does not properly belong. He is the heir to a brewery of great proportions but spends his time otherwise: he 'went Abroad, kept Company, hunted much, and lov'd it exceedingly' (7).[4]

---

[4] Peterson points out that the 'Fool Husband' is a recurring figure in Defoe's journalism. Following the exemplary pattern of marriage Defoe describes in his didactic works, Peterson argues that Roxana's husband is responsible for her moral decline 'because his marriage did not permit growth, by family instruction, in the

Except for the inappropriate hunting, those socially aspiring activities are precisely the ones that provide Roxana years later with her greatest moments, the ones she spends the most time and detail on and the ones she is referring us to in her opening summary of herself as a young girl. Those triumphs occur when she returns to England after profitable years on the Continent as a mistress and a merchant. She aspires, she tells us, to 'nothing less than of being Mistress to the King himself' (161). And it is at this point in her narrative that she issues her most forthright personal manifesto when an eminent merchant proposes marriage. Harassed by proposals from 'Lovers, *Beaus*, and *Fops* of Quality, in abundance' (171), Roxana repeats 'that nothing less than the *KING* himself was in my Eye' (172).

That ambition, or something like it, is realized shortly afterwards. The specific occasion Roxana describes is the ball she gives at which she astounds the company of courtiers (among whom, masked, is the king) with her 'Turkish' dance and costume. Roxana explains that both the costume and the dance are fraudulent, personal adaptations designed to please. The costume is indeed Turkish, but the diamonds with which it is decorated are fake: 'and on both Ends where it join'd, or hook'd, [it] was set with Diamonds for eight Inches either way, only they were not true Diamonds; but no-body knew that but myself' (174). The dance is new and French, learnt in Paris, but 'being perfectly new, it pleas'd the Company exceedingly, and they all thought it had been *Turkish*; nay, one Gentleman had the Folly to expose himself so much, as to say, *and I think swore too*, that he had seen it danc'd at *Constantinople*; which was ridiculous enough' (175–6). That delight in deception is a characteristic Roxana shares with Defoe's other narrators. But in this context the deception is an aggressive exposure of the artificiality of social forms by a natural self. Roxana pleases others by dancing but pleases herself by tricking them, revealing their artificiality in her mastery of the art of creating arti-

---

knowledge of good'. (See 'The Matrimonial Theme of Defoe's *Roxana*', *PMLA*, 70 (1955), 170.) We might wonder why Defoe's narrative neglects to mention even the possibility of that 'family instruction' which is the title of one of his didactic works, indeed why there is never any 'family life' in Defoe's narratives. I suppose the intense individuality the narrators require denies that kind of moral possibility and reminds us how special and limited the self and those around it have to be in Defoe's fiction.

ficial social forms. Roxana pleases by combining the strange
with the familiar, the Turkish with the French, demonstrating
the power she has over those categories by creating a new thing
which exists only in her imagination. The incident is thus an
epitome of Roxana's career as a whole: she makes herself into a
brilliant social event but remains herself behind that event and
renders that event, in truth and in the reality we are privy to,
different from its public appearance.[5] All of this activity points
to the defining insight of the book: the 'natural' self exists
primarily in its manipulative relationship to the artificial social
forms and the selves that are entirely within them. That natural
self is not simple nature, never mere self-expression or spontaneous assertion. That emphasis is added by the sequel to
Roxana's first triumph, a second ball which she gives a week
later by popular demand. There some ladies try to steal her
thunder by presenting a strange oriental dance, which fails to
please because it is exactly that, nature untouched for social
effect: 'They danc'd three times all-alone, for no-body indeed,
cou'd dance with them: The Novelty pleas'd, truly, but yet
there was something wild and *Bizarre* in it, because they really
acted to the Life the barbarous Country whence they came; but
as mine had the *French* Behaviour under the *Mahometan* Dress, it
was every way as new, and pleas'd much better, indeed' (179).[6]

What is striking and even frightening about Roxana among

[5] Commentators have tended to see this scene as part of Defoe's satiric attack
on the immorality summed up for readers of the time in the Restoration court and
directly epitomized in the overtly decadent social and sexual licence of Roxana's
lavish masquerade. (See David Blewett, '*Roxana* and the Masquerades', *MLR*, 65
(1970), 499–502.) Even the heavily emphasized artificiality of Roxana's las-
civiously hybrid dance has been identified by M. E. Novak as part of the satiric
mechanism. It represents, he says, 'not so much a theory of aesthetics as a moral
commentary, for Defoe frequently drew upon primitivistic ideas in attacking the
vices of society'. (See 'Crime and Punishment in Defoe's *Roxana*', *JEGP*, 45 (1966),
462.) Once again, I have to argue simply that the satire fails, or is at least mixed
in with an admiration for Roxana's immoral energy, which articulates it so clearly
that the energy quite overwhelms the moral intent.

[6] It is at this point in her narrative that Roxana hints that she then spent three
years and one month as a royal mistress, living 'retir'd, having been oblig'd to
make an Excursion, in a Manner, and with a Person, which Duty, and private
Vows, obliges her [*sic*] not to reveal, at least, not yet' (181). Her pseudo-discretion
at this moment is such that it is hard to tell whether she is still speaking or whether
an 'editor' has taken over and speaks in the third person. That discretion at such a
moment is as appropriate as it is disingenuous. We are turned into an audience
like the one at her dance, mystified into belief in her authenticity by her manipulation of a social form, that is, the indiscreet 'discretion' proper to a royal mistress.

Defoe's narrators, then, is her awareness of the necessity of withdrawal from experience that she shares with some of them but which she alone masters with total self-consciousness and nearly complete confidence. She locates the source of contradiction in the society around her, pin-pointing it from her beginnings with her foolish husband. His 'foolishness' is defined very precisely if implicitly by Roxana's narrative. He mistakes society for nature, operates as if natural impulse were licensed by social status. Roxana notes that she had 'five Children by him; the only Work (perhaps) that Fools are good for' (10). The courtesan's sexual evaluation of her husband so wickedly clear in the 'perhaps' indicates a perspective which treats sexuality as a treacherous natural urge, undirected towards true self-assertion, unaware of the necessary instrumentality of mere nature in the context of artificial social realities like marriage and financial survival. The special kind of natural self that Roxana comes to possess is defined by its awareness of that social context surrounding mere impulse and able to act accordingly, that is, to interact dialectically with social realities and thereby rearrange and master them.

Roxana's initial dilemma is designed to illustrate the helpless irrelevance of the merely natural and undialectical self faced with social circumstances, not only her husband's bankruptcy and desertion but her own social limitations as a middle-class matron. Reduced to pawning valuables to live, she tells us that she would have worked, 'but to think of one single Woman not bred to Work, and at a Loss where to get Employment, to get the Bread of five Children, that was not possible, some of my Children being young too, and none of them big enough to help one another' (15). Perhaps the most striking aspect of Roxana's helplessness in this opening sequence is her 'silence'. She is the most voluble of Defoe's main characters, the one who uses speech most effectively to define herself, indeed the one with the wittiest and most personalized style. Yet here within her narrative she is reduced to silence several times, a silence that is pointed to as the only response that she can muster. When her old aunt and another old woman visit her in her distress, Roxana is 'sitting on the Ground, with a great Heap of old Rags, Linnen, and other things . . . looking them over, to see if I had any thing among them that would Sell or Pawn for a little

Money' (17). She bursts into tears, there is nothing else she can do: 'The Truth was, there was no Need of much Discourse in the Case, the Thing spoke it self' (17). In short, Roxana's narrative emphasizes the natural inevitability behind what seems to be a social event. The dreadful implications of mere nature begin to arise: 'we had eaten up almost every thing, and little remain'd, unless, like one of the pitiful Women of *Jerusalem*, I should eat up my very Children themselves' (18).

In the middle of all this, Roxana's tearful silence is pointedly and repeatedly corrected by the cunning articulations of her maid, Amy. Amy is, in anybody's reading of the story, a disturbing character, perhaps the most gratuitously self-assertive figure in all of Defoe's books. There seems to be no clear precedent in the narrative convention for Amy's singular ferocity. Maids in such stories are normally useful for carrying messages to lovers or undermining enemies by domestic espionage. Tools rather than allies, they never need to possess Amy's self-conscious aggression. Her particular kind of aggressive amorality in the service of her mistress is, however, simply given rather than explained. As we have seen, Defoe's other heroes tend to have significant relationships with subsidiary figures who influence them or push them into action. One function of those characters is clearly to absorb a good deal of the responsibility for morally dubious or unacceptable actions, to act as a bridge between the world of compelling circumstances and the central self, thereby to ratify the desires of the self by placing them in another form of circumstance. Like William the Quaker pirate, Moll's governess, Colonel Jack's Captain Jack and the other urchins, Amy functions in these ways. But the relationship she has with Roxana is also much more intimate than any that the others are allowed to have with their masters. To use psychological terms, one would have to call Amy some kind of *alter ego*, a locus of those energies that Roxana will gradually acquire and perfect, and even in the end attempt to reject by giving them back to Amy. More important, in the context *Roxana* provides, Amy is the classless naturalism that Roxana needs in order to survive but which she cannot simply possess at once or in Amy's simple-minded and straightforward way. Amy's intelligence and low cunning are, therefore, necessarily gratuitous, natural responses to an inequitable social situation, informed and practical responses which contrast with Roxana's tears and cannibalistic fantasies. The logic of the narrative here demands Amy's controlled and classless naturalism as the opposite of Roxana's class-bound naturalism, at this point in her story chaotic and self-destructive, within the limitations of society rather than beyond them.

Thus, Amy's extraordinary performance in this sequence is consistently the logical correction of Roxana's failure, as Amy literally becomes her mistress, adopts her social position in order to dramatize it and thereby modify it to advantage. Amy 'puts' it into Roxana's 'thoughts' to send for her aunt. She is out pawning a silver spoon when that lady arrives, but she enters into the midst of Roxana's tears and dreadful fantasies with 'a small Breast of Mutton, and two great Bunches of Turnips, which she intended to stew for our Dinner' (18). It is Amy who tells the visiting ladies about Roxana's circumstances, not only correcting Roxana's sobbing silence but dramatizing it, setting it 'forth in such moving Terms, and so to the Life, that I could not upon any Terms have done it like her myself' (18). At last, Roxana retreats entirely and leaves the house and the management of the disposal of her children to Amy and her allies, the two women who are conscripted into Roxana's cause by Amy's eloquence. They contrive a strategy for leaving the children with their aunt, a plan which combines brutal desertion (Amy leaves the two children at the door and runs away) and elaborate rationalization and persuasion (the aunt enters and tells a fabricated story of Roxana's eviction). This plan is carefully devised in the context of legal provision for pauperized children. Roxana is to disappear and her children are then the responsibility of the parish. The object is to avoid the notorious fate of parish children by threatening Roxana's relatives with that possibility for the children. Social arrangements are manipulated and exploited by Amy's strategem for natural advantage for Roxana and her children. These very precisely charted movements within social circumstances constitute the recurring pattern of the book. The entire plot is presented, moreover, with Defoe's characteristic dramatic underlining, in extensive dialogue between the aunt and the relatives. Roxana herself is made to reiterate her non-participation and, in the middle of it all, to stress the art with which the scheme is carried out:

This was all acted to the Life by this good, kind, poor Creature; for tho' her Design was perfectly good and charitable, yet there was not one Word of it true in Fact; for I was not turn'd out of Doors by the Landlord, nor gone distracted; it was true, indeed, that at parting with my poor Children, I fainted, and was like one Mad when I came to myself and found they were gone; but I remain'd in the House a good while after that; as you shall hear. (22)

Roxana's initial innocence is extreme: tears, fearful fantasies, fainting, near madness. Like Moll, she begins with an extreme so that she may pass convincingly to the other. Ideological movement in Defoe's narratives obeys quasi-physical laws of motion rather than psychological ones. But the transition in *Roxana* from innocent trust in benevolent social exteriors to the practical certainty of malevolent natural realities beneath them is by nature a slow revelation and, as such, parallel to the narrative's unfolding subversive perspective on social realities. The relative gradualness of Roxana's conversion is a means of dramatizing not only the arbitrary and artificial nature of social realities but their dense interconnection with natural desires. Amy's classless naturalism and simple morality of survival are not really sufficient to save Roxana from the precisely complicated social dilemma in which she now finds herself. Roxana passes from silence and hysteria to voluble and mournful hesitation and useful analysis. That is to say, the melodramatic simplicities of survival do not endure at all in this kind of social world for someone in Roxana's social position.

Thus, Roxana's first encounter with pretence in her Landlord is an elaborate examination of that interaction between desire (in the broadest self-assertive sense) and social and moral conventions—both she and the eager landlord are married. Implicit in the inexhaustible casuistry that she and Amy and her suitor bring to bear upon the situation is the search for a natural reality which can coexist with the inhibiting social forms represented by marriage. Finally, of course, Roxana will control for her own pleasure and power those forms and the restrictions they imply. But this sequence is crucial in the ideological pattern of the narrative; it establishes the importance of the complete and complex world of social and moral forms as a ground for the self. That comprehensive grasp of moral and social circumstances establishes the authority of the narrative in such matters and dramatizes again the impossibility of a purely 'natural' solution in an extraordinarily socialized world. What we as readers experience along with Roxana is the eventual necessity not simply of survival but of negating the negation of those forms by exploiting them from within, that is, from that full realization of their arbitrary and therefore malleable nature which this opening sequence of social survival provides.

This sequence with the landlord is the second and more difficult half of Roxana's survival scene. Having disposed of her children, Roxana is still left with herself and Amy to feed, ironically caught in her 'great House' faced with the purest of natural needs. The landlord is the carrier of that opposing non-natural world; he and the house he owns and Roxana lives in represent that tricky interaction of social circumstances and natural need which *Roxana* is out to dramatize. He appears and restores quite directly the social order from which Roxana has fallen: he buys meat, orders wine and beer ('poor *Amy* and I had drank nothing but Water for many Weeks' (26)), hires a gardener, orders furniture, and arranges for Roxana to take 'Summer Gentry' (32) as lodgers. Roxana sees, then, that she has no real choice when he asks to become one of those lodgers: 'I told him, he ought not to ask me Leave, who had so much Right to make himself welcome; so that the House began to look in some tollerable Figure, and clean; the Garden also, in about a Fortnight's Work, began to look something less like a Wilderness than it us'd to do; and he order'd me to put up a Bill for Letting Rooms, reserving one for himself, to come to as he saw Occasion' (33). His final touch is to provide an elaborate contract for cohabitation, complete with substantial indemnification for Roxana in case of abandonment or death. The landlord arranges his desire with social forms; he modifies social restrictions by counter-arrangements of his own.

To be sure, we are led to see that such counter-arrangements come from messy natural needs, that as Amy puts it more than once his 'charity' begins in 'Vice'. The landlord ratifies his arrangements with a wonderful sexual thrust which implicitly reveals the source and target of his measures:

Now, my Dear, is this not sufficient? Can you object any thing against it? If not, as I believe you will not, then let us debate this

Matter no longer; with that, he pull'd out a silk Purse, which had three-score Guineas in it, and threw them into my Lap, and concluded all the rest of his Discourse with Kisses, and Protestations of his Love; of which indeed, I had abundant Proof. (42)

In short, we are led by Amy's cynical analytic chorus and by Roxana's own rendition of the end of his arrangements to see that his social forms are merely instruments for his personal desires. Roxana is outside all that. Her monitory asides as she tells us about all this, her insistence that she sinned out of fear ['the Terrors behind me look'd blacker than the Terrors before me' (43)] and in full possession of her guilt, establish her as a 'natural' self caught in a double world of unnatural arrangements, those which lead her to her initial dilemma and those which the landlord invents in transparent parody of social forms. She is victimized here, indirectly of course, not by direct natural necessity but by means of those unnatural arrangements, that order of things represented by the landlord, his house, garden, wine, furniture, and generous contract; and in the ultimate past, by the social arrangements which put her in that ordered circle of things and then arbitrarily shifted her to its desperate perimeter.

Roxana notes that her landlord believes in his devices as she clearly cannot: 'he either was before of the Opinion, or argued himself into it now, that we were both Free, and might lawfully Marry' (43). The guilt and uncertainty which Roxana dwells on free her from his social arrangements, declare in fact that she exists somewhere between a denial of social forms such as Amy exemplifies and advises and a deluding self-appropriation of them such as the landlord represents.

I say but too justly, that I was empty of Principle, because, as above, I had yielded to him, not as deluded to believe it Lawful, but as overcome by his Kindness, and terrify'd at the Fear of my own Misery, if he should leave me; so with my Eyes open, and with my Conscience, as I may say, awake, I sinn'd, knowing it to be a Sin, but having no Power to resist; when this had thus made a Hole in my Heart, and I was come to such a height, as to transgress against the Light of my own Conscience, I was then fit for any Wickedness, and Conscience left off speaking, where it found it cou'd not be heard. (44)

That is, Roxana is careful to adopt neither Amy's pure naturalism which saved them initially nor the pure social artifice and
self-rationalization the landlord uses. Her guilt here seems to
establish her moral superiority over both of them, but it is
clearly as we read a means of establishing a self-asserting power
which involves much more than moral superiority, which
paradoxically allows her to be much worse than either of them.
Roxana understands and accepts the realities of her present
position, not a wife but a whore, in a way that is beyond the
capacities of her two saviours. Both of them have participated in
a curious alliance in persuading Roxana to cohabit; both of
them (from different perspectives) assume the existence of a
natural mode of behaviour. Roxana acts, as we have seen, with
difficulty at this point in her narrative, trying to balance the
natural and the social imperatives her tempters offer her. But
having acted, Roxana proceeds in chilling fashion to exert her
power not just over Amy and the landlord but over the ideological positions they represent. She proceeds towards a mode of
behaviour which is neither merely natural nor merely social but
a creative manipulation of both these categories.

Throughout (and perhaps here more than elsewhere),
Roxana has to attend to the penitential superstructure of her
story. Thus she tells us in a conspicuously brief paragraph that
they lived 'surely, the most agreeable Life, the grand Exception
only excepted, that ever Two liv'd together' (45). But the bulk
of her account of their early life is her putting Amy to bed with
her landlord. In a way, that remarkable scene is simply part of
the sensational revelation this type of book must deliver. But it
is also a way of taking Amy at her amoral word and of exposing
the invalidity of the landlord's contract. He is easy and calls her
wife; Amy wonders out loud that her mistress is not with child
yet. Roxana's response shows us how well she understands the
power implicit in her moral position and how well she understands Amy's naturalism and her landlord's easy structures:

*Law*, Madam, *says Amy*, what have you been doing? why you have
been Marry'd a Year and a half, I warrant you, Master wou'd have
got me with-Child twice in that time: It may be so, *Amy, says I*, let
him try, can't you: No, *says Amy*, you'll forbid it now; before I told
you he shou'd with all my Heart, but I won't now, now he's all
your own: O, *says I, Amy*, I'll freely give you my Consent, it will be

nothing at-all to me; nay, I'll put you to Bed to him myself one
Night or other, if you are willing: No, Madam, no, *says Amy*, not
now he's yours.

Why you Fool you, *says I*, don't I tell you I'll put you to Bed to
him myself.

Nay, nay, *says Amy*, if you put me to-Bed to him, that's another
Case; I believe I shall not rise again very soon.

I'll venture that, *Amy, says I*. (45–6)

Roxana insists on exercising power within the pseudo-structure
in which she now lives. She forces Amy to act out her naturalism, that is, to become the true whore in their strange tri-
angular relationship. And when she strips Amy and thrusts her
into the landlord's willing embrace, Roxana's comment tells us
that she is in effect dramatizing his lack of authenticity and her
power over the real terms of their relationship. '*Here*, says I, *try
what you can do with your Maid* Amy' (46). Roxana explains quite
explicitly that the purpose of such a scene is to separate herself
from those who have hitherto arranged her survival, to expose
by her own arrangements the inadequacy of those who have
arranged and defined the moral world she now lives in. 'I need
say no more; this is enough to convince any-body that I did not
think him my Husband, and that I had cast off all Principle,
and all Modesty, and had effectually stifled Conscience' (46).

This is an important moment in the upward curve of the
book's action. Both Amy and the landlord lose their respective
claims on Roxana as ideological masters. They are both exposed as untrue to the ideological positions they occupy: Amy
reduced for a time to extravagant penitence (certainly more
extravagant than that she chided her mistress for earlier), and
the landlord's specious social forms exposed as mere excuses for a
promiscuity that he hates afterwards. Roxana is the victor in all
this because she is absolutely inside her new reality, attracting
others into its destructive and self-exposing elements and
allowing (nay forcing) them to absorb the shocks: 'Had I
look'd upon myself as a Wife, you cannot suppose I would have
been willing to have let my Husband lye with my Maid, much
less, before my Face, for I stood-by all the while; but as I
thought myself a Whore, I cannot say but that it was something
design'd in my Thoughts, that my Maid should be a Whore
too, and should not reproach me with it' (47). Roxana succeeds

in a very thorough way not simply in gaining moral equality with Amy (and with the landlord) but in acquiring ideological superiority. An earlier Amy had replaced Roxana, literally speaking for her and managing her survival, urging her then into the connection with the landlord and indeed offering to sleep with the landlord for her. Amy now replaces Roxana again but on the latter's own terms, caught in the same opposition between natural inclination and social restraints that Roxana suffered from earlier. Roxana is now the master of that same opposition which began her narrative. She forces Amy into that opposition and asserts her power not only over Amy but over the opposition itself, as Amy's simple naturalism is corrupted by social and moral guilt. So, too, the Landlord began as the master and manipulator of social forms, taking over in the house and presiding over its social realities as Roxana once did. He is now the victim and the fool of those forms, believing in his own contrivances even after this convincing demonstration of their mere instrumentality: 'he was quite alter'd, for he hated her heartily, and could, I believe, have kill'd her after it, and he told me so, for he thought this a vile Action; whereas what he and I had done, he was perfectly easie in, thought it just, and esteem'd me as much his Wife as if we had been Marry'd from our Youth' (47). Just as Amy's naturalism yields to its moral opposite in Roxana's force field, so too the landlord's social security yields to its natural opposite, sexual guilt. Roxana, in that context, has no guilt; her act transfers it to them. The landlord and Amy are caught in their moral oppositions; they reveal their inability to sustain their positions in the dialectic between artificial social relationships and natural satisfactions. Roxana presides by means of her purposeful voyeurism, and her organization of this scene is the first of many such dispositions she will stage in order to reside in that dialectic of the social and the natural without ever succumbing to its destructive movements. She will, that is, preside over pleasure and power, making them interact without reacting on herself. Her voyeurism is thus the perfect beginning to her career, out of a cool sensuality and social agnosticism manipulating and directing social forms and those who are in them and perplexed by them, gaining pleasure and power from those forms by exploiting them internally without belonging to them.

Her pleasure, in effect, flows from that power and not from within the pleasurable acts themselves.

The virtue of such an understanding of the book and of this quite astonishing scene in particular is that we are able to avoid the customary superficial psychologizing and to convert the psychological manœuvres of the scene into part of a coherent structural pattern. We are able to see, in other words, that psychological movement in the context of a narrative is also a means of social movement whereby the self performs for its readers and asserts and defines itself in ways that involve the pleasure of order that fiction always gives.[7] To be sure, moments of intense coherence such as this scene are necessarily rare. Having definitely established herself and her power, Roxana can then quickly summarize her uneventful life thereafter with the landlord, pausing only to remind us that she had occasional 'dark Reflections which came involuntarily in, and thrust in Sighs into the middle of all my Songs; and there would be, sometimes, a heaviness of Heart, which intermingling itself with all my Joy, and which would often fetch a Tear from my Eye' (48). Such consciousness of guilt and residence in contradiction (Roxana also declares herself happy at times) continue the superiority established by the stripping scene, as Amy and the landlord quickly lose their guilt and return to their complacency.

Structurally, that superiority is nothing less than Roxana's ability to *move* through her narrative (at this point, to cohabit with her landlord) and to *remain* outside it (that is, to affirm her guilt as a form of resistance to that movement). That balance of movement and stability is precisely enacted in the transition from this first part of the narrative to its second part. After the next two years (and three paragraphs), the landlord has occasion to go to France on business for two months. His uneasiness as he presents his plan to Roxana emphasizes several

---

[7] Samuel Monk calls this scene a 'glance into hell' and 'the most appalling scene in serious eighteenth-century fiction, except for one or two in *Clarissa*'. (See *Colonel Jack* (Oxford English Novels, 1965), Introduction, p. xvii.) That would be a fair description of the moral and psychological weight of the scene, if Roxana went on to perform other acts of like depravity, if she continued to be a *voyeuse* or to follow the sexual pathology implicit in voyeurism. But her act is so clearly a matter of self-assertive strategy that it is not repeated and its implications for Roxana's sexual personality are completely ignored.

things: the fragile illegality of their relationship, Roxana's utter dependence and financial helplessness, and the air of social necessity and risk that surrounds both of them.

> Well, my Dear, *says I*, and how shall I make you easie?
> Why, by consenting to let me go, *says he*, upon which Condition, I'll tell you the Occasion of my going, that you may judge of the Necessity there is for it on my Side; then to make me easie in his going, he told me, he would make his Will before he went, which should be to my full Satisfaction. (49)

This language of affection is quasi-diplomatic. She and her landlord deal with one another, negotiate their movements within their relationship, as their relationship is itself a negotiated, special, and precarious pact. Roxana accepts and 'offers' to go along with him: 'He was so pleas'd with this Offer, that he told me, he would give me full Satisfaction for it, and accept of it too' (50). Such manœuvring establishes in us as we read the balance between affection and protection that marks successful human relationships in *Roxana*. The rare and striking thing about *Roxana* is its honesty about that balance. Roxana moves to France, to great profit and grand living, and eventually to great risks; but she first acquires a stable base, the monetary equivalent of the moral coin of despair and guilt she has spent in her first part. The landlord's generous will (£1,000 with interest from his death, plus household effects) provides her with the concrete stability which makes the new and accelerated tempo of part two possible.

The France in which Roxana and her landlord settle is quickly established as a dangerous place, but social dangers have replaced the moral snares of previous scenes. This shift can be seen as a version of Defoe's characteristic strategy of replacing a social environment with a natural one in which morality is easily suspended for the purposes of survival. Only here one social environment is replaced by another one which is different because it is more rather than less social. Instead of being naturalized to excuse action, society is 'artificialized' towards the same end. Thus, Roxana emerges as a social being in various new ways; before the landlord's death she lives 'in a very good Figure, and might have liv'd higher if I pleas'd' (51), and after his death she appears in a distinct social role, widely known 'by the Name of *La Belle veuve de Poictou*; or, The pretty Widow of *Poictou*' (57). But at the same time that she lives well in society, she remains, as her public epithets imply, somehow secret and known only to herself and to her privileged readers. Moreover, that separation from social reality is enforced by her spectacular premonition of her landlord's death:

> I star'd at him, as if I was frighted, for I thought all his Face look'd like a Death's-Head; and then, immediately, I thought I perceiv'd his Head all Bloody; and then his Cloaths look'd Bloody too; and immediately it all went off, and he look'd as he really did; immediately I fell a-crying, and hung about him, My Dear *said I*, I am frighted to Death; you shall not go, depend upon it, some Mischief will befal you. . . . (52–3)

Social heights are balanced by personal depths; bones, blood, and the first emotionally charged moment (that we are given) with the landlord act as a natural compensation or counter-balance for the pleasant illusion of social movement. The emotional intensity of Roxana's participation in her landlord's murder earns her, in the dynamics of the narrative, the right to her distanced manipulation of Parisian society. Indeed, her anticipation of the murder's exact form certifies her natural worthiness even more explicitly.

Roxana herself sees her new predicament as a repetition with an important variation on her initial problem: 'a dreadful Disaster . . . threw me back into the same state of Life that I was in before; with this one happy Exception however, that whereas before I was Poor, even to Misery, now I was not only provided for, but very Rich' (51). Such an announcement verges on cynicism; critics lie ready to pounce on such statements as examples of Defoe's moral irony. Roxana saves herself from such moral readers with her horrible vision and her attempts to persuade her landlord not to go on his trip, like all excursions in Defoe's narratives, a journey for profit and power. Roxana's own trip takes up her landlord's profitable movement and refines it as well. She practises, we read with pleasure, a more efficient secrecy than he, buries him and advances herself with a double motion of personal secrecy and public advertisement which is to become her signature as we read on. She has him buried by bribing someone to represent the dead man as a

Catholic: 'Upon all which, *tho' not one Word of it was true*, he was Buried with all the Ceremonies of the *Roman* Church' (54). Then, there are several paragraphs of grief and a recurrence of her vision, followed immediately by the rewards of grief and the self-assertive movements which preserve them:

These things amaz'd me, and I was a good-while as one stupid; however, after some time, I began to recover, and look into my Affairs; I had the Satisfaction not to be left in Distress, or in danger of Poverty; on the contrary, besides what he had put into my Hands fairly, in his Life-time, which amounted to a very considerable Value, I found above seven Hundred Pistoles in Gold, in his Scrutore, of which he had given me the Key; and I found Foreign-Bills accepted, for about 12000 Livres; so that, in a Word, I found myself possess'd of almost ten Thousand Pounds Sterling, in a very few Days after the Disaster. (55)

What saves Roxana through all this from simple and un-interesting hypocrisy or moral shallowness as we read is the precision of the narrative's underlying structure and the dynamic exactness of Roxana's movements within that struc-ture. She is given enormous substance by circumstances she has tried to forestall. But given those circumstances, like Defoe's other agile and alert narrators, she moves to exploit them. She writes immediately to Amy back in London with precise in-structions for securing the landlord's effects there against his relations or his real wife's friends. Quite suddenly she is the master of self-aggrandizing and only superficially legal manœuvres: 'I order'd her to convey away all the Plate, Linnen, and other things of Value, and to secure them in a Person's Hands that I directed her to, and then to sell, or dis-pose the Furniture of the House, if she could; and so, without acquainting any-body with the Reason of her going, withdraw; sending Notice to his Head Manager at *London*, that the House was quitted by the Tennant, and they might come and take Possession of it for the Executors' (55). She moves in precisely the same way her landlord moved when he saved her, but she adds a secrecy and quickness all her own. He, we are told quite specifically, has been murdered because he lacked secrecy, because he allowed it to be known 'that he generally carried a shagreen Case in his Pocket, especially when he went to Court, or to the Houses of any of the Princes of the Blood, in which he

had Jewels of very great Value' (51). His attackers knew this,
Roxana informs us, and he died because they knew it: 'They
were suppos'd to kill him, because of the Disappointment they
met with, in not getting his Case, or Casket of Diamonds, which
they knew he carry'd about him' (53). Roxana exploits the
public facts that have betrayed her hapless landlord. She gives
it out that the jewels were stolen when they are in reality in her
possession; she passes as the bereaved but innocent victim of the
landlord's bigamy, his French widow surprised to hear of his
English one. Finally and most triumphantly, she acquires a new
lover in the very nobleman to whom it was reported her landlord was carrying the jewels he was killed for. This splendid
'Prince' calls to offer condolences, gives her a generous gift, and
offers her a pension for as long as she resides in Paris. What
makes all this so marvellous is that we are made conscious as
readers all along of the balance Roxana manages between circumstances and manipulation. She controls without controlling, she exploits the compulsions of chance and the structures
of society without ever violating them, working within them,
extending them, and modifying them.

The long affair with the Prince constitutes a new section of
Roxana's career and, in the context of the traditional secret
history, represents a revision of its conventions close to inversion.
Like other and lesser books of its kind, *Roxana* presents a great
deal of aristocratic hardware: jewellery, china, clothing, houses,
equipage, and servants and parties are rolled out frequently for
our delight. The secret history tends to colour all its fascination
with slick moralizing. Perhaps the most truly frightening aspect
of *Roxana* is the book's implicit attitude towards the gorgeous
paraphernalia of the genre. All these objects are presented as
examples of Roxana's power rather than for their own sweet
selves. Normally, those objects and habits constitute a compelling environment against which the heroine struggles in vain.
Readers are encouraged to cheer her struggle and enjoy the
instruments surrounding her fall. The complexity of Roxana's
consciousness allows her to occupy a position like that of the
hypothetical reader of secret histories. She enjoys it all but
stands outside it all and marvels at the sight of others all around
her caught in the dynamics of that world.

The apartness which gives her that privileged view lies

primarily, of course, in the accumulated force of the narrative so far. But again, that apartness is reinforced by a structural pattern in the events as they appear to us in Roxana's presentation. Partly, this is obviously a matter of repeated moralizing, which exists, strikingly, next to overt pleasure in the very actions under scrutiny. Most important, it is also a matter of maintaining that opposition between the natural and the artificial that Roxana has mastered. At one point, for example, the Prince asks Roxana in a moment of post-coital tenderness to dress herself in her best suit of clothes. She has just received three splendid ones from him, one of silk figured with gold, another with silver, and a crimson one. Roxana promises to wear the suit which he likes best, offering to guess at his preference. She chooses the silver one and appears dramatically, in her rendering, 'out of my Dressing-Room, which open'd with Folding-Doors into his Bed-Chamber' (71).

He sat as one astonish'd, a good-while, looking at me, without speaking a Word, till I came quite up to him, kneel'd on one Knee to him, and almost whether he would or no, kiss'd his Hand; he took me up, and stood up himself, but was surpriz'd, when taking me in his Arms, he perceiv'd Tears to run down my Cheeks; My Dear, *says he*, aloud, what mean these Tears? My Lord, *said I*, after some little Check, for I cou'd not speak presently, I beseech you to believe me, they are not Tears of Sorrow, but Tears of Joy; it is impossible for me to see myself snatch'd from the Misery I was fallen into, and at once to be in the Arms of a Prince of such Goodness, such immense Bounty, and be treated in such a Manner; 'tis not possible, my Lord, *said I*, to contain the Satisfaction of it; and it will break out in an Excess in some measure proportion'd to your immense Bounty, and to the Affection which your Highness treats me with, who am so infinitely below you. (71–2)

As readers we are in the unique position to understand the complexity of Roxana's 'satisfaction', as she calls it, and we alone know the total source of its true force on her at this point. Her satisfaction is compounded of a delight in social ritual and personal power. Roxana arranges a tableau in which she stars, using the props and costumes that social relationships and the extraordinary personal accidents of her career provide. Her delighted self-dramatizing in this scene interacts beautifully with the aristocratic *mise en scène* provided for her. Moreover, she uses those pointedly artificial things to create a palpably 'natural' scene, consisting of her tears and his astonishment (their muteness is noted several times). Roxana presents herself as pure and happy victim, brought by the Prince's bounty to tears she cannot suppress. She is 'below' him in the social scale but is, in effect, reminding him of her natural equality. That equality, in addition, allows her to mimic the social rank she does not possess, dressed in the perfect gown (indeed his favourite, it turns out) and making a perfect appearance framed by the folding doors of his bedroom.

That equality, finally, becomes a natural superiority in the rest of this scene. The Prince goes to wipe her tears 'but check'd his Hand, as if he was afraid to deface something; I say, he check'd his Hand, and toss'd the Handkerchief to me, to do it myself' (72). Roxana quickly arranges her culminating ritual, designed to demonstrate her total naturalness. She first expresses an italicized wonder that the Prince should think she was '*Painted*' and then has him rub her face as hard as he can:

> He appear'd surpriz'd, more than ever, and swore, which was the first time that I had heard him swear, from my first knowing him, that he cou'd not have believ'd there was any such Skin, without Paint, in the World: *Well, my Lord*, said I, *Your Highness shall have a farther Demonstration than this; as to that which you are pleas'd to accept for Beauty, that it is the meer Work of Nature;* and with that, I stept to the Door, and rung a little Bell, for my Woman, *Amy,* and bade her bring me a Cup-full of hot Water, which she did; and when it was come, I desir'd *his Highness* to feel if it was warm; which he did, and I immediately wash'd my Face all over with it, before him; this was, indeed, more than Satisfaction, that is to say, than Believing; for it was an undeniable Demonstration, and he kiss'd my Cheeks and Breasts a thousand times, with Expressions of the greatest Surprize imaginable. (72–3)

This extravagant demonstration is a self-conscious reversal of what Roxana herself identifies as the 'Romance' she seems to be in. Beautiful heroines are usually such on sight and provide no verification for their lovers. Roxana performs within the conventions of the romantic cliché, establishing her natural uniqueness in a context of common and conventional artifice, moving the Prince explicitly from mere belief to demonstration. Her command of nature places her outside it to the extent that she can stage it in her own sequence and for her own maximum profit. She can use her nature to move the Prince to a state of surprise where he is effectively as much out of control as she is in command. And Roxana goes on immediately to remind us of her transformation, reviewing for exemplary purposes her initial condition and stressing her incredible social progress as much as anything else: 'that I should be caress'd by a Prince, for the Honour of having the scandalous Use of my Prostituted Body, common before to his Inferiours; and perhaps wou'd not have denied one of his Footmen but a little while before, if I cou'd have got my Bread by it' (74). It is, in short, the Prince who is degraded by the connection and loses his control and his status, who provides the best moral in the whole sequence: 'a Man enslav'd to the Rage of his vicious Appetite; how he defaces the Image of God in his Soul; dethrones his Reason; causes Conscience to abdicate the Possession, and exalts Sence into the vacant Throne; how he deposes the Man, and exalts the Brute' (75).

Throughout, Roxana is exceedingly careful to define her freedom within these arrangements. Her self-justifying moral strategy is one we have seen before in Defoe's narratives but perhaps never so explicit in admitting singularity as sufficient cause for action. Roxana reasons that though she is a whore, she was 'the Queen of Whores' (82), and though a mistress, she is independent and secret, that is, a private rather than a public mistress. She secures independence and secrecy because unlike other 'Women in such Circumstances', she explains, she never asked anything of her prince, neither for herself nor for others. She has power without exercising it directly, the appearance of virtue without its limitations. In short, her career represents a self-conscious and crucial modification of the normal pattern of such relationships. She makes it clear in word and deed that she does not occupy a position; she presides over it, inside her social reality as aristocratic mistress but far beyond or above it by virtue of her natural reality as a private intelligence. This satisfying connection between secrecy and power is the recurrent discovery in Defoe's narratives, but it is nowhere more overt than here. His other narrators tend to be defensive in their secrecy, using it to cover their natural and therefore vulnerable selves. Roxana, as we have seen, uses her natural self, indeed her singular body itself, to promote her social self, exploits carefully selected aspects of her naturalness to achieve social power without ever giving up that natural self. In fact, she never reveals her authentic and total natural self, which we readers experience not as the ordinary and libidinal self that desires normal pleasure and wealth but the special and more exquisite self that desires autonomy and self-possession.

The moral serenity that seems to prevail at this point in the narrative indicates just how perfect such a structural balance is for Defoe's narrative sensibility and just how the narrative reveals its secret concern to promote a controlling self rather than a controlled libidinal self. The moralizing diminishes considerably as Roxana's actions become totally smooth and professional. She even puts herself in a position to exercise moral superiority when her brewer husband turns up suddenly as a member of the French Horse Guards. From her privileged social position she spies on him and determines 'that he was the same worthless Thing he had ever been'. Had he proved worthy, she claims, she would have returned 'to *England* again, send for him over, and have liv'd honestly with him' (93). She herself is alive to the moral symmetry of the situation, and her rhetoric takes an explicit delight in the social and moral power that she now possesses: 'Seeing therefore, no Remedy, I was oblig'd to withdraw my Hand from him, that had been my first *Destroyer*, and reserve the Assistance that I intended to have given him, for another more desirable Opportunity' (94). Our pleasure as readers comes from the paradoxically smooth justice of Roxana's claims and the symmetry she institutes out of what could have been destructive coincidence. Such a sequence lets us see that Roxana is now in total control to the extent that she makes a novel of secret and orderly power for the self out of the turbulent materials of romance and secret history, typified in this coincidental and potentially melodramatic *rencontre* with her husband.

Perhaps the ultimate pleasure this scene offers us as readers is the movement of the self, Roxana's tireless energy in keeping her self and her story moving, that is, constantly showing us the marvellous space between her narrating and acting intelligence and the world in which that intelligence operates. All Defoe's narratives exist to give us this particular sense of novelistic

movement, to enact that space of consciousness and power
between the self and the world. The problem they all face is that
such movement has no goal except itself, that novelistic character is by definition concerned only with perpetuating its own
movement and thereby its proper being. Northrop Frye has
remarked that all narrative has two fundamental movements:
'a cyclical movement within the order of nature, and a dialectical movement from that order into the apocalyptic world
above'.[8] Roxana's narrative seems to describe movement of the
first sort, with the social and moral circumstances providing the
cycles Frye speaks of and the ostensible centre of our interest.
But I think that *Roxana* eventually (if fitfully) escapes that
world and achieves a mastery which clearly approximates at
times the autonomy proper to Frye's second kind of movement.
Frye's terms are necessarily not exactly ours in this case. In
*Roxana*, the 'apocalyptic world above' is the interior world of the
self's superior knowledge and supervising position; the self
remains in a vivifying dialectic with the world of events without ever desiring or envisaging what we would call transcendence. The apocalyptic world is in this case alongside the world
or even within it.

   I think, in other words, that it is correct to speak of a progression in *Roxana* from a concrete involvement of the self in
events to an increasing abstraction of the self whereby events
are exploited or even created ('arranged' is the more neutral
term) to assert the self, where Roxana is not simply in control of
herself but where that self we speak of when we name her and
her narrative is defined by that control itself, even to the extent
of exploiting what Roxana tells us is her conscious resolve to do
otherwise. That she assigns to the category of mysterious inner
compulsion that which suits her prosperity and continuity as a
character is a clear sign of the absolute control and apartness as
moral and social transcendence that is behind the narrative.
Fredric Jameson has observed that for Sartre middle-class
man's illusion of being takes the form of regret and remorse, or
more often the fear of regret and remorse.[9] Roxana's narrative,
as can be seen very well as we approach this point in it, tries to
certify its main character by regret and remorse but keeps

---

[8] *The Anatomy of Criticism* (Princeton, 1957), p. 161.
[9] *Marxism and Form* (Princeton, 1971), p. 277.

slipping off that safe ledge into actions in which Roxana achieves identity by denying regret and remorse or marvelling over their inadequacy after the exciting and expansive fact.

Such emerging and always tentative autonomy is a matter of degree. Roxana is always to some extent primary in her narrative, but she spends her first hundred pages or so working her way out of the restrictions imposed by the format of the secret history: poverty, seduction, and financial settlement. She works, as we have seen, within that format by manipulating her 'natural' self, learning to advance herself with it in the context of social artificiality which the secret history provides. She rises from being the victim of financial and sexual necessity to become the master of courtly sexuality at its most profitable in her long affair with the French prince. That affair ends only when the prince's princess dies and he is struck with guilt over his past indifference and infidelity. Like the book's other transitions so far, this one is precipitated by natural disaster, and Roxana again finds herself alone. But this time she is also wealthy and powerful; the disaster does not diminish her at all. Indeed, just before the break we have learned that Roxana has triumphed over the Prince's other mistresses, as she hears from his old servant and procuress 'what was, you may be sure, to my particular Satisfaction, *viz.* that, as above, I had him all my own' (107). Clearly, then, Roxana exists as a character in that 'Satisfaction' she speaks of here, in that sense of power, that is, of apartness from the natural self which is exploited within her personal and social relationships.

She resolves to return to England: 'there, I say, I thought I cou'd better manage things, than in *France*, at least, that I would be in less Danger of being circumvented and deceiv'd; but how to get away with such a Treasure as I had with me, was a difficult Point, and what I was greatly at a Loss about' (111). Roxana's problem is, for the first time, not survival but a question of maintenance and continued economic growth. Part of her fortune consists of the valuable diamonds left in her possession by her late landlord, and those diamonds are not legally hers, since she was never married to him and they were reported stolen by his murderers.

At this point in her narrative, Roxana is no longer the embattled heroine of the secret history. By virtue of her circumstances, she is fully the most powerful outsider in Defoe's narratives, travelling through society at its highest levels, without any legal status in it. Her solution is to transform herself, as she remarks a bit later, 'from a Lady of Pleasure' into 'a Woman of Business, and of great Business too, I assure you' (131). Such a transformation is entirely appropriate to the deeper transformation that I am concerned with tracing. Economic activity of any magnitude is always illegal or nearly so in Defoe's narratives; it serves, by definition, no purpose except sheer display of the self's ability to perform and to accumulate far beyond the needs of survival. Roxana begins at this stage in her career to define herself by her skill in such large transactions, by in fact converting everything into a transaction, that is, by her ability to separate herself entirely from a good deal of the human substance in her relationships with others. Where before she has exploited aspects of her 'natural' self, her body and her vivacity, by a process of self-dramatization and effective display; she now uses herself as a social and therefore artificial entity or commodity, a rich and attractive woman who can afford to reserve the natural self she has so far depended on for survival. That natural self interested in survival and security gives way to a self which cares more and more for the pure pleasures of secrecy and apartness, for those satisfactions that define and delimit a self as such. The narrative moves into the most abstract sequences in all Defoe's fiction, and Roxana's increasing sense of evil and damnation that critics have noted is a sign of an abstract, and to that extent 'inhuman', urge to pure apartness. We, however, are in a fair position to see Roxana's compulsive urge to separation as the result of her social perception of herself as a 'commodity', that is, as someone having exchange value in the world through which she moves. Her apartness becomes for us as readers the enjoyment of an entirely free and personal dimension of her character which she holds apart from her social identity and which corresponds to her substance. Our enjoyment is guaranteed by Roxana's continual return to the social realities of being a commodity; that is, we enjoy her substance because it is constantly extracted for us from the buzz of social relationships and economic contingencies. She thereby acquires that dialectical reality which is this novel's version of moral substance.

Her return to England, for example, is made possible by an alliance with a Dutch merchant who warns her that a Jew has recognized the illegally held jewels she is trying to sell and plans to seize them. Roxana returns to Rotterdam subsequently and finds grounds for doubting her benefactor's motives when she perceives 'that he resolv'd to *make Love to me*' (138). She listens (amused) as he circles around and finally makes his proposal. She submits after a 'seeming Resistance' (143), but refuses his offer of marriage the next day. Her reasoning is that she has paid her debt to him for saving her from the Jew by sleeping with him, saving herself in the bargain a thousand Pistoles she had previously offered him as a reward.

> But he drew himself into it, and tho' it was a dear Bargain, yet it was a Bargain of his own making; he cou'd not say I had trick'd him into it; but as he projected and drew me in to lye with him, depending that it was a sure Game in order to a Marriage, so I granted him the Favour, as he call'd it, to balance the Account of Favours receiv'd from him, and keep the thousand Pistoles with a good Grace. (144)

The wonderful trick that Roxana herself points out for us in all this lies in her adaptation of herself from a female commodity into an aggressive purchaser. She has acquired a bargain by tricking the buyer, pretending to sell herself and her fortune and in reality buying independence at the cheapest price possible. Roxana justifies herself to the astonished merchant by eloquent bursts of feminist ideology, which he denounces as subversive singularity on her part. Indeed, Roxana is herself surprised by her instinct for independence, and she tells us that part of her wants to marry her earnest merchant. She finds herself at length pregnant and alone, marvelling at her own moral turpitude in refusing him as he, finally, leaves her to go to Paris.

> ... I cry'd four and twenty Hours after, almost, without ceasing, about it; and yet, even all this while, whatever it was that bewitch'd me, I had not one serious Wish that I had taken him; I wish'd heartily indeed, that I cou'd have kept him with me; but I had a mortal Aversion to marrying him, or indeed, any-body else; but form'd a thousand wild Notions in my Head, that I was yet gay enough, and young, and handsome enough to please a Man of

Quality; and that I would try my Fortune at *London,* come of it what wou'd. (161)

The entire sequence is the central and recurring one of the book, here at its clearest. Roxana passes from amoral and clear-headed triumph to turbulent moralizing and near repentance and then back to surprised self-possession. She tells us that remorse wears off gradually as time and the business of managing her considerable fortune co-operate to make her forget. Curiously for us, perhaps, Roxana is not saved at this point by her eloquent ideology of feminist independence, even though she has certainly earned it and proved its point in her initial experience with her brewer husband. What saves her first is not thought but action, her discovery of a self that surfaces in action, emerging irresistibly in the exact techniques of financial solidification—movement itself in short, movement in spite of the hesitations of the moral self. A self is revealed and reasserted in these sequences which is somehow apart from and stronger than Roxana's moral will as she dramatizes it, stronger even than the libidinal self she describes. The question of whether Roxana is lying about her hesitations here and throughout the book is a classic and irrelevant one. What matters for us as readers of such a sequence is that Roxana's substance as a dynamic will that defines itself in the process of securing apartness and moving financially and socially supersedes the illusion of static moral or social substance. What we see is not Roxana and her society, but rather Roxana, her society, and a third term which presides over that dyad, which understands through action the relationship which constitutes the opposition called Roxana and society. The *form* of the sequence is the working loose of that energy, just as *Roxana* itself in its most involving moments such as this is a working out of the reality that character in the fiction that Defoe wrote consists of the concrete energy which operates upon the inert illusions of substance contained in words like self and society.

Roxana's greatest triumph at the ball where she gains her name and (perhaps) a royal lover is thus the coherent climax of such an emerging process. It is the moment in which she most clearly and overtly presides over those artificial pseudo-entities called society and self, where she plainly extracts the character called Roxana by action which shows a deep under-

standing of the ways in which society and the individual interact. The crucial point is that Roxana's story as a whole exemplifies the free individual who is somehow free precisely to the
extent that he understands social necessity. For the free individual like Roxana, social necessity can be manipulated to
create freedom. And in this middle section of the story when she
lives first for three years 'with a Person, which Duty, and private
Vows obliges her not to reveal, at least, not yet' (181), and then
as the mistress of a Lord at £1,500 a year, Roxana tells us
often enough to bore us that her freedom involves staggering
accumulation, income virtually without reciprocal participation in the market. For the recurring boast she makes is that
her income is never spent but added to her capital. 'In a word, I
had now five and thirty Thousand Pounds Estate; and as I
found Ways to live without wasting either Principal or Interest,
I laid up £2,000 every Year, at least, out of the meer Interest,
adding it to the Principal; and thus I went on' (182).

Such freedom, as we all know, involves an obvious if exhilarating contradiction. Defoe's narrative never faces that
contradiction, for society and the social self remain to the end
mere instruments of the individual's freedom and self-develop-
ment. The necessity the narrative chooses to introduce is the
only necessity that the bourgeois novel at this stage in its
existence can tolerate: 'nature'. Roxana's slow decline from
this point into more and more convincing remorse and regret
comes out of her decisions to find her original five children by
her brewer husband, to become a private person, and to marry
out of relative affection her Dutch merchant. This is not to
say that her ability to manipulate social forms diminishes, but
rather that natural affections distract Roxana from the satisfactions of social mastery. Roxana is eventually defeated not by the
impossibility of maintaining her powerful identity above social
realities but by what the narrative presents as the self-contained
and inevitable moral-psychological laws of nature. The psychology of guilt which the narrative more and more examines
is thus an effective way of dispersing the social and economic
contradictions at its imaginative centre and asserting in a final
way the primacy of the self. What historical critics have identified as the presentation of a moral-theological state near despair is in the economy of the novel a means of staging an

evasion of historical necessity by shifting the scene to the natural world of the interior self. Roxana remains existentially free for us as readers in a special way by running deliberately into her own moral-psychological necessity.

Even in following her maternal impulses and beating a social retreat, Roxana continues to delight us by feats of social movement, by various transformations of herself within society as she effects that retreat. For example, she leaves her Lord and moves to Kensington, and then, giving it out that she is returning to Rotterdam, she moves into a court in the Minories, lodging with Quakers and turning herself into a Quakeress:

> When all was ready, I dress'd myself in the Dress I bought of her, [her Quaker landlady] *and said*, Come, I'll be a QUAKER to-Day, and you and I'll go Abroad; which we did, and there was not a QUAKER in the Town look'd less like a Counterfeit than I did: But all this was my particular Plot to be the more compleatly conceal'd, and that I might depend upon being not known, and yet need not be confin'd like a Prisoner, and be always in Fear; so that all the rest was Grimace. (213)

But Roxana is for the first time uneasy. The transformation is drastic, and the rich courtesan feels 'like a Fish out of Water' (214). When the Dutch merchant she had earlier refused to marry and about whom she has sent Amy to inquire suddenly appears in London, she is confused, wonders about his financial 'disappointments', and carefully suppresses what she tells us is her natural affection for him. Amy sends a report at this point that her Prince may want to marry her. Just as she is about to dismiss her merchant, news arrives from Amy that the Prince has been wounded, perhaps mortally, in a hunting accident. Roxana holds her ground, and Amy soon arrives with further news that the Prince has turned penitent after his accident and wants nothing more to do with Roxana. Throughout this familiar kind of exceedingly careful negotiation for advantage, Roxana has described herself as struggling between gratitude and affection for her merchant and ambition to be a Princess, 'truly craz'd and distracted for about a Fortnight, as most of the people in *Bedlam*, tho' perhaps, not quite so far gone' (234). Roxana returns several times to that self-analysis, insisting that social ambition has possessed her to the point of madness:

So fast a hold has Pride and Ambition upon our Minds, that when once it gets Admission, nothing is so chimerical, but under this Possession we can form Ideas of, in our Fancy, and realize to our Imagination: Nothing can be so ridiculous as the simple Steps we take in such Cases; a Man or a Woman becomes a meer *Malade Imaginaire*, and I believe, may as easily die with Grief, or run-mad with Joy, (as the Affair in his Fancy appears right or wrong) as if all was real, and actually under the Management of the Person. (238–9)

What Roxana understands at this point (or better, what we experience as her readers) is the destructive illusion of social mastery, the necessarily private megalomania of social ambition in a rigid class structure. Now, we know that Roxana has already successfully invaded and manipulated that class structure to tremendous advantage, that she has been the mistress of a Prince and a Lord, probably a royal mistress, and is now (in Amy's phrase) 'as rich as Crassus' (238), and finally that these things have in our reading of them been 'actually under the Management of the Person'. That her satisfied apartness should now turn to near megalomania is part of the process of gracefully turning the narrative over to the exploration of a psychology of guilt and frustration. That shift is obviously in the service of various truths about the rhythms of power and possession; perhaps such a reversal is a psychological inevitability. But it is also clearly a means of balancing Roxana's elaborate feats of social mastery, that is, of evading the necessity to retract them as fantasies. Rather than succumbing to any precise limitations within the social and economic world, the self destroys itself according to its own laws, by means of its own mysteriously gratuitous excesses. Indeed, there is a marvellous ideological economy in the reversal. Society remains an inert entity which by its rigid artificiality induces madness; the self asserts its naturalness by its very madness. Roxana finds her bewilderment in the demands made by her ambitious self upon her affections, which tend towards her merchant and her children, and the opposition between the natural and the social is invoked. That ambitious self is aligned, in effect, with society, which excites ambitions it can never satisfy. Having been exploited to the full, society can now take the blame for Roxana.

Roxana is temporarily saved by marriage to her merchant and the legal acquisition of a title. Her husband buys a baronetcy and she becomes Lady —— in London and a Countess at The Hague. With Roxana's acquisition of legal status, the narrative faces certain problems. To be interesting and affecting, Roxana must in some real sense be outside society, somehow beyond its essential artificiality. So even in these her most staid pages Roxana continues to play at reduced and private versions of her former games. She dresses up in her Turkish costume for her husband, making good her boast that he will not recognize her in it. She delights in the privacy of their establishment, a baronet and his lady living quietly with their Quaker landlady, 'and the Privacy of our Mirth, greatly added to the Pleasure of it' (246). And she gives her Quaker landlady 100 guineas and an income of £40 a year, pointing heavily as she does to the exact parallels between that lady's situation and her own at the beginning of her narrative (the Quaker lady has been deserted by her husband and left with four children). All of these activities are signs of her undiminished power and apartness, the last especially a reminder of how she can now forestall the same social disaster she began with and preside benevolently (like Crusoe near his end) over a repetition of her initial catastrophe. But paradoxically, it appears at first, the real source of her apartness is her recurring guilt, which now may be said to dominate the narrative in the attention given to Roxana's troublesome daughter.

It used to be said frequently that the guilt exhibited by Defoe's heroes is the cheap price they pay for their secular achievements. It is truer to say that their guilt is a way, still another way, of asserting themselves as separate and therefore superior entities. Roxana's guilt is a means of maintaining her dynamic relationship to the essentially static world around her. The world of legal status and secure wealth is not simply possessed. It is maintained in tension with guilt and remorse, held with a difficulty which once again dramatizes the dynamic nature of the self in Defoe's sensitive narratives:

And let no-body conclude from the strange Success I met with in all my wicked Doings, and the vast Estate which I had rais'd by it, that therefore I either was happy or easie: No, no, there was a Dart struck into the Liver; there was a secret Hell within, even all the while, when our Joy was at the highest; but more especially *now*, after it was all over, and when according to all appearance, I was one of the happiest Women upon Earth; all this while, *I say*, I had such a constant Terror upon my Mind, as gave me every now and then very terrible Shocks, and which made me expect something very frightful upon every Accident of Life. (260)

Roxana's career is over, as she notes, but the self carries on, finding in effect a new way to be itself in being once again something radically other than appearances. The fear and trembling of this passage coexists with a continuing participation in an expanding economic world, for her new husband turns out to be 'immensely rich' and she details their careful monetary arrangements, including a 'revelation' scene where Roxana lists her wealth for her astonished merchant (omitting a few thousand in cash to provide for her daughters). But our pleasure by now is located in Roxana's maintaining herself apart and those giddy arrangements serve as counterpoint, as a means of dramatizing the radical disparity between appearance and personal reality over which the self presides with some insistence: 'there was a secret Hell within, even all the while, when our Joy was at the highest.'

That remorse is quite minor, of course, next to what Roxana undergoes in the last pages of the book when her daughter appears again unexpectedly and guesses who she is. The antithesis that informs this last sequence is clear. Nature, in the most elemental fashion, gathers its forces and begins to expose Roxana. Society, we may notice, is quite irrelevant. Roxana's elaborate career of social manipulation is threatened only by that very nature she has spent the last quarter of her narrative serving. Again, that threat is a way of isolating her and continuing her certification as a dynamic entity apart from her social appearances. The nature that she had to renounce and abstract as an instrument of social movement now returns with all the compulsive instability we associate with natural forces and with a concreteness without parallel in the narrative since Roxana's initial encounter with nature at the beginning of the book. Roxana is dining with the captain of the ship which will take her to Holland, when the captain's wife's sister appears. Roxana's ambivalent reactions point to the true function of this sequence.

I cannot but take Notice here, that notwithstanding there was a secret Horror upon my Mind, and I was ready to sink when I came close to her, to salute her; yet it was a secret inconceivable Pleasure to me when I kiss'd her, to know that I kiss'd my own Child; my own Flesh and Blood, born of my Body; and who I had never kiss'd since I took the fatal Farewel of them all, with a Million of Tears, and a Heart almost dead with Grief, when *Amy* and the Good Woman took them all away, and went with them to *Spittle-Fields:* No Pen can describe, no Words can express, *I say*, the strange Impression which this thing made upon my Spirits; I felt something shoot thro' my Blood; my Heart flutter'd; my Head flash'd, and was dizzy, and all within me, *as I thought*, turn'd about, and much ado I had, not to abandon myself to an Excess of Passion at the first Sight of her, much more when my Lips touch'd her Face; I thought I must have taken her in my Arms, and kiss'd her again a thousand times, whether I wou'd or no. (277)

Of all the secret emotions that Roxana has in her narrative, this is the most explosive. It is the moment in the book that she comes closest to losing control of herself in public, and it is the most specifically physical passage in the book. By contrast, her sexual career must strike every reader as generalized and dispassionate, for sexual emotions have no place in the conquest of society, only sexual movements. It is mainly here that Roxana takes the trouble to record physical sensations that come near the compelling turbulence of sexuality. The point is that she returns to this version of the natural as a way out of her narrative, as a way of ending it with a resonant vibration guaranteed to keep her alive past her last page. The enemy is still society, for it is fear of being revealed as the Lady Roxana that keeps her from acknowledging her daughter. Such a pattern brings us back to the denaturalization of the social environment which is the narrative's major strategy.

Nature works by returning us to origins, by re-establishing unities. Society, Roxana's fear shows us, works by denying origins and establishing separate classes and persons. In truth, Roxana is a character who enacts desires that we are in a position to recognize as socially derived; she may be said to embody a cluster of energies we can see as the constituents of individualist ideology. But that ideology involves the denial of society as a source of individual motive and of the personal movement we call character, and their replacement by that extra-historical and hypostatized version of the self located in 'nature'. Society, a monstrous artificial construct, prevents Roxana from re-entering the natural world of maternal affection. But she does, in another sense, re-enter it by lying painfully just outside it, by the strength of her desire in a passage like this and in the last sequence of guilt and perhaps murder which closes the narrative but keeps the case of Roxana wide open.

Such a reading of this controversial and dark last part of *Roxana* resolves some traditional problems. Critics have long had good cause to wonder about the heroine's contradiction at this point, since like all readers they have sensed that in spite of her vile plot against her daughter she remains quite as attractive a character as ever. Her energy to negotiate and to remain apart is undiminished, and these concluding pages are as full of stratagems enforcing the secret consciousness of power as they are of intense remorse and fear. If we accept that contradictory experience, we are able to see that the moral content which causes the contradiction is really a form, that Roxana's intense participation in her own moral ambivalence is novelistically a drastic means of self-assertion, the only variation left to her in the light of her career and its total success.

An acceptance of content as form is implicit in all my readings of Defoe's narratives, for their natural tendency as mimic autobiographies is towards the conversion of the material and therefore inert facts of a life to the recurring pattern of biography. It seems to me that such a pattern is inevitably the 'self' finding the 'other' which continually threatens and simultaneously defines the self. As we have seen, Roxana has nowhere to turn at her end but to herself for an 'other'. That guilty internal self is the last resource of the self when it senses that all other externals have been neutralized. The *Roxana* we actually read is thus more than a superficial exercise in the psychology of guilt, much more than a half-hearted exposé of middle class hypocrisy. It is nothing less than a presentation of the form of an eighteenth-century individualist consciousness as it converts, in Coleridge's phrase, truth into power.

Roxana's own words at her end can serve as proof and conclusion. Her daughter is apparently murdered by Amy, and Roxana is beset by ghastly images of that death. She resolves to go to Holland but tells us that she reserves the whole truth from her Quaker landlady: 'there was no need of that Part being expos'd; and it was always a Maxim with me, *That Secrets shou'd never be open'd, without evident Utility*' (326).

# VII

## Epilogue: *A Journal of the Plague Year* as Epitome

. . for the face of things so often alters, and the situation of affairs in this great British Empire gives such new turns, even to nature it self, that there is matter of new observation every day presented to the traveller's eye.

Defoe, A Tour Through the<br>Whole Island of Great<br>Britain, I.

AMONG Defoe's longer narratives, *A Journal of the Plague Year* is *sui generis*. His other narrators are autobiographers who place themselves at once in the middle of events, shaping and altering their surroundings from act to act. Their task is to present themselves at the expense, finally, of the world, to extract free-dom from various kinds of necessity. In place of these expansive conquests, the *Journal* offers a detailed and carefully compelling picture of necessity in the ultimate human forms of disease and death. The semi-anonymous H. F. lives at the contemplative edge of that necessity, mysteriously immune to the plague so that he can record the inscrutability of natural process. Defoe's other narrators appropriate their environments, converting them from historical and geographical entities into emanations of the infinitely resourceful self. The saddler's account is rooted in and limited by the historical moment of the plague, and it is surrounded as well by the verifiable documents and maps of an actual London.[1]

---

[1] F. Bastian has asserted that Defoe's major source was his own experience and 'a considerable mass of first-hand information, critically sifted by an acute mind'. (See 'Defoe's *Journal of the Plague Year* Reconsidered', *RES*, 16 (1965), 166.) The traditional praise of the book has involved marvelling over Defoe's powers of literary reconstruction and research, so Bastian's affirmations mark an important if exaggerated critical shift. Freed as it is from the conventions of popular narrative format, the *Journal* is free to make use of Defoe's own experience of walking the streets of London as a private citizen. Manuel Schonhorn has reinforced that

These differences are hardly surprising. The *Journal* is pseudo-history in the service of expert political propaganda,[2] and the saddler is necessarily an adjunct to these purposes, a witness to events whose reactions support rather than convert their reality. But as Louis Landa has remarked and as every reader of the book can affirm, H. F. 'achieves a measure of individuality, enough at least to insinuate concern for his fate into a reader's mind'.[3] It seems to me, moreover, that our concern for the saddler's fate is never a matter of crude anxiety over his survival. That, after all, is given from the start. The source of our concern and what we participate in as readers is the process of ordering an unprecedented intrusion of natural chaos called the plague, and what the saddler leads us to fear is the dominance of disorder. In short, the saddler is not a lesser Crusoe; he is an intensified and almost abstract version of the ordering self that we have seen in Defoe's other narratives.

The plague is an extended moment of total uncertainty, an exaggerated, nearly metaphysical version provided by history of the random destructiveness of an environment. Perfectly, one can add, that environment is both natural and social. The plague is a natural disaster attendant upon commerce and urban crowding, perpetuated and complicated by the conditions of social life. What we are delighted witnesses to as readers is the simultaneous resolute stillness and efficient movement of the saddler in the plague. The special trick he manages is what all Defoe's narrators aspire to achieve in the larger spaces and more extensive rhythms of their lives: to balance the claims of action and submission and to extend that pattern to their environments. The saddler stays because he has a hunch. His inactivity is a form of action which reconciles movement and stillness in a perfect manner. Moreover, his solution to the problem set by the plague is entirely personal, private. Others did well to fly.

---

common-sense view of the matter by pointing out that although Defoe reconstructed in his narrative the topography of an older London, he concentrated on those locations and structures still a part of the London scene in 1720. (See 'Defoe's *Journal of the Plague Year*: Topography and Intention', *RES*, 19 (1968), 387.)

[2] J. R. Moore says that the *Journal* and *Due Preparations for the Plague* were published in 1722 to create support for Walpole's unpopular Quarantine Act. (See *Daniel Defoe: Citizen of the Modern World* (Chicago, 1958), p. 320.)

[3] *The Journal of the Plague Year* (Oxford English Novels, 1969), Introduction, p. xxxiv. All further references in the text are to this edition.

Upon the foot of all these Observations, I must say, that tho'
Providence seem'd to direct my Conduct to be otherwise; yet it is
my opinion, and I must leave it as a Prescription, (*viz.*) *that the best
Physick against the Plague is to run away from it.* I know People encourage themselves, by saying, God is able to keep us in the midst
of Danger, and able to overtake us when we think our selves out of
Danger; and this kept Thousands in the Town, whose Carcasses
went into the great Pits by Cart Loads; and who, if they had fled
from the Danger, had, I believe, been safe from the Disaster; at
least 'tis probable they had been safe. (197–8)

Note the last qualifying phrase. The saddler is nothing if not
reasonable. He rejects 'Turkish Predestinarism' (193) and its
extremes of trust and careless fatalism in favour of Christian
moderating action; he refines the plague from the direct
visitation of an angry God to the result of natural causes. And
yet he sympathizes with those who are distracted nearly to
belief in the consoling clarity of such simplicities. All this
reasonableness and more serve to obscure that initial irrationality, the decision to stay. Like Crusoe, H. F. presents a detailed
brief for the existence of personal providential signals. He
surrounds his decision to stay with circumstances which confirm his initial inclination to stay. He thought of going away
but could get no horse, resolved to walk and sleep in a tent but
his servant left him. He opens his Bible at random and the
91st Psalm advises him to trust in God, advice we might add
maliciously to be found almost everywhere in that book. All
these details add up to 'Intimations from Heaven of what is
his unquestion'd Duty to do' (10), even though the saddler's
brother tells him that Providence does not work through such
trivial and particular means. The theological question of particular Providences remained in doubt in the early eighteenth
century,[4] but the needs of narrative are always clear.
The central self must in some way assert itself at the expense
of the other, and H. F. must stay if we are to have a book
to read. That fact is both cause and effect of the narrator's
power over what he sees and experiences. The sheer necessity

[4] R. M. Baine notes that in Defoe's day the doctrine of particular Providence
'was beginning to weaken', and sees its defence as a pervasive theme in Defoe's
works, especially in the *Journal*, where 'the pattern of Providence is most frequently
felt and most variously apprehended'. (See *Daniel Defoe and the Supernatural* (Athens,
Georgia, 1968), pp. 3, 6.)

of wanting and having this kind of first-person observer (in events and yet outside them) involves not just journalistic efficiency but a fundamentally superior self that can participate in the world with involvement but without loss. We have forgotten how important such truisms are and how coherently and intensely Defoe's narratives work them out. In so far as we are readers, the theological arguments are thereby after the fact, a handy ideological justification of what is given by the functional and structural requirements of the narrative. The special privilege of the narrator in the novel is given, to return to Lukács's phrase, in the 'affirmation of a dissonance' between the immanence of being and empirical life.[5] In other forms, says Lukács, that situation is a prelude to form; in the novel it is the form itself. The *Journal* is an almost pure articulation of that form implicit in the situation which may be said to create the novel as a genre.

The saddler's search for justification is the first indicator in the narrative of his essentially gratuitous resistance to the demands of empirical life raised to the nth power by the plague. Gratuitous at least at first, for the narrator's function is to protect himself from the formlessness of that horrendous physical reality. It is only paradoxical at first glance that he has to stay in the middle of death and disorder in order to live and establish the order of his narrative. More overtly and clearly than Defoe's other narratives, the *Journal* allows us to see that the self does not so much resist disorder as exploit it to create its own order.

H. F.'s narrative is the unfolding of a mystery and its reduction to facts—statistics, measurements, causes, and effects. He explains at the very beginning that there were no newspapers to give false reports, so he thought that official documents like the weekly Bills of Mortality could be used and trusted. But even they are unreliable, invaded by 'Knavery and Collusion' (6), and H. F. depends upon his own observations for the truth of the spreading infection. Those observations are impelled by what he repeatedly calls his 'curiosity'. In turn, the plague in all its exact details compels the saddler: 'I mention'd above shutting of Houses up; and it is needful to say something particularly to that; for this Part of the History of the Plague is very

---

[5] *The Theory of the Novel,* p. 72. See above, Chapter I.

melancholy; *but the most grievous Story must* be *told'* (36). H. F.'s horror is consistently coupled with an exactness which is obviously a means of controlling and intensifying that horror at a measured pace. The narrating self is a measuring intelligence whose strength is expanded by that exactness. Thus the description of the great pit at Aldgate begins with measurements, an engineer's survey: 'it was about 40 Foot in Length, and about 15 or 16 Foot broad; and at the Time I first looked at it, about nine Foot deep; but it was said, they dug it near 20 Foot deep afterwards, in one Part of it, till they could go no deeper for the Water' (59). But that order is less than the truth, and he goes to see it at night to count the bodies it conceals. What he sees is a sort of authentic disorder:

It was about the 10th of *September,* that my Curiosity led, or rather drove me to go and see this Pit again, when there had been near 400 People buried in it; and I was not content to see it in the Day-time, as I had done before; for then there would have been nothing to have seen but the loose Earth; for all the Bodies that were thrown in, were immediately covered with Earth, by those they call'd the Buryers, which at other Times were call'd Bearers; but I resolv'd to go in the Night and see some of them thrown in. (60)

The saddler's 'curious' enumeration of these things precludes, of course, the inarticulate horror which is the natural reaction to them. He admits as much: 'This may serve a little to describe the dreadful Condition of that Day, tho' it is impossible to say any Thing that is able to give a true Idea of it to those who did not see it, other than this; that it was indeed *very, very, very* dreadful, and such as no Tongue can express' (60). Such clumsy underlinings mark the end of his attempts to render his feelings about the plague and to concentrate solely on his relationship to it. After the great pit at Aldgate, the saddler tells us he is 'almost overwhelm'd', and his narrative shifts noticeably about this point towards description of what others did about the plague. His 'curiosity' continues, but leading now in more positive directions to the discovery no longer of pure horror but of resourceful ordering by others in the face of the plague. In Defoe's other stories, the narrators are the only ones permitted to function that way; they observe themselves. Here the saddler becomes a pure and disinterested intelligence who has earned the right by staying in the middle of disorder to claim the rewards of order around him. He claims those rewards in the sense that the novelistic narrator tends to appropriate for himself and for us what he sees, claims them in the novelistic sense that to narrate is to supply the perception which supplies being. Having stayed by himself and for his own inscrutable reasons, he presides over the order he discovers in the absolute middle of the plague. The narrative sequence is such that a powerful apartness such as we have seen at times achieved by Defoe's other characters with great labour is the saddler's privilege, the result of his actively staying still in the centre of the whirlwind. Having endured disorder, having looked steadily into it, and having done that for no reason except a sense of secret and special destiny, the saddler discovers that the plague is the source of an order greater than that which prevailed before the plague struck. That pattern stands from our perspective on Defoe's narratives as a remarkable epitome of their imaginative strategies.

The saddler finds virtue, courage, and ingenuity: in the Waterman whose family is stricken and then provided for by means of a large flat stone, in those who have taken refuge aboard ships in the harbour, in the biscuit-baker, sail-maker, and joiner who establish with their skills a community of survival for themselves in the middle of it all. London itself is a source of joyful satisfaction as a model of order, 'a Pattern to all the Cities in the World for the good Government and the excellent Order that was every where kept, even in the time of the most violent Infection; and when the People were in the utmost Consternation and Distress' (155). Order and decency, he records, are preserved to such an extent that nothing extraordinary is seen during the day, 'not the least Signal of the Calamity to be seen or heard of, except what was to be observ'd from the Emptiness of the Streets, and sometimes from the passionate Outcries and Lamentations of the People, out at their Windows, and from the Number of Houses and Shops shut up' (186). As Manuel Schonhorn has observed, the book is a tribute to the city itself,[6] but that tribute must be read as a means of

---

[6] 'Defoe's *Journal of the Plague Year:* Topography and Intention', *RES,* 19 (1968), 398.

enlarging and solidifying the observing self which has remained in the city. H. F. combines personal experience, anecdote, and socio-political observation in such a way that they co-operate to place him beyond confusion or ideological simplification. He examines questions of origins and effects with informed nicety. He establishes physical contagion over miasma and natural causes (tempered by awareness of ultimate providence) over supernatural intervention. The individual depravity of the sick in spreading the infection is proved to be the understandable defence of the hard-pressed provincial towns. The validity of his observations and opinions as well as their consonance with Defoe's opinions are interesting but irrelevant questions for the purpose of grasping the imaginative base of the book. Those observations function as an endorsement of the narrative self. The act of discovery that we read about is what matters, the transition from the natural chaos of the plague and the brief uncertainty of the self that it engenders to the serene contemplation of an extended human order.

The ultimate step in that contemplation, in logic if not quite in sequence, is the overt realization that the plague is a fruitful crisis, a set of circumstances which made men forget their sectarian alliances: the Test Act is voided in practice. And finally, the economic disaster wrought by the plague produced, like the Great Fire before it, tremendous prosperity afterwards. Though offered pages apart from each other, those two consolidations explain the special sort of transforming privilege the narrator now has. He is able to see on the one hand how the plague restores natural conditions, encourages the survival of the resourceful, and destroys artificial distinctions in the brotherhood of survival. On the other, he can see that the plague co-operates with what we might call the normal business cycle and is as much a metaphor for social-economic conditions as a hyperbolic version of natural conditions. The natural and the social interact in the *Journal* with a quiet perfection nowhere else achieved in Defoe's narratives; the 'truth' of human nature resides in the natural environment, and in the privileged moment elaborated by the narrator's intelligence that environment and the social-economic setting where that truth is normally obscured coalesce. The narrator possesses that unique resolution of the antithesis between the natural and the social by virtue of his obstinate or perhaps singular and privileged refusal to run.

The saddler concludes by spending a good number of his last pages in sorrow at the return of careless disorder. The plague subsides and people forget the danger of contagion and return to normal religious strife. The plague, then, is a brief moment of clarity when nature and society coincide and allow the self to observe and to order, to act without moving. History presented Defoe with the materials to solve the problem that his other narratives confront in overtly personal and therefore quite impossible ways. *A Journal of the Plague Year* remains a thickly factual, even grossly truthful, book. But the imagination which flares up occasionally and dominates those facts is the secret and smiling and still quite impossible self for which we read Defoe.

# Index

Addison, Joseph, 174
Alter, Robert, 77, 79
Amadis de Gaul, 15
Andersen, Hans, 5n.
Arendt, Hannah, 24n.
Austen, Jane, 18
autobiography, 35, 48–9

Baine, R. M., 1–2n., 6n., 235n.
Barthes, Roland, 32, 151, 152
Bastian, F., 233n.
Baxter, Richard, 5
*Bildungsroman*, 151, 171
Blewett, David, 201n.
Bond, Clinton S., 1–2n.
Boswell, James, 3, 174
Boyce, Benjamin, 3n.
Brooks, Douglas, 113n.

capitalism, 14–15, 23, 25–7
casuistry, 6–7, 8
Cervantes, Miguel de, 12–13
Chalmers, George, 1n.
*chronique scandaleuse*, 192–4
circumstantial realism, 9
Coleridge, S. T., 231
Collins, Wilkie, 23
Cumberland, Richard, 5

Dampier, William, 77
Defoe, Daniel, Works:
  *Captain Singleton*
    compared with *Robinsoe Crusoe*,
      63–4
    and pirate legend, 63–5, 93
    sources of, 65, 76–7
    compared with *The King of the
      Pirates*, 65, 76–7, 84, 85, 88
    compared with picaresque, 77–8,
      79
    narrator's initial nullity, 77–9
    freedom and circumstances in,
      80–3
    narrator's assertion of competence,
      84–5
    self-conscious and separate nar-
      rator in, 80–1, 84–5

function of complication in, 85–6
and market society, 86
survival and accumulation in, 86–7
typical of Defoe's stories, 87
significance of details in, 88–90
active and passive reconciled in,
  90–1
function of William the Quaker in,
  91–2
disguise and transformation in,
  92–3
*Colonel Jack*
  sentimentalism in, 146
  compared with Defoe's other nar-
    ratives, 146–8, 149, 158, 162, 166
  compared with *Bildungsroman*, 151,
    171
  stylistic analysis of, 147–8
  hero's gentility, 148–50, 157, 159,
    170
  doubles and surrogates in, 150,
    162–4, 171–3
  self-assertion and development of
    hero, 151–2, 183–4
  secret and separate narrator in,
    152–3, 159–60, 164–6, 175–7
  transformations of criminal ac-
    tivity in, 153–62
  multiple identity as recurring
    pattern in, 161–2
  private and public roles in, 166–
    170, 175–7, 178–9
  relationship to history of hero,
    169, 174–5, 185–8, 189–91
  stability as narrative theme, 170–
    171
  pseudo-repentance of hero, 171–3
  hero as 18th-century spectator,
    174–5
  amorous adventures in, 177–83
  class implications of marriages,
    179–80
  transformation of marriage, 180–1
  military adventures in, 183–7
  self and circumstances in, 181–2,
    186–7
  hero as prosperous trader, 189–91